The Passport
That Does Not
Pass Ports

THE PASSPORT
THAT DOES NOT
PASS PORTS

AFRICAN LITERATURE OF TRAVEL IN THE TWENTY-FIRST CENTURY

EDITED BY Isabel Balseiro AND Zachariah Rapola

Michigan State University Press | *East Lansing*

Michigan State University Press
East Lansing, Michigan 48823-5245

LIBRARY OF CONGRESS CATALOGING-IN-PUBLICATION DATA
Names: Balseiro, Isabel, editor. | Rapola, Zachariah, editor.
Title: The passport that does not pass ports : African literature of travel
in the twenty-first century / edited by Isabel Balseiro and Zachariah Rapola.
Other titles: African humanities and the arts.
Description: East Lansing : Michigan State University Press, 2020.
| Series: African humanities and the arts | Includes bibliographical references.
Identifiers: LCCN 2019049197 | ISBN 978-1-61186-373-4 (paperback)
| ISBN 978-1-60917-647-1 | ISBN 978-1-62895-408-1 | ISBN 978-1-62896-409-7
Subjects: LCSH: Africa—Description and travel. | Travelers' writings. | Africa—Literary collections.
Classification: LCC DT12.25 .P37 2020 | DDC 960.3—dc23
LC record available at https://lccn.loc.gov/2019049197

Book design by Charlie Sharp, Sharp Designs, East Lansing, Michigan
Cover design by Erin Kirk New.
Cover art: El Anatsui, *Untitled*, 1983, copyright © El Anatsui (used with the artist's permission).

Michigan State University Press is a member of the Green Press Initiative and is
committed to developing and encouraging ecologically responsible publishing
practices. For more information about the Green Press Initiative and the use of
recycled paper in book publishing, please visit www.greenpressinitiative.org.

Visit Michigan State University Press at *www.msupress.org*

Contents

vii   ACKNOWLEDGMENTS

ix   INTRODUCTION, *Isabel Balseiro*

I. Theories of Travel

3   Bye, Bye Babar, *Taiye Selasi* (Ghana/Nigeria)

7   Afropolitanism, *Achille Mbembe* (Cameroon)

II. Traveling Fictions

15   The Wanderer, *Hassouna Mosbahi* (Tunisia)

27   The Start of the Affair, *Nuruddin Farah* (Somalia)

45   Presidential Portraits, *Zachariah Rapola* (South Africa)

53   A Private Experience, *Chimamanda Ngozi Adichie* (Nigeria)

63   Weight of Whispers, *Yvonne Adhiambo Owuor* (Kenya)

97   Murambi (Excerpt from *Murambi, The Book of Bones*), *Boris Boubacar Diop* (Senegal)

103   Homeland (Excerpt from *Far from My Father*), *Véronique Tadjo* (Côte d'Ivoire)

113   Abdar and Terhas (Excerpt from *African Titanics*), *Abu Bakr Hamid Khaal* (Eritrea)

III. Memoirs

121   Photography Is Like Hunting (Excerpt from *A Stranger's Pose*), *Emmanuel Iduma* (Nigeria)

125   Hargeisa Snapshots, *Doreen Baingana* (Uganda)

129   Zanzibar, circa 1996, *Heidi Grunebaum* (South Africa)

133   Fugee, *Hawa Jande Golakai* (Liberia)

149   2010 World Cup (Excerpt from *One Day I Will Write about This Place*), *Binyavanga Wainaina* (Kenya)

161   Tending the Backyard: Port Harcourt (Excerpt from *Looking for Transwonderland*), *Noo Saro-Wiwa* (Nigeria)

183   Trapdoor (Excerpt from *The Return: Fathers, Sons and the Land in Between*), *Hisham Matar* (Libya)

193   ABOUT THE CONTRIBUTORS

Acknowledgments

For the beautiful metaphor that gives this book its title, I would like to express heartfelt gratitude to Souleymane Bachir Diagne. Deep gratitude as well goes to Zachariah Rapola, who generously invited me to join his multivolume book project on contemporary African arts and culture years before our ideas distilled into this collection. At Michigan State University Press, we would like to thank Catherine Cocks and Kenneth Harrow for their support. Many dear friends put away pressing work to offer comments on the metamorphosing introduction in its early and late stages. Warmest thanks to Carli Coetzee, Brenda Cooper, Heidi Grunebaum, Tobias Hecht, Ntongela Masilela, Pamela Nichols, and Mark Sanders. I would like to thank, as well, those friends who lent a hand in trying to reach a number of authors: Harry Garuba and Lola Shoneyin, Sheila Walker and Matthew Randolph, as well as Makhosazana Xaba and Iyunolu Osagie. Without generous research grants and publishing subventions, copyright fees would have been out of reach. I hereby acknowledge the support lent by the Beckman Endowment Funds, the Brian Butler '89 Faculty Enhancement Fund, the Humanities, Social Science, and Arts Department, as well as the Dean of Faculty Office at Harvey Mudd College, of the Claremont Colleges. Last and most appreciatively, I would like to recognize the steadfast collaboration of three consummate research assistants: Bonny Chen, Lillian Liang, and Isaiah Fujii Bresnihan.

Isabel Balseiro

My deep and most profound thanks to Isabel Balseiro for the collaborative effort. I will forever be indebted to her for the time and extraordinary effort invested in ensuring the realization of this anthology. Seeing this transatlantic project taking shape and coming to fruition has been one of the most enriching creative experiences.

Zachariah Rapola

This book is dedicated to the memory of scholar and poet Harry Oludare Garuba, a traveler in Africa and in the world, whose ways knew no boundaries and who moved so many of us.

Introduction

Isabel Balseiro

A boom in travel writing by Africans has been recognized for a few years now.[1] This flourishing includes authors who may have been born on African soil but have grown up in the diaspora (for example, Yaa Gyasi, Noo Saro-Wiwa), those who, despite frequent returns, make their living outside of Africa (Alain Mabanckou, Teju Cole), or even some who enjoy the privilege of shuttling between the United States and the continent (Chimamanda Ngozi Adichie). While their lives reflect the migratory movement that characterizes not only Africa but the global South more generally, the focus of this book is on writers who live in and travel within Africa.

Despite the subtitle *African Literature of Travel in the Twenty-First Century*, the narratives in this volume are not meant as a guide to travel destinations. Readers expecting to embark on a voyage of discovery, and those in search of previously unknown African travel writers, run the risk of being disappointed. The selection of pieces here casts a wider net, as the book aims for an audience with varying degrees of familiarity with two vast fields: African literature and travel writing. Those for whom this volume may be an initiation into them are as welcome as those who would accept an invitation to reconsider accounts of African travel from a new perspective. To situate an audience for this book, imagine scholars designing syllabi with titles like "World Literatures: Travel Writing," "African Literature: A Post-na-tional Approach," "Language and Literature in a Glocal World," "Transnational Africa," or "Borders, Exile, Language," as well as students with a craving for such offerings. The literature of travel in Africa today deserves all the readers it can garner.

The concept of travel proposed by this book is based on the acuity of vision particular types of travelers exhibit: travelers for whom a mother tongue finds embers across linguistic borders, for whom a strange land isn't necessarily foreign since in it they manage to perceive vestiges of the familiar. These are authors for whom the act of traveling extends a canvas on which to paint, through recourse to words, someone else's reality—a reality never too distant from one's own. Against the tropes of travel writing, this volume posits literature of travel.

These writers' fictions and theories, their ponderings and judgments tell us what good literature has always been: "Creative writing seems to derive from the need to cross boundaries, to be out of place in the world," as Kenyan author Simon Gikandi has suggested.[2] That is what makes these writers coalesce: reflection about the act of being in motion, about reconfiguring place; a consciousness of how geography redirects the focus of one's gaze and, in turn, how that altered gaze filters inward. In doing so, the self, having absorbed the landscape, inhaled the scents, paid heed to accents, accepted the condition of being out of place, reconstitutes individual consciousness and joins a collective sense of existing beyond borders. Place inhabits this renewed sense of self, literature enables its expression. It is not only spatial but conceptual terrain these authors traverse as they move. The visual, the aural, the tactile, all sensorial differences are subsumed within this transforming self and distilled into narratives that could not have been imagined by the travelers anywhere other than elsewhere. This collection offers travel writing as theorized, written, and memorialized by authors from across the continent, representing a total of thirteen countries of origin and at least twelve countries of destination.

In Part I, titled "Theories of Travel," two pieces foreground the conceptual framework that charts some of the terrain a number of the contributors to the book navigate. In Part II, "Traveling Fictions," the imaginative worlds recreated by the eight authors take us on journeys sought and feared, obligatory and unexpected, while in Part III, "Memoirs," seven writers reminisce.

To introduce the reader to some of the polemics involved in writing about, from, and outside Africa, two well-known theoretical pieces open the collection: "Afropolitanism" and "Bye, Bye Babar." Including them side by side here serves to foreground some of the controversies in African cultural debates today. Both are directed as much to outsiders as to continental insiders and help us consider ways of repositioning an African-centered world—which this collection of writings about intra-African travel endorses. At a time when exclusion and closed borders are fast becoming the pattern in the global North, one of the thorniest debates taking place on the continent is who counts as African. The two pieces, unequivocally, answer that debate with a resounding acceptance of all forms of being African: multiracial, diasporic, local, individuals who travel and live between African countries, as much as those who shuttle within and out of the continent. In short, Africans at home in more than one national space and unafraid of being in motion. Yet the positions from which the arguments are made by each author differ from one piece to the next. As Parts II and III of the book suggest, it is the journeys of African writers within Africa that matter here. In a defiant tone, the October 2018 issue of *Chimurenga Chronic* asks, "What is the African imagination of a borderless world? What are our ideas on territoriality, borders and movement?"[3]

Portraying African cultures and histories as imbued with mobility, itinerancy, and displacement, "Afropolitanism" by Achille Mbembe asserts that colonization sought to freeze this phenomenon through the erection of borders. Yet the idea of autochthonous people versus nonnatives was the virulent backlash in which the "victim's violence was seldom directed at the actual torturer."[4] This is relevant to Africans writing about intra-African travel because, with the pretense of defending cultures under threat, the resurgence of nativism in some corners is both worrisome and risky. It bears remembering that some "autochthonous" cultures were "invented not by the actual autochthons but by missionaries and settlers."[5] The internecine violence of the recent past in Rwanda is evoked in this collection as a painful reminder by Senegalese Boris Boubacar Diop and Kenyan Yvonne Adhiambo Owuor. The idea of Afropolitanism, unlike Pan-Africanism or negritude, is portrayed as "an aesthetic and a particular poetic of the world . . . refusing on principle any form of victim identity—which does not mean that it is not aware of the injustice and violence inflicted on the continent."[6] Undeterred by borders, Afropolitanism is in fact a revival of intellectual life based in the reality that many African artists and thinkers live outside Africa or in African countries other than those of their birth. "They are developing, sometimes without their knowing it, a transnational culture which [Mbembe] call[s] 'Afropolitan' culture." As a variant of cosmopolitanism, Afropolitan culture requires the kind of cross-pollination that being at home in more than one African country affords.

While the jury is still out on who coined the term, the concept of "Afropolitan" culture was picked up by London-born Ghanaian-Nigerian Taiye Selasi. Her "Bye, Bye Babar,"[7] the first theoretical piece in this book, paints a portrait of what she calls the "Afropolitans," the newest generation of African emigrants. Their genealogy is traced from the mass emigration of young Africans in the 1960s to the unlikely scholarship opportunities ushered in by the political divisions of the Cold War. "Afropolitan" identity is explored as it is being formed, and the author wonders what these new emigrants can look forward to as they dance in European capitals to the beat of Fela Kuti. Whereas the elders claimed a country as home, the younger "Afropolitans" invent a home in bits of claimed heritage, concessions to the affect of where they have lived, racial identities that are more a matter of politics than of pigment.[8]

In response to a talk titled "Translation, Checkpoints, Sovereign Borders," Senegalese philosopher Souleymane Bachir Diagne expressed objections to the idea of travel as a bourgeois activity, one in which everyone partakes in the mobility promised by a globalized and cosmopolitan world.[9] Diagne focused his remarks on a kind of sojourn that precludes airport-hopping, perusing duty-free shops, or the luxury of VIP lounges. Instead, he directed the audience toward contemporary travel that is interrupted after encountering impediments at every turn and checkpoint en route to destination.

After a number of decades of "traveling under his Senegalese passport … [h]is passport, he said, … does not pass ports—it is a devalued document whose bearer is generally to be considered suspect."[10] And this from a respected West African scholar at an Ivy League school who was described by *Le Nouvel Observateur* as one of the fifty thinkers of our time. In his response, Diagne continued his thoughts by linking his travels to those of thousands of other migrants, raising the ghosts of the tragedy at Lampedusa.[11] Two historic losses took place in the Mediterranean in October 2013. On October 3, a fishing boat carrying over five hundred asylum seekers from Eritrea, Ghana, and Somalia capsized, leaving a staggering death toll of over 360; on October 11 a second embarkation, also carrying migrants from the Libyan coast, shipwrecked, causing thirty-four casualties. Both boats sunk near the southern Italian island of Lampedusa. The European Union called for concerted and greater search and rescue efforts, and Operation Mare Nostrum was set in motion by the Italian government to prevent the loss of life of such magnitude.[12] But unseaworthy rafts, of course, are not the only way Africans travel in the twenty-first century.

In *A Stranger's Pose*, Emmanuel Iduma writes, "Photography is a charismatic medium. Sometimes it takes five decades for a photograph to unravel itself." The allusion is to a black-and-white photograph taken in 1963 by the iconic Malian artist Malick Sidibé. A couple dances on a worn floor; she is barefoot and festively dressed, he wears a light-colored suit. Her animated, lifted right limb mirrors his across the few paces between them. Their arched backs, flexed knees convey the pulsating rhythm to which they move—heads in such close proximity that they almost touch. The unity of their bodies, the half-conscious, bashful smiles this image projects, reveals "the fulcrum of desire" Iduma recognizes. On a visit to the celebrated photographer, in Sidibé's latter years as his eyes begin to fail, Iduma realizes that what he might have seen in a glossy magazine growing up in Nigeria becomes more real by the encounter with its creator in Bamako. The photograph unravels. "Photography is like hunting," Sidibé confides to the younger man. In the excerpt of the book included here, Iduma offers us a powerful glimpse of the precision and indeterminacy with which a photographer's, and a hunter's, hand steadies a shot. A glimpse into the exact moment when someone or something in motion is truncated.

In *African Titanics*, Abu Bakr Hamid Khaal tells the story of African migrants attempting to cross the ocean to European shores. Leaving behind their lives in Eritrea, Abdar and Terhas migrate through Northern Africa in hopes of making it to the coast of the Mediterranean and then across to Europe. In the excerpt of the novel included in this book, they prepare to undertake the uncertain journey aboard an African "Titanic." As they wait for traffickers to bring them to the ship, Abdar and Terhas notice what has been left behind by previous travelers in the holding house—letters that never reached their intended recipients, personal objects, and a wall of heartbreaking graffiti. The journey of Abdar and Terhas is not unlike that of thousands of other migrants attempting to make the crossing from Africa into Europe. *African Titanics* keeps some of those stories from drowning, inscribing exodus against oblivion and rendering decipherable what seems opaque. Whose lives are these? one might ask.

In Hassouna Mosbahi's atemporal short story "The Wanderer," the life depicted is that of a Bedouin who has wandered since he was a child, at first attempting to find the precise place of his birth. Yet there is no going back. That place can only be evoked in the stories he grew up listening to, stories of other wanderers on the mysterious paths that headed in different directions, particularly of those who took the Camel Road, including his ancestress Mahbuba. One day he sets off on a journey in the other direction, away from his origins, taking with him nothing but a wanderlust. He embarks on one journey, to the capital and then beyond, to the West, but also on another, a journey into books and the mind. In "Weight of Whispers," Yvonne Adhiambo Owuor spins a harrowing tale of an aid worker hearing a whispered conversation among refugees in a Nairobi camp. Louis Boniface Kuseremane (Bonbon) tries to escape from Rwanda to Europe with his mother, wife, and sister after a missile attack on a plane kills the presidents of his country and of neighboring Burundi. Bonbon had whispered that the perpetrators must be hunted down. The whisper echoes in the form of "hoarse murmurs, eyes white and wide with an arcane fear" and into the confusion of the ensuing genocide. In their flight, the family makes a stop in Kenya, where they check into a first-class hotel, expecting to leave in a few days, only to run into countless setbacks—one more tragic than the next—while attempting to continue on to Europe. As their luck dwindles, readers are taken on a dizzying journey through corruption, cruelty, and indifference, with these members of the Rwandan elite ultimately joining the ranks of the most downtrodden of refugees, where the privileges of social class dissolve.

Nuruddin Farah, for his part, paints a lurid portrait of a retired professor of politics turned Johannesburg restaurateur who develops an infatuation with a young Somali asylee with a mysterious past. James MacPherson, the retiree, pursues Ahmed slowly, learning his life story and offering him different forms of support—starting with free meals from his restaurant and, eventually, a bed in his house. Empathy and curiosity become enmeshed with a powerful tale of sexual intrigue and imprecise relations of power and subjugation, as McPherson relentlessly seeks his prey. In Hawa Jande Golakai's "Fugee," an epidemiologist offers a self-lacerating account of her experience of the Ebola virus as she tries to travel home to Monrovia but runs into immigration troubles that briefly land her in jail on accusations of fraud. Once home, she evokes life in a city in crisis. A different kind of traveler is presented by Chimamanda Ngozi Adichie in "A Private Experience." The story relates the unlikely encounter between two women escaping a violent street riot. One is an urbanite, an Igbo-speaking Christian visiting relatives up in the north during a school vacation, the other a rural market woman whose Hausa-inflected English and headscarf, under other circumstances, would have made her an enemy. Yet only through the help the Muslim woman grants does Chika find her way out of a situation far more dangerous than any pro-democracy rally she has ever attended at university. In the context of Nigeria, traveling between south and north can amount to going as much distance as crossing into a foreign country.

Return to the homeland after the death of a parent lends an elegiac mood to travel. Against the civil war that tore Côte d'Ivoire apart, Véronique Tadjo reveals the inner turmoil of a daughter flying to Abidjan to attend her father's funeral. After years of living elsewhere on the continent, the woman intuits that the country once left behind no longer welcomes but alienates. Guilt about having been absent during the illness and death of Dr. Kouadio Yao permeates her growing sense of shifting identity. In carving out a space of memory for the loss of family, self, and country, Tadjo reminds us of the importance of maintaining filial ties, however tenuous. That is something Hisham Matar's entire oeuvre has grappled with since the publication of his first novel. In an excerpt from his memoir *The Return*, the author finds himself in the Cairo airport waiting for a connecting flight to Tripoli. The Egyptian capital stirs painful memories, as this is where Jaballa Matar was last seen alive before being abducted, flown to Libya, and imprisoned. The absence of his father marks the beginning of the fragile universe Matar's narrative inhabits. Shrouded in the mystery of a disappearance that never lets up, wedged between his mother and his American wife, a photographer, in that airport lounge, Matar threads a measure of continuity despite the persistence of uprootedness.

These are the lives, the sights and sounds, brought to us by the twenty-first-century African travelers in this book, who evoke memories, heritage, sexual desire, and landscapes, and embrace the literature of travel as part of African narrative traditions of self-making. Emmanuel Iduma reconstitutes self through time, Abu Bakr Hamid Khaal describes the displacements of contemporary African selves through migration; Hassouna Mosbahi and Yvonne Adhiambo Owuor develop the same theme; Véronique Tadjo and Hisham Matar write the transformed self on return, intimating an impossible return. These seventeen writers have much to say about African countries other than their own, or, as in the case of "A Private Experience," about nations with sharp divisions between north and south. When crossing national borders, voluntarily or not, on journeys to neighboring states or further afield, these authors see past hackneyed images, and their glances capture, in narrative, realities that defy definition. Writing is sometimes at its best when authors make this sense of estrangement and discomfort a source from which cultural translation emanates. Most pieces in the book cohere into literary renditions that could have been written only from the position of an outsider who isn't entirely nonnative, someone who locates in shifting ground the only certainty—"when the object of analysis [is] out of place . . . [and the writer pursues a] continuous questioning of the geographies and traditions that authorize it."[13]

The circulation of people, art, commodities, ideas, and treasures within and beyond Africa has a long history. This collection invites readers to follow the steps taken by creative artists in search of literary routes leading to the pulse of a contemporary literature of travel. The journeys depicted involve arrivals and departures, passports, checkpoints, and, at times, unintended destinations, all within the continent. The subject of travel writing in Africa is old but the genre has been gaining in popularity if we consider the proliferating blogs dedicated to it[14] as well as an expanding list of titles.[15] The seventeen authors included here affirm, and root themselves in, the realities of a continent aware of the world in the offing while standing ready to find their gravitational center within their own. What does this repositioning of an Africa-centered world tell us?

A provocatively named website, Africa Is a Country,[16] treats the continent, comprising fifty-four states, more than two thousand languages, and a billion inhabitants, as being too vast, too intricate, and too diverse to fit into any simplistic label. This book offers the possibility of looking at Africa through the eyes of artists for whom national, linguistic, and cultural boundaries blur—if not into the expansiveness of a Pan-Africanist contour, at least in contempt of cartographies of old, those drawn from another center. In addition to calling themselves citizens of discrete countries within the diversity afforded by societies such as Nigeria, Tunisia, South Africa, or Cameroon, these theorists, fiction writers, and memorialists traverse cultural spaces of their own making, borrow with abandon, defy nomenclature—and will not be contained by the deceptively simple designation "African." Furthermore, while some would embrace it, others might reject the presumption of a shared "Africanity." And yet in their differences and commonalities, unsurprisingly, all cross into the terrain that Gikandi reminds us is the obligatory destination of creative writers: "to be out of place in the world."

Against a presumption of single origin, this book is organized around the argument that these African travelers hold a particular vision of the cultural moment, dynamic and inchoate because it remains in the making. The narratives, leading in many directions, transgress generic, spatial, religious, and sexual boundaries. But being African centered requires making a choice: privileging the African imagination, transcending facile assumptions, and proposing new ideas about territoriality, borders, and bodies in movement. The focus is within, not outside Africa, in contrast to "an enormous amount of contemporary African writing—sometimes it seems like most of it—which is concerned with the experiences of emigration to Europe or North America, dealing both with the often extreme difficulties of Africans establishing themselves abroad and with the process of a growing Afro- or cosmopolitanism. [This book] is also restricted to twenty-first-century writing."[17] Generational shifts, say from Chinua Achebe to Chimamanda Ngozi Adichie, Ngugi wa Thiong'o to Binyavanga Wainaina, Esk' ia Mphahlele to Phaswane Mpe, have given way to a different sense of social and literary values. "Africa" is a name under which the amalgamation of fifty-four states, two thousand languages, and a billion people occurs—and through which, for far too many, all these become indistinct from one another. African writers are transnational by virtue of their pluralistic societies and their wealth of languages, by the choices they make against internal and external pressures to conform to established boundaries.

Once one might have embraced the term "African" to reject colonially demarcated geographical borders, stereotypes endorsed by European travel literature, or neocolonial allegiances built through the rapaciousness of one-party states in which dissent would be crushed summarily. Since the publication of Chinua Achebe's classic *Things Fall Apart* (1959), where the inner fissures of an Igbo village prior to the arrival of British missionaries are evoked, literature in Africa has evolved independently of the legacy bestowed by colonialist writing. If Joseph Conrad gave Europe the enigmatic *Heart of Darkness*, Ama Ata Aidoo returned the favor when she replied by means of a querulous love letter to her fellow Pan-Africanists, *Our Sister Killjoy*. In that hybrid narrative, Aidoo dissects the corpse Europe became against the backdrop of the Berlin Conference and through an unflinching forensic gaze cuts open the wounds of the "brain drain" that C. L. R. James diagnosed as one of the lingering and deepest tragedies of postindependence.[18]

But the authors in this book are not concerned principally with colonialism, nor with creating a counternarrative to the notion of Africa as a country. All travel depicted is intra-African, and the connections from one piece to the next rest much less on having reached a consensus regarding what Africa *is* than on what it *is not*. The pieces are put in conversation with one another through the conviction that the center around which the traveling pivots is anchored in the distinct, if not fully apprehensible, dynamic realities of the countries on which each writer's gaze rests. Even as the gaze is that of a stranger, it is endowed with the emotional acuity of someone for whom the encounter's translation of being out of place *is* home—for these authors writing *is* home. The awareness of being estranged, the distinct foreignness that displacement instills, nudges these seventeen writers toward language as a map onto which the peculiarity of encounters with other strangers are drawn.

To return to the piece on photography by Emmanuel Iduma, the effect of travel on perception tells us much about a viewer's position in space. What has been observed from afar seldom matches its actual image, what has been learned through reference often differs from firsthand experience. Travel sears the distance between subject and object. What was once remote becomes tangible as the subject shifts positions. What if a traveler's eyes met the unknown with the clarity of vision only movement permits—blurring the focus, recalibrating, blending distinctions, lowering the eyelid just enough to apprehend that indeterminacy which unbounding oneself of the familiar brings? These are the strivings of the new African literature of travel presented here. Free of routines, surrounded by the music of strange sounds, tasting food whose novelty is not lost on the tongue, these travelers, their senses alert, imaginations avid, render Africa anew with the precision that comes from knowing one's place in the world. Surrendering atavistic understandings of self and capturing landscapes through restless eyes, these seventeen writers unravel in motion.

The Passport That Does Not Pass Ports asks readers to question certain myths about the conditions of journeying for Africans—be they about the means through which travel occurs or the utopian presumption that ultramobility will become the norm any time soon. Beyond diversity, however, these authors offer an altered image of the center and the certainty of having reframed the punctum. In the twenty-first century, to travel in and write about Africa requires the vision of those for whom being abroad and being at home entail a certain mental borderlessness, gaze opening inward to reflect and commit to the act of seeing and inscribing others—no matter the distance.

NOTES

1. Maureen Moynagh, "Afropolitan Travels: Discovering Home and the World in Africa," in *New Directions in Travel Writing*, edited by Julia Kuehn and Paul Smethurst (New York:

Palgrave Macmillan, 2015), 281–296.

2. Simon Gikandi, "Introduction: Another Way in the World," *PMLA* 131.5 (2016): 1198.

3. "On Circulations and the African Imagination of a Borderless World," *Chronic Chimurenga*, October (2018): 2.

4. Achille Mbembe, "Afropolitanism," translated by Laurent Chauvet, in *Africa Remix: Contemporary Art of a Continent*," edited by Njami Simon and Lucy Durán (Ostfiderm, Germany: Hatje Cantz, 2005), 28.

5. Ibid.

6. Ibid.

7. Carli Coetzee raises an intriguing possible link between this title and the collection *Should We Burn Babar?* by Herbert R. Kohl. In that book, Kohl derides "the green-suited elephant, Babar, as a celebratory and Eurocentric narrative of assimilation." See Carli Coetzee, "Afropolitanism: Reboot," *Journal of African Cultural Studies* 28.1 (2016): 101–103. In contrast to Mbembe's philosophical gravitas in his piece on the subject, Selasi's lighthearted tone has led a number of critics to accuse her of turning African identity into a commodity.

8. For further discussion on "Afropolitanism," see the section titled "Contemporary Conversations" in *Journal of African Cultural Studies* 28.1 (2016). Half the issue is devoted to the controversy surrounding the embracing or vehement rejection of the term.

9. Http://africasacountry.com.

10. Ibid.

11. Sarah Stillman, "Lampedusa's Migrant Tragedy, and Ours," *New Yorker*, October 10, 2013, http://www.newyorker.com.

12. Ibid.

13. Gikandi, "Introduction," 1998.

14. Ktravula, Invisible Borders, MzansiGirl, the Pilgrimages Project launched by the Chinua Achebe Center for African Writers and Artists at Bard College in collaboration with Chimurenga, Kwani Trust and Kachifo, DynamicAfrica, Pelo Awufeso's Waka-About, and Akinmade, among others.

15. Travel writing by African writers in the continent of Africa abounds. See Tabish Khair, Martin Leer, Justin D. Edwards, and Hannah Ziadeh, eds., *Other Routes: 1500 Years of African and Asian Travel Writing* (Bloomington: Indiana University Press, 2006); Olaudah Equiano, *The Interesting Narrative of the Life of Olaudah Equiano, or Gustavus Vassa, the African* (1789; London: Heinemann, 1989); Leo Africanus, *The History and Description of Africa: And of the Notable Things Therein Contained* (1896; Cambridge: Cambridge University Press, 2010); Edward W. Blyden, *From West Africa to Palestine.* (1873; Freetown,

Sierra Leone); Nnamdi Azikiwe, *My Odyssey: An Autobiography* (London: C. Hurst, 1970); Tété-Michel Kpomassie, *An African in Greenland* (New York: NYRB Classics, 2001); Maureen Stone, *Black Woman Walking: A Different Experience of World Travel* (Bournemouth: BeaGay Publications, 2002); Aedín Ní Loingsigh, *Postcolonial Eyes: Intercontinental Travel in Francophone African Literature* (Liverpool: Liverpool University Press, 2009); Ivan Vladislavić, *Portrait with Keys: The City of Johannesburg Unlocked* (New York: W.W. Norton, 2009); Sihle Khumalo, *Heart of Africa: Centre of My Gravity* (Cape Town: Umuzzi, 2009); Sihle Khumalo, *Dark Continent, My Black Arse* (Johannesburg: Penguin Random House South Africa, 2010); Sihle Khumalo, *Almost Sleeping My Way to Timbuktu* (Cape Town: Umuzzi, 2013); Kofi Akpabli, *A Sense of Savannah: Tales of a Friendly Walk through Northern Ghana* (Accra: TREC, 2011); Kofi Akpabli, *Tickling the Ghanaian: Encounters with Contemporary Culture* (Accra: TREC, 2011); Noo Saro-Wiwa, *Looking for Transwonderland: Travels through Nigeria* (Berkeley: Soft Skull Press, 2012); Binyavanga Wainaina, *One Day I Will Write about This Place: A Memoir* (Minneapolis: Graywolf Press, 2012); Daniel Metcalfe, *Blue Dahlia, Black Gold: A Journey into Angola* (London: Hutchinson, 2013); Pelu Awofeso, *Tour of Duty: Journeys around Nigeria* (Torrance: Homestead Publishing, 2013); Teju Cole, "Water Has No Enemy," *Granta 124: Travel*, 6 August 2013; Teju Cole, *Every Day Is for the Thief* (New York: Random House 2015); Emmanuel Iduma, *A Stranger's Pose* (London: Cassava Republic, 2018); Lerato Mogoatlhe, *Vagabond Wandering through Africa on Faith* (Johannesburg: Jacana Media, 2018).

16. Self-described as "one of the leading intellectual voices in the African online media sphere" (http://africasacountry.com/).

17. For these observations I thank an anonymous external reviewer of this book.

18. C. L. R. James, *Nkrumah and the Ghana Revolution* (Westport, CT: L. Hill, 1977).

Theories of Travel

1

Bye, Bye Babar

Taiye Selasi

t's moments to midnight on Thursday night at Medicine Bar in London. Zak, boy-genius DJ, is spinning a Fela Kuti remix. The little downstairs dance floor swells with smiling, sweating men and women fusing hip-hop dance moves with a funky sort of djembe. The women show off enormous afros, tiny T-shirts, gaps in teeth; the men those incredible torsos unique to and common on African coastlines. The whole scene speaks of the Cultural Hybrid: kente cloth worn over low-waisted jeans; "African Lady" over Ludacris bass lines; London meets Lagos meets Durban meets Dakar. Even the DJ is an ethnic fusion: Nigerian and Romanian; fair, fearless leader; bobbing his head as the crowd reacts to a sample of "Sweet Mother."

Were you to ask any of these beautiful, brown-skinned people that basic question—"Where are you from?"—you'd get no single answer from a single smiling dancer. This one lives in London but was raised in Toronto and born in Accra; that one works in Lagos but grew up in Houston, Texas. "Home" for this lot is many things: where their parents are from; where they go for vacation; where they went to school; where they see old friends; where they live (or live this year).

Like so many African young people working and living in cities around the globe, they belong to no single geography, but feel at home in many.

They (read: we) are Afropolitans—the newest generation of African emigrants, coming soon or collected already at a law firm/chem lab/jazz lounge near you. You'll know us by our funny blend of London fashion, New York jargon, African ethics, and academic successes. Some of us are ethnic mixes, e.g., Ghanaian and Canadian, Nigerian and Swiss; others merely cultural mutts: American accent, European affect, African ethos. Most of us are multilingual: in addition to English and a Romance language or two, we understand some indigenous tongue and speak a few urban vernaculars. There is at least one place on The African Continent to which we tie our sense of self: be it a nation-state (Ethiopia), a city (Ibadan), or an auntie's kitchen. Then there's the G8 city or two (or three) that we know like the backs of our hands, and the various institutions that know us for our famed focus. We are Afropolitans: not citizens, but Africans, of the world.

It isn't hard to trace our genealogy. Starting in the 60s, the young, gifted, and broke left Africa in pursuit of higher education and happiness abroad. A study conducted in 1999 estimated that between 1960 and 1975 around 27,000 highly skilled Africans left the Continent for the West. Between 1975 and 1984, the number shot to 40,000 and then doubled again by 1987, representing about 30% of Africa's highly skilled manpower. Unsurprisingly, the most popular destinations for these emigrants included Canada, Britain, and the United States, but Cold War politics produced unlikely scholarship opportunities in Eastern Bloc countries like Poland, as well.

Some three decades later this scattered tribe of pharmacists, physicists, physicians (and the odd polygamist) has set up camp around the globe. The caricatures are familiar. The Nigerian physics professor with faux-Coogi sweater; the Kenyan marathonist with long legs and rolled r's; the heavyset Gambian braiding hair in a house that smells of burnt Kanekalon. Even those unacquainted with synthetic extensions can conjure an image of the African immigrant with only the slightest of pop culture promptings: Eddie Murphy's "Hello, Babar." But somewhere between the 1988 release of *Coming to America* and the 2001 crowning of a Nigerian Miss World, the general image of young Africans in the West transmorphed from goofy to gorgeous. Leaving off the painful question of cultural condescension in that beloved film, one wonders what happened in the years between Prince Akeem and Queen Agbani?

One answer is: adolescence. The Africans that left Africa between 1960 and 1975 had children, and most, overseas. Some of us were bred on African shores then shipped to the West for higher education; others born in much colder climates and sent home for cultural re-indoctrination. Either way, we spent the 80s chasing after accolades, eating fufu at family parties, and listening to adults argue politics. By the turn of the century (the recent one), we were matching our parents in number of degrees, and/or achieving things our "people," in the grand sense, only dreamed of. This new demographic—dispersed across Brixton, Bethesda, Boston, Berlin—has come of age in the 21st century, redefining what it means to be African. Where our parents sought safety in traditional professions like doctoring, lawyering, banking, engineering, we are branching into fields like media, politics, music, venture capital, design. Nor are we shy about expressing our African influences (such as they are) in our work. Artists such as Keziah Jones, *Trace* founder and editor Claude Gruzintsky, architect David Adjaye, novelist Chimamanda Adichie—all exemplify what Gruzintsky calls the "21st-century African."

What distinguishes this lot and its like (in the West and at home) is a willingness to complicate Africa—namely, to engage with, critique, and celebrate the parts of Africa that mean most to them. Perhaps what most typifies the Afropolitan consciousness is the refusal to oversimplify, the effort to understand what is ailing in Africa alongside the desire to honor what is wonderful, unique. Rather than essentialising the geographical entity, we seek to comprehend the cultural complexity; to honor the intellectual and spiritual legacy; and to sustain our parents' cultures.

For us, being African must mean something. The media's portrayals (war, hunger) won't do. Neither will the New World trope of bumbling, blue-black doctor. Most of us grew up aware of "being from" a blighted place, of having last names from countries which are linked to lack, corruption. Few of us escaped those nasty "booty-scratcher" epithets, and fewer still that sense of shame when visiting paternal villages. Whether we were ashamed of ourselves for not knowing more about our parents' culture, or ashamed of that culture for not being more "advanced," can be unclear. What is manifest is the extent to which the modern adolescent African is tasked to forge a sense of self from wildly disparate sources. You'd never know it looking at those dapper lawyers in global firms, but most were once supremely self-conscious of being so "in between." Brown-skinned without a bedrock sense of "blackness," on the one hand, and often teased by African family members for "acting white" on the other—the baby-Afropolitan can get what I call "lost in transnation."

Ultimately, the Afropolitan must form an identity along at least three dimensions: national, racial, cultural—with subtle tensions in between. While our parents can claim one country as home, we must define our relationship to the places we live; how British or American we are (or act) is in part a matter of affect. Often unconsciously, and over time, we choose which bits of a national identity (from passport to pronunciation) we internalize as central to our personalities. So, too, the way we see our race—whether black or biracial or none of the above—is a question of politics, rather than pigment; not all of us claim to be black. Often this relates to the way we were raised, whether proximate to other brown people (e.g., black Americans) or removed. Finally, how we conceive of race will accord with where we locate ourselves in the history that produced "blackness" and the political processes that continue to shape it.

Then there is that deep abyss of Culture, ill-defined at best. One must decide what comprises "African culture" beyond pepper soup and filial piety. The project can be utterly baffling—whether one lives in an African country or not. But the process is enriching, in that it expands one's basic perspective on nation and selfhood. If nothing else, the Afropolitan knows that nothing is neatly black or white; that to "be" anything is a matter of being sure of who you are uniquely. To "be" Nigerian is to belong to a passionate nation; to be Yoruba, to be heir to a spiritual depth; to be American, to ascribe to a cultural breadth; to be British, to pass customs quickly. That is, this is what it means for me—and that is the Afropolitan privilege. The acceptance of complexity common to most African cultures is not lost on her prodigals. Without that intrinsically multidimensional thinking, we could not make sense of ourselves.

And if it all sounds a little self-congratulatory, a little "aren't-we-the-coolest-damn-people-on-earth?"—I say: yes it is, necessarily. It is high time the African stood up. There is nothing perfect in this formulation; for all our Adjayes and Adichies, there is a brain drain back home. Most Afropolitans could serve Africa better in Africa than at Medicine Bar on Thursdays. To be fair, a fair number of African professionals are returning, and there is consciousness among the ones who remain, an acute awareness among this brood of too-cool-for-schools that there's work to be done. There are those among us who wonder to the point of weeping: where next, Africa? When will the scattered tribes return? When will the talent repatriate? What lifestyles await young professionals at home? How to invest in Africa's future? The prospects can seem grim at times. The answers aren't forthcoming. But if there was ever a group who could figure it out, it is this one, unafraid of the questions.

Afropolitanism

Achille Mbembe

Whether it is about literature, philosophy, or the arts, African discourse has been dominated, for almost a century, by three politico-intellectual paradigms that, as it happened, were not mutually exclusive.

First, there were a number of variations of anticolonial nationalism. They had a deep influence in the spheres of culture, politics, economics, and even religion. Second, there were various reinterpretations of Marxism from which many forms of "African socialism" derived. Finally, there was a pan-African sphere of influence that gave special place to two types of solidarity—a racial and transnational solidarity, and an international and anti-imperialist solidarity.

At the beginning of the twenty-first century, we can say that this intellectual pattern has not fundamentally changed even if, behind the scenes, important social and cultural reconfigurations are in progress. The gap between the real life of societies, on the one hand, and the intellectual tools by means of which societies understand their future, on the other, is not without risk for thought and culture. The three politico-intellectual paradigms have indeed become institutionalised

Translated from the French by Laurent Chauvet. Reprinted with permission from Achille Mbembe. All rights reserved.

and ossified to such a degree that, today, they no longer make it possible to analyse transformations in process with the slightest bit of credibility. The institutions embodying these paradigms operate, almost without exception, like "guaranteed incomes." Moreover, they hinder the renewal of cultural criticism and artistic and philosophical creativity, and reduce our ability to contribute to contemporary thought on culture and democracy.

Worlds in Movement

Of all the reconfigurations in progress, two in particular could weigh heavily on the cultural life as well as aesthetic and political creativity of the coming years. First of all, there are those that deal with new answers to the question "Who is African and who is not?"

For many, to be "African" is to be "black" and therefore "not white," with the degree of authenticity being measured on the scale of raw racial difference. Thus, all sorts of people have a link with or, simply, something to do with Africa—something that gives them the right ipso facto to lay claim to "African citizenship." There are, naturally, those called Negroes. They were born and live in African states, making up their nationals. Yet if Negro Africans form the majority of the population in Africa, they are neither the sole inhabitants nor the sole producers of art and culture of the continent.

From Asia, the Middle East, and Europe, other population groups have settled in various parts of the continent in various periods of history, and for various reasons. Some came as conquerors, traders, or missionaries, like the Arabs and Europeans. Fleeing all sorts of misfortune, seeking to escape persecution, simply filled with the hope for a peaceful life, or driven by their thirst for wealth, others settled under more or less tragic historical circumstances, like the Afrikaners and the Jews. Yet others, who came essentially as servile labor, settled down and started families in the context of labor migration, like the Malays, Indians, and Chinese in southern Africa. More recently, Lebanese, Syrians, Indo-Pakistanis, and some hundreds or thousands of Chinese have made an appearance. They all arrived with their different languages, customs, eating habits, clothing fashions, ways of praying—in other words, their ways of being and doing. Today, the relations between these various diasporas and their societies of origin are complex. Many of their members see themselves as full-fledged Africans, even if they also belong somewhere else.

While Africa has for long been a destination for all sorts of population move-ments and cultural flows, the continent has also, for centuries, been a point of departure to other regions of the world. This ancient process of dispersal took place on horseback throughout what is usually referred to as modern times, and followed the three routes of the Sahara, the Atlantic Ocean, and the Indian Ocean. The creation of Negro diasporas in the New World, for example, is the result of such a dispersal. Slavery, which as we know not only involved the European-American world but also the Arab-Asian world, played a decisive role in this process. As a result, traces of Africa cover the face of the capitalist and Islamic worlds from one end to the other. In addition to the forced migrations of the previous centuries, there have also been migrations driven by colonisation. Today, millions of people of African origin are citizens of various countries of the world.

When discussion arises about aesthetic creativity in contemporary Africa, and even knowing who and what is "African," the political and cultural critics tend to pass over in silence this historical phenomenon of worlds in movement.

Seen from the viewpoint of Africa, the worlds-in-movement phenomenon has at least two sides: that of dispersion, as already mentioned, and that of immersion. Historically, the dispersal of populations and cultures was not just about foreigners coming to settle in our backyard. In fact, the precolonial history of African societies was a history of people in perpetual movement throughout the continent. It is a history of colliding cultures, caught in the maelstrom of war, invasion, migration, intermarriage, of various religions we make our own, of techniques we exchange, and of goods we trade. The cultural history of the continent can hardly be under-stood outside the paradigm of itinerancy, mobility, and displacement.

It is this very culture of mobility that colonisation once endeavored to freeze through the modern institution of borders. Recalling the history of itinerancy and mobility means talking about mixing, blending, and superimposing. In opposition to the fundamentalists preaching "custom" and "autochthony," we can go as far as to assert that, in fact, what we call "tradition" does not exist. Whether one is talking of Islam, Christianity, ways of dressing, trading, speaking, or even eating, none has survived the bulldozer of miscegenation and vernacularisation. This was the case well before colonisation. There is, indeed, a precolonial African modernity that has not yet been taken into account in contemporary creativity.

The other aspect of the worlds-in-movement phenomenon is immersion. It affected in various degrees the minorities that, coming from far, ended up settling and starting families on the continent. Over time, links with their countries of origin (whether European or Asian) became remarkably complex. Through contact with a new geography, climate, and people, they became cultural hybrids even though, because of colonisation, Euro-Africans in particular continued to aspire to racial supremacy, and to mark their difference from and even their contempt for anything "African" or "indigenous." This is very much the case with the Afrikaners, whose name even means "Africans." We find the same ambivalence among Indians, and even the Lebanese and Syrians. Most of them express themselves in the local languages, know and even practice certain national customs, yet live in relatively closed communities and do not marry outside of them.

Thus, it is not simply that a part of African history lies somewhere else, outside Africa. It is also that a history of the rest of the world, of which we are inevitably the actors and guardians, is present on the continent. Our way of belonging to the world, of being in the world and inhabiting it, has always been marked by, if not cultural mixing, then at least the interweaving of worlds, in a slow and sometimes incoherent dance with forms and signs that we have not been able to choose freely, but which we have succeeded, as best we can, in domesticating and putting at our disposal.

Awareness of the interweaving of the here and there, the presence of the elsewhere in the here and vice versa, the relativisation of primary roots and memberships and the way of embracing, with full knowledge of the facts, strangeness, foreignness, and remoteness, the ability to recognise one's face in that of a foreigner and make the most of the traces of remoteness in closeness, to domesticate the unfamiliar, to work with what seem to be opposites—it is this cultural, historical, and aesthetic sensitivity that underlies the term "Afropolitanism."

The Nativistic Reflex

The second type of ongoing reconfiguration has to do with the rise in power of the nativistic reflex. In its mild form, nativism appears as an ideology glorifying differences and diversity, and fighting to safeguard customs and identities perceived as threatened. According to nativistic logic, identities and political struggles are founded on the basis of a distinction between "those who are from here" (autochthons) and "those who came from outside" (nonnatives). Nativists forget that, in their stereotyped forms, the customs and traditions to which they claim to adhere were often invented not by the actual autochthons, but by missionaries and settlers.

Thus, during the second half of the century, a form of bio-racism (autochthons vs. nonnatives) appeared almost everywhere on the continent, politically nurtured by a particular idea of victimisation and resentment. As is often the case, the victim's violence was seldom directed at the actual torturer. Almost every time, the victim turns against an imaginary torturer who, coincidentally, always happens to be weaker, that is, another victim who often has nothing to do with the original wound. This can be seen in many countries, and not only in Africa, where a genocidal impulse always inhabits victimisation ideologies. These create a culture of hatred, with an incredible power of destruction, as we have seen in Rwanda and elsewhere.

Afropolitanism is not the same as Pan-Africanism or negritude. Afropolitanism is an aesthetic and a particular poetic of the world. It is a way of being in the world, refusing on principle any form of victim identity—which does not mean that it is not aware of the injustice and violence inflicted on the continent and its people by the law of the world. It is also a political and cultural stance in relation to the nation, to race, and to the issue of difference in general. Insofar as African states are pure (and, what is more, recent) inventions, there is, strictly speaking, nothing in their essence that can force us to worship them—which does not mean that we are indifferent to their fate.

As for African nationalism, it represented originally a powerful utopia with an unlimited insurrectionary power—a temptation for self-understanding, for facing the world with dignity, as beings endowed with a human face. But as soon as nationalism turned into the official ideology of a state become predator, it lost any ethical heart, and became a demon "who roams at night and flees the light of day." It is this human face and human figure that nationalism and nativism keep coming up against. Racial solidarity as advocated by Pan-Africanism does not escape from these dilemmas. As soon as contemporary Africa awakens to the forms of multiplicity (including racial multiplicity) that are constituents of its identity, rejecting the continent on the basis of a form of Negro solidarity alone becomes untenable. Moreover, how can we not see that this so-called solidarity is deeply harmed by the way in which the violence of brothers against brothers, and the violence of brothers against mothers and sisters, have occurred since the end of direct colonisation?

Broad-Mindedness

Thus we need to move on to something else if we want to revive intellectual life in Africa and, at the same time, the possibilities of an art, a philosophy, an aesthetics that can say something new and meaningful to the world in general. Today, many Africans live outside Africa. Others have decided of their own accord to live on the continent but not necessarily in their countries of birth. More so, many of them have had the opportunity to experience several worlds and, in fact, have not stopped coming and going, developing an invaluable wealth of perception and sensitivity in the course of these movements. These are usually people who can express themselves in more than one language. They are developing, sometimes without their knowing it, a transnational culture that I call "Afropolitan" culture.

Among them, we find many professionals who, in their daily business, must continually measure up against not the village next door, but the world at large. Such "broad-mindedness" is found more deeply still among a great number of artists, musicians and composers, writers, poets, painters—workers of the mind who have been aware since the beginning of the postcolonial era. On another level, a small number of metropolises can be counted as "Afropolitan." In West Africa, Dakar and Abidjan played this role during the second half of the twentieth century. The Senegalese capital represented the cultural counterpart of Abidjan, the business centre of the subregion. Today, Abidjan is unfortunately undermined by the cancer of nativism. In East Africa, the position was once held by Nairobi, business centre and the regional seat of several international institutions.

But the centre of Afropolitanism par excellence is, nowadays, Johannesburg in South Africa. In this metropolis built on brutal history, a new form of African modernity is developing. It is a modernity that has little to do with what we have known up to now. Johannesburg feeds on multiple racial legacies, a vibrant economy, a liberal democracy, a culture of consumerism that partakes directly in the flows of globalisation. It is where an ethic of tolerance is being created, likely to revive African aesthetic and cultural creativity, in the same way as Harlem or New Orleans once did in the United States.

Traveling Fictions 2

The Wanderer

Hassouna Mosbahi

He betrayed his Bedouin forbears in everything except their love of nomadic wandering. When he was a child his mother used to point to the broad plains and the bare hills. "I gave birth to you over there," she would say.

He gazed at her long, pale face, her slender body, and her light green wraparound: she was like an olive tree in a season of drought.

"Whereabouts exactly?" he asked.

She always pointed at the plains and the hills and repeated her words as if she had not heard the question.

"I gave birth to you over there."

He too looked at the distant horizon, where the hills seemed to be like waves or clouds of thick, grey dust. He clung to her dress.

"But where exactly?" he pleaded. "Tell me, whereabouts exactly."

"I can't remember exactly," she said, as if talking to herself. "You know, we had to move camp from time to time, depending on the time of the year. But you were born at the beginning of autumn. I think I gave birth to you near the great Camel olive

---

"The Wanderer," copyright © by Hassouna Mosbahi, translated and abridged from the Arabic by Peter Clark.

tree, but no . . . no, I think it was in the week of the afreets. At the foot of the Red Mountain. Or maybe . . . Oh, I've forgotten. Memory is as faithless as a man, my boy."

He spent days wandering over the plain and in the hills looking for the place where he had first seen light. He despaired of ever finding it, went back to his mother, and plucked at her dress.

"Where was it exactly?" he insisted. "Exactly where?"

On one particular autumn day when the flies were buzzing and the air was heavy with the yellow dust that had been brought in by the scorching winds from the south, his mother got fed up with his questions, shook a stick in his face, and shouted at him.

"Just stop asking questions, wretched child," she said, "or your head will meet this stick. I've told you a thousand times, I can't remember. I simply can't remember. Haven't you heard what I said?"

He curled up in a corner, trembling. She stood there, her bosom heaving. Beads of sweat glistened on her long, pale face. She tossed the stick aside.

"I can't remember the spot," she said, somewhat distracted. "But I do remember it was a difficult birth, and that when I was in labour Salim al-Ahmar was killed by a bomb left behind by the Germans during the war, and that a lot of donkeys and other animals died from some disease nobody knew anything about."

He was scared of the thick stick and shaken by the tales of disaster his mother had told so briskly. He did not dare ask any more questions. But they stayed in his mind as he sat reciting the Koran to his feeble one-eyed teacher. He used to spend half the day wandering over the plain. He climbed up the foothills of the mountains, and wandered aimlessly through the parched, sandy wadis looking for some clue to the place of his birth. One day, exhausted, he stretched out in the shade of the Camel olive tree and turned things over in his mind. Thoughts galloped through his mind like horses at the races held to celebrate weddings. By sunset he had come to the conclusion that all things around him, great and small, were also totally unaware of their place of birth. They gave the question no importance whatsoever. All that concerned them was moving on. People were on the go all the time. In times of heat and in times of cold. On mountains and in deserts. At night and in the daytime. They ate as they moved on. They sang as they moved on. They quarrelled as they moved on. Anything happened as they were on the move or were preparing to be on the move. His cousin Zainab gave birth when she was gathering corn in the middle of the afternoon. And Shaykh al-Hudhaili dropped dead as he was eating couscous and talking to guests. And Mabruk fell in love with Salima from the Masa'id tribe on his way back from some long journey to the north. And Hajj Salih, so it was said, walked to the holy city of Mecca and died there after having completed the rites of the pilgrimage. They were always on the move, like the wind. They were on the move as they sniffed the air for the smell of water or of fresh pastureland, like wolves sniffing out the scent of sheep. As his father used to say, "We're Bedouin. We only cease being on the move when we're thrown into the grave."

From then on he no longer thought about the place of his birth. But he wandered in his imagination, dreaming of the moment when he could set off beyond the mountains and return with wondrous tales of maids with shocks of fine hair who wandered barefoot through gardens of jasmine irrigated by rivers of milk and pure honey.

He then became fascinated by the tracks left by herds of goats in the hills, or the footprints of the shepherds in the wadis. Or the paths that led through the olive groves, tracks that spread out and joined up like a spider's web. But most of the tracks that stimulated his imagination were those that led far away, beyond the mountains. There another world began, a world his soul yearned for.

These tracks all had names, like human beings. The track that headed south was called the Long Road because it stretched out until it was lost in the far distance. From this track on cold winter days came beggars wrapped in light-coloured, shabby burnouses. They looked like pathetic donkeys in a state of collapse. They wandered through our village and to the rhythm of tambourines chanted praise to God, with the aim of obtaining alms from the people.

At sunset people brought them bowls of couscous and meat. All night you could hear them, their voices rising and falling with the sighing of the wind and the beat of the tambourines.

The path that headed eastwards was called the Red Road, from the colour of the soil. From this track came men with tall, gaunt frames, with faces as sharp as knives, sporting proud moustaches. They had tiny suspicious eyes, full of cunning. People would whisper to each other that they were thieves from the Mahafiz tribe who stole animals from the western tribes to sell in the markets of the east after dyeing them a different colour.

The path that headed northwards was called the Snakes' Road because of the number of poisonous snakes that could be found in the sulphurous crannies in hills crossed only by the bold and determined. Along this path came scowling tar merchants riding ugly mules. He loathed them and used to hide in a haystack as soon as he saw them coming. He once dreamed that they took him through the village tarred and naked, cracking their whips on his skull, with people around clapping and singing as if they were at the wedding.

———————

But the most famous path was the Camel Road. First it led slowly and uncertainly through the wadis to the west of the village. It then suddenly rose, like a horse rearing its head in preparation for a fight. It climbed into the hills that divided their tribe from the Masa'id tribe. It then became lost in the black wilderness of the Empty Canyon. It derived its name from the fact that it was the camel caravan route to and from the west. In times of drought and hardship the caravans would fill the road with their cries and songs day and night. As they headed west he would climb up the lofty Camel olive tree. From its branches he would watch the caravan as it disappeared and became a dark blotch beneath a cloud of dust. That blotch remained in the middle of nowhere, apparently motionless, and then disappeared completely in that stretch of land called the Empty Canyon. It would leave the memory of its heavy groaning movements. People told strange and scary stories about the Camel Road. They said it was haunted by ghouls and spirits. Shaykh al-Ashhab, who was always on the move, used to tell various stories, full of detail, tales that could frighten old and young alike.

"Listen, my friends," one story started. "You know that from my youth I have travelled day and night, summer and winter. You know that I fear none but God the All-Knowing, the All-Capable. But I have unquestionably encountered fear more than once on the Camel Road. Yes, only on the Camel Road, and on no other road at all."

Shaykh al-Ashhab cleared his throat. His eyes scoured the horizon for a few minutes.

"One moonlit night, my friends," he resumed, "I was traversing the Empty Canyon. My mind was calm and I was moving slowly. Now and then I hummed some song. Then I sensed I heard the sound of a human in great distress. I stopped and listened carefully. There was no sound in this wilderness but the rustle of leaves and the rush of the wind. I murmured a prayer against Satan and continued my journey. Then a few paces on I heard a woman crying piteously for help.

"'God, please do not kill me. Brother, do not make my little ones orphans.'

"I took my knife out and had my stick in my hand. Cautiously I headed in the direction of the voice. Suddenly I heard the woman's cry for help again. But this time it came from another direction. I went towards it. The cry came again but I could not work out where it was coming from. I stopped in the middle of the track, my stick raised high. I stayed like that for some time, listening for anything apart from the beating of my own heart. I moved again, and again the woman's voice was quite near me. It seemed to be between my feet.

"'Dear God, please do not kill me. Brother, do not make my little ones orphans.'

"It is not easy, my friends, to describe my feelings during those moments. Fear can, you know, blind a man and take his mind away. I recall only that I ran straight ahead, the woman's cries now between my feet, now behind me, now in front of me, to my left, to my right. She did not give up until a Masa'id dog started barking."

Shaykh al-Ashhab fell silent. He stared at the silent faces of the men around him.

"On one other occasion," he went on, "it was broad daylight, yes, in the middle of the day; I was making my way down the Wolves' Slope and suddenly came upon a woman of the most unparalleled beauty. Friends, she was as fair as the full moon. She was walking along, her face uncovered, her dark tresses cascading to her waist. She hastened to be right at my side.

"'Are you of mankind, or are you a djinn?' I asked.

"'I am of mankind, one of the best.'

"'Where are you from? Who are you? What are you doing here, all alone in this deserted place?'

"'I am from the Masa'id, and have come out for a particular reason.'

"'How is it that your people let so fair a maid as yourself come uncovered and alone into such a wilderness?'

"'This is a secret I will disclose to nobody,' she laughed.

"Then she quizzed me about my background and my life. Charmed by her laughter and her sweet manner, her beautiful voice and her gracious way of moving, I replied. Then for some unknown reason I looked down at her feet. What I saw amazed and terrified me. This most gorgeous woman had the hooves of a mule. Yes, the hooves of a mule. I said to myself, 'Maybe heat and exhaustion have got to me, and sapped my wits.' I rubbed my eyes hard and stared at her again. I found myself facing a creature who had the head of an owl as well as the hooves of a mule. I don't know what I did after that. All I remember is that when I regained consciousness I was lying on the ground with men from the Masa'id tribe around me, sprinkling water on my face and invoking the name of God."

He betrayed his Bedouin forbears in everything except their love of nomadic wandering.

He grew up listening to wonderful stories. The most enchanting was the tale of his ancestress Mahbuba. That story was told all the time, especially in the winter when it got really cold and folk gathered around the fire. Or on summer nights when they stayed up, stretched out on the threshing ground beneath a sky made bright by the most beautiful moon ever seen.

"It was in a year of severe drought," it was related, "when the Reaper had taken his generous harvest. The survivors of the tribe packed their few possessions onto camels, on donkeys and mules, left their homeland, and set off to the distant east. They travelled day and night for months, fleeing dust, hunger, and thirst. One night they rested at the foot of a mountain. At dawn they rose and resumed their trek. But one woman, Mahbuba, was accidentally left behind. Her husband had died on the road, leaving her with twin boys, Sa'ad and Sa'id. It was in the middle of the morning when she woke up and found they were all alone in this vast emptiness. She was panic-stricken and ran around as one possessed, her two little ones babbling away on her back. She tired herself out, sat by the track, and wept bitter tears. But God is merciful to his faithful people. He allows none to be forsaken. So, not long before the sun went down the poor woman saw before her a proud man with a face full of compassion. He asked her some questions.

"'I've lost my way, good sir,' she said, fighting back her tears. 'I've lost my family and my fellow travelling companions.'

"She then told him her story in detail. He invited her to his house. He treated her respectfully, letting her forget that she was a stranger and a widow. She entered his service loyally and honorably.

"When the twins grew up the good man summoned them.

"'You are now two handsome young men,' he told them. 'From this day on you must show people what you are made of.'

"He then gave each one of them a plot of fallow land on which there were only stones and thorns.

"'If you put this land to good use,' he said, 'God will put you to good use.'

"The twins toiled night and day, in heat and in cold, until that barren piece of land became green and fertile, and full of good things. When the wise old man saw this, he summoned them to him once more.

"'God has prospered you in what I had you undertake,' he said. 'You are entitled to take half what is due to you.'

"He then married them to two wondrously fair young women from among his relations, arranging such a wedding party that people talked of it for many years afterward."

At this point, the listeners fell silent, sat up in their seats, their skull-caps askew, and took a sip of their tea. One man sighed.

"God was merciful to our ancestress," he said, "as was the shaykh who looked after her and provided this fine wedding feast."

They then closed their eyes and sank into silence or into sleep. But our hero, in his fantasies, wandered far afield. He was himself like Mahbuba, lost in the deserts where no man trod, where no bird flew. Nothing but stones, thorns, mirages. He was walking, walking, walking, crossing deserts, mountains, and wadis, until he reached the land of ghouls. There he met ferocious robbers who would steal even the teeth of dogs as they barked. He met snakes that would swallow a man in an instant as if he were a fly. And crocodiles who could devour the sultan's army. And evil grey-haired witches who could turn men into monkeys or rats. After a fierce struggle he plunged his sword into one ghoul and returned on the back of a green horse that had wings of light, accompanied by a princess veiled by her long hair and carrying a scented apple that could restore youth and raise the dead.

He betrayed his Bedouin forbears in everything except their love of nomadic wandering.

On cold mornings he went to the Koranic teacher who chanted softly *"Glory to Him, who carried His servant by night from the Holy Mosque[1] to the Further Mosque."*[2] He would repeat these strange words until he became totally oblivious to the cold, the thorny cactus plants, and the evil one-eyed teacher whose stick hovered over their heads all day long. He saw himself standing in the desert with the most beautiful horse in the world—it had the face of a human, a mane of moist pearls alternating with luminous sapphire, ears of emerald, and eyes like lustrous stars. It was grey-white, with three white feet and on its fourth an anklet studded with pearls. An unknown voice whispered to him, "Mount and ride." And so he mounted and rode. The steed flew with him beyond the mountains surrounding his homeland. He looked down on people who were like ants. Then in one second they were in the seventh heaven. He looked below to see the earth and all that was on it as small as a drop of water.

Then one day he set off on his first journey. His mother stood on the doorstep, murmuring prayers to herself. His father leapt onto the back of their grey mule and issued instructions about the animals and about household matters. He jumped up behind and they set off. Behind them his mother poured out a bucket of water, saying not a word. At the edge of the village they found other men on mules waiting for them. They all set off slowly on the Camel Road. It was towards the end of an autumn day. Shadows covered the plain, the slopes, and the mountains. The scent of fresh wild figs was in the air and the land had been stripped after the harvest. The sun set before they had traversed those bare wadis that divided them from the lands of the Masa'id. The darkness gradually thickened until the hills and mountains were transformed and they seemed suspended in space. At one point they were attacked by wild dogs but the men took no heed of them.

Mabruk Ould 'Amir told stories about his stingy grandfather that made them shake with laughter on the backs of their mules. Every now and then one of them would call out, "Tell us another, Mabruk. May you live long!"

They started to descend a rough slope. A cold wind, bearing the scents of pine, wormwood, and juniper, brushed against them. The mules slowed down their ambling pace. The path straightened up. Shadowy trees intertwined above their heads.

As they went deeper into the forest it got colder and colder. As night drew on, Mabruk's enthusiasm waned. Anecdotes became fewer and the gaps between them increased. They then stopped completely. His father and the other men were silent. All he could hear was the tramp of the hooves of the mules on the ground. Silence took such possession that he felt totally separated from his father and the other men. It was as if he was left floundering alone in the eternal darkness. Suddenly they heard a strange noise, and suddenly all was silent again. The forest then moved as if wild horses were charging through it. There were bizarre groans, and distressed bleats as of a camel about to be slaughtered. It seemed to the boy that the darkness was full of those spirits and ghouls and she-demons they had been talking about. He was about to cry out in terror, and then heard Mabruk:

"Dawn has broken, my friends."

It was while he was travelling with his father in the villages of the north that he became fascinated with atlases.

August. The horizons were lit up with the heat of mirages. He was puffing like a wild dog. His father was snoring loudly in a corner of the tent. His mother was grinding wheat and repeating those sad songs that recalled the motion of caravans as they made their slow, heavy way towards the north. He knew that she would shortly burst into tears. Grief gathered in her heart like dust on a track. He slipped away with a huge atlas that he had won as a school prize for outstanding work. He stretched out in the shade of the Camel olive tree. Bliss! The branches chattered with those affecting songs that made him forget the grief-laden songs of his mother. As soon as he opened the book he forgot about everything else. He wandered through countries, crossed seas and oceans. Penetrated jungles. Here near the arm of his own country that stretched into the sea was the island of Sicily, shaped like the sheepskin that his mother would spread for visitors. Sardinia was shaped like an old tortoise. Beyond were the snow-covered Alps over which Hannibal's armies rumbled like a wild storm. To the left lay Gibraltar. Above lay the land of Al-Andalus, drenched in the blood of defeated Arabs. Below that, red Marrakesh with its veiled sultans and the roads to Timbuktu. He repeated to himself the name *Timbuktu, Timbuktu, Timbuktu*, as if he were repeating a favourite song. He traced with his fingers the desert roads that meandered and linked up in the places where troupes of blacks sang, their teeth as sparkling bright as stars on a dark night. Further down he could smell the African jungle, where crocodiles and lions were as much at liberty as the donkeys in his home village. At the heart of Africa was the Congo, blown up like the body of a ghoul. Then far away were the Magellan Straits where fierce storms blew all the year round. After wandering in those lands scattered on the edge of the world—Australia, the Philippines, Singapore, Malaysia, Ceylon—he turned back and looked at the Nile as it sauntered through the desert.

He was now not far from the land of revelation. *Glory to Him, who carried His servant by night from the Holy Mosque to the Further Mosque.* He pondered over the effects of the remarkable stories of the Koran. Here Moses cast his staff that turned into a snake. There was the pit into which Joseph was thrown. Here Abraham contemplated sacrificing his son, Ishmael. And here was the dry palm tree to which Mary resorted at the time of her labour. There are the wells of Zamzam, the cave of Hira where Gabriel addressed the Prophet one dawn. He returned to Khadija in a feverish sweat, crying, "Cover me up, cover me up."

Once more an old dream recurs, and he sees himself as a traveller, a staff in his hand, like Moses. He goes into the desert at night and the road is lit up for him as far as the eye can see. He is thirsty and his staff guides him to a well and he draws up water in a bucket. He needs food and strikes the ground and, lo and behold, before him is a table spread with all that is good and tasty. He wants some fruit. He strikes the ground again and at once a fruit-bearing tree springs up. He passes by a difficult mountain. He strikes the ground and a path opens up. He wishes to cross a river and dry land opens up before him.

He was in this dream world when the young lads of the village turned to him. "What have you been reading in that book?" they ask.

When he was fifteen years old he saw the sea for the first time. From that moment on he was so enchanted by the blue of the sea and the music of the crashing waves, that he developed a feeling of loss when he went back to the village. Over the course of time this sense of alienation intensified. He felt constrained by the desert winds, by the flies and the intense heat, the locusts, the crows that screeched on peaks, and by the snakes that hissed in the rocky hills when it was hot and by the lice that fed on the unwashed scalps of young people, by the snuff the Bedouin used to cram into their cheeks and up their noses, by the drought that destroyed man and beast and by the yellow dust that blinded people in the month of May.

This was indeed a break. He entered the capital by its southern gate one autumn afternoon when the sky was clear and the air was fresh. He dropped off his suitcase and wandered by himself among the bookshops near Bab al-Bahr and experienced a yearning for those books he had heard of but had not yet read: *Journey to the End of Night*, *À la recherche du temps perdu*, *A Portrait of the Artist as a Young Man*.

"I must devour all these as soon as I can," he said to himself as he carried a bundle of books to the small room he shared with a huge student called Jum'a. He never tired of reading Che Guevara's memoirs or *The Little Red Book* of Mao Tse-tung. He dreamed of a new revolution that would bring workers and peasants to power. As for himself, he said to himself as he listened to Jum'a's fiery talk, "You are a Bedouin and have got to work hard to be a writer. Isn't this what you've wanted since you became besotted with atlases and ancient legends?" He closed his eyes and let his imagination wander. He could see his own books lining the windows of bookshops and people rushing to buy them. He saw himself sitting in Café Paris with city notables, smoking a pipe and replying calmly and eloquently to journalists' questions. Jum'a would bring him up sharp and shout: "You're betraying your class. You should be ashamed of yourself."

Then he met Yassin. He too liked to eat macaroni with spicy sauce in Maltese restaurants. He liked the stories of old Mahmoud in the port bar, the girls of La Marsa and La Goulette in their summer swimming costumes. He enjoyed the films of Eisenstein, De Sica, Bergman, Pasolini, Jean-Luc Godard, and Youssef Chahine. The poetry of Baudelaire, Rimbaud, Abu Nuwas, Lorca, Mayakovsky, Eluard, and Adonis. The obsessions of Mersault on the beach of Algiers and Bloom in the brothels of Dublin. Like Yassin he loved Jewish songs and the music of al-Hadi al-Juwaini.

But it was his wanderlust that was stronger than anything else. He felt that the capital, the whole country, was too confined for his dreams. One restless day he and Yassin were drinking beer slowly at the Café des Nègres.

"I'm going to travel," he announced.

"Where to?"

"I only want to get away to the West."

"What about the East?"

"That's like some old whore's cunt."

After that he crossed the seas and again there was a break in his life.

For many years he wandered from country to country. In Paris he sought out what remained of the surrealists. He loved Chantal, who dreamed of life amongst the Tuareg. In Madrid late one night he met a feeble old man who told him the details of Lorca's death. In Dublin he drank Guinness until he staggered about like a hero of Joyce. In Amsterdam he fell in love with a blonde girl who loved hashish, Berber songs, and Arabic music. In New York he lived with the blacks and looked for traces of Henry Miller in Brooklyn. In Rome he shared foul wine and smelly cheese with revellers. In Copenhagen he heard that the security forces back home had killed hundreds in clashes with the trade unions. In Ronda he stayed quietly in the hotel Rainer Maria Rilke used to stay in. In Prague he was haunted by Kafkaesque nightmares. In Athens he dreamed that Socrates, wearing the clothes of an imam, chased him into the wilderness with a cudgel shouting: "Go back where you came from, go back, you rogue!" In Berlin he fathomed the pessimism of Schopenhauer: life is like a pendulum, swinging from right to left, between pain and boredom.

NOTES

1. Holy Mosque of Mecca.
2. Further Mosque of Jerusalem.

The Start of the Affair

At a fire sale a few years ago, James MacPherson, a retired professor of politics at Wits, Johannesburg, known for his seminal work on the Frontline States' war of attrition against the apartheid regime, bought a restaurant in Pretoria specializing in North African cuisine. His knowledge of Africa was extensive, a result of having lived in various places around the continent for a number of years, most notably Zambia and Tanzania, and of having travelled frequently to the neighboring states.

Now he spends much of his time at a corner table in the restaurant, surrounded by the papers on which he has scribbled notes for a book he intends to lick into shape. He seldom interferes with the business side of the restaurant, allowing the manager, Yacine, a Moroccan, full authority to deal with most problems. And, on the rare occasion that Yacine seeks his input, James defers to him, saying, "It is your call."

James has thickened with age, gaining much weight. His once slim body has ballooned outward, and his paunch extends far ahead of him. His feet are swollen, as if he were diabetic. His doctor recommends regular workouts. And, because he

---

"The Start of the Affair" was first published in *The New Yorker*. Reprinted by permission of Nuruddin Farah and Aragi Inc.

does not feel sufficiently motivated to walk to the local gym, James has set up a mini-gym in the basement of his house. The last time he hired a personal trainer to come to his home, to help stretch his inflexible body, the young man spoke rudely to him, because he could barely bend forward to touch his toes. In addition, James has a weak left eye and he is forced, at times, to turn his entire body in order to catch sight of a person or a thing.

James has the habit of arriving at nine in the morning, just as the restaurant is opening, not only because he loves the grainy coffee that the chef, a Turk, makes but also because he derives great joy from being in the restaurant and from the companionability of the young men and women who work in the offices nearby and come in for breakfast meetings. He revels in the bodies coming and going, and feels there is a purpose to the noisy activity here, a meaning to the bustle of waiters taking orders, chefs and sous-chefs preparing the food, and the manager doing the sums, printing the bills after payment, the customers engaging one another in conversation and, as is common among Africans, touching freely. James observes the young men with keener interest than he does their female colleagues or clients.

He has lately, however, shown obvious keenness in one particular young man, who emerged from the staff door at lunchtime one day, carrying what looked to him like a doggie bag with food in it. Possibly the glimpse of the youth stirred something in James's memory—he was a handsome fellow, with an uncanny likeness to the preteen son of a Somali family James had known in Tanzania. This family, from whom he used to buy his provisions, had owned a general store adjacent to James's hotel. The boy's father was exceptionally kind to James whenever he went round to the store, and the two would chat about Somali politics in broken Swahili. The mother, for her part, was by far the prettiest woman James had ever set eyes on. He became close enough to the family for the wife to invite him home for meals on festive occasions and for the husband to lend him cash a couple of times when a money order had been delayed. And, when James took ill and the hotel management did nothing, the boy's father sent a Somali doctor to attend to him. James was so beholden to the boy's parents that he could not bring himself to take advantage of the young thing on the various occasions when he and the boy were alone at the swimming pool to which he had invited him. James, though tempted, chose not to abandon himself to his unreasoning passion.

He remembers all this now that he has learned from the kitchen staff that the young man he saw is, indeed, Somali. Eyebrows are raised, and the staff starts gossiping when, on subsequent days, James asks what the young man's name is, what he does for a living, where he lives, and how long he has been in the country. The kitchen staff cannot seem to decide whether his curiosity is innocent or not, the Turk saying that James's eyes light up, like those of a teenager in love, whenever Ahmed comes into view.

One morning, on his way to the restaurant after a dentist's appointment, James makes a detour, entering a nearby store, which Ahmed manages. It is not clear in James's mind if he will speak to Ahmed, and, if he does, whether he will ask about Ahmed's visits to the restaurant or find out if he is related to the young Somali boy James knew in Tanzania. James is a sensitive soul, and he is loath to infringe on anyone's sense of privacy if he can help it; likewise, he won't pester his employees with queries that might embarrass them. He just wants to have a feel for the store, and to make the young man's acquaintance.

Immediately, he can tell that there is no roaring business here. There are only five people in the place, two women in full-body tents and a third wearing headgear similar in style to a nun's, and an old man sitting on a low stool who is chatting with the young man and occasionally helping to retrieve items that are placed high up in the stacks. James takes his time. He has no interest in purchasing any of the items on display. But he hangs around; he wants to exchange a few words with Ahmed in the proper manner, reasoning that he likes the look of the young man, loves the way he concentrates on what he is doing, and senses, too, that his movements are those of a young man who has said yes to hard work.

James finds himself gazing at the fellow's handsome face, his sweet smile, his delicately carved features. He is relieved to confirm that Ahmed is not the preteen, now a young man, to whose parents he was beholden in Tanzania, and of whom he had not taken advantage. He can now afford to think ahead to the day when he can fill his eyes with Ahmed's naked body, given the chance. He wishes he were an artist and Ahmed a nude subject, posing to be drawn. Sadly, though, the clothes on Ahmed prove to be an encumbrance. They are so badly designed. What is more, the sleeves of his shirt are too short, and there is visible dirt around the neck, plus curry-type stains here and there, and the trousers are too baggy. The fellow could do with a cleaner set of clothes, laundered and pressed. James can't recall seeing him wearing any clothes other than the ones in which he is now standing. But all that could be fixed in less than half an hour's shopping—and James is prepared to foot the bill to dress him in clothes that would bring his features to the fore. Still, he doubts that their conversation today will move much beyond swapping names.

Then, as luck would have it, and because James has stuck around longer than he initially intended to, he and Ahmed are alone and the young fellow is asking, "What can I sell to you?"

James's thoughts are suddenly cluttered with the detritus of memories, feelings for which he cannot find adequate explanation. Had he the guts to answer the question honestly, he might have replied that he was interested not in buying any of the trinkets and cheap clothes from China but in him, and only him. In other words, since everything has a price, how much would Ahmed's "company" cost in monetary terms? How much to hold him in an embrace?

"My name is James MacPherson," he says.

Then, smiling serenely, he moves a step closer.

"Yes-hello-James-welcome," the Somali says, speaking the words in such a way that James can't help imagining that, in Ahmed's head, they form a single hyphenated word.

"What is your name?"

"My name is Ahmed Ali-Mooryaan," the Somali says.

James, wanting to know how to address him, asks, "So, which is your Christian name?"

"I have no Christian name."

James realizes right away that he has made a faux pas. And so, in an attempt to charm him, he offers his hand, formalizing the ritual of their encounter with a handshake. As he takes the young man's slender hand—the hand of a pianist, James thinks—he expounds, "I know that you Somalis have one name, which is your given name, another which is your father's name, and a third, which is your paternal grandfather's. So whose name or nickname is Mooryaan?" James is aware that descriptive nicknames are often bestowed on people bearing the commonest of names. Presumably, there are thousands of men called Ali, and the idea is to distinguish one Ali from another. Hence Ali-Mooryaan.

"My name is Ahmed."

"And your father's name?"

"His name is Ali. But everybody calls him Mooryaan."

James puts on the delightful smile of a man determined to redeem himself. "Mooryaan is a beautiful name, isn't it?"

"My dad is a beautiful man."

"A beautiful name for a handsome man."

"My dad is handsome, a man's man."

James is uncertain what he means by this, but wonders if the phrase "a man's man" is no more than a literal translation from Somali into English. And he lets it pass. However, he asks, "Is it an Arab name from the Koran or purely a Somali name?"

James intends to impress Ahmed; he wants the young man to know that he has a modicum of knowledge about his traditions.

"My father is famous in Mogadishu," Ahmed says.

James asks, "What is your father famous for?"

"You say his name, everybody knows him."

Pressing, he repeats, "But what's he famous for?"

"Mooryaan is just a nickname."

"But what does Mooryaan mean, in Somali?"

"Just a nickname between him and his friends," Ahmed explains. "He is good-looking, and is now powerful, rich, and blessed with fifteen children—twelve boys, three girls—and four wives. Mooryaan is his famous nickname."

"And the nickname has stuck?"

"Stuck, what means 'stuck'?"

James wonders if Ahmed's command of the language becomes dishevelled whenever he feels ruffled. Or could it be that he has only "street English," as an Arabic speaker might put it?

"And what made you leave your father in Somalia and come to South Africa?"

"South Africa is good, the best in Africa."

"But why not Europe or the U.S.A.?"

"My applications were denied."

"Why?"

"Politics," Ahmed replies.

"Politics, how?"

"My dad upset America."

"To upset America, your dad must be a big man."

"In Somalia, he is big, my dad."

"How did you come here?"

"There were five of us, and we started our journey from Mogadishu by plane to Nairobi," Ahmed replies. "At Nairobi airport, we bribed the immigration officials. From there, we travelled to Tanzania, where we encountered lots of trouble, then more trouble, and were imprisoned. We were accused of illegally entering the country. Three of my friends were raped in prison, first by prison guards and then, again and again, by the prisoners."

"Why were you spared?"

"Because I had money to give and I did."

"Then what happened?"

"Four of us were allowed to leave."

"And the fifth?"

"He is still in detention."

"Why?"

"He is the second 'wife' of the prison warden."

"And from Tanzania you came to what country?"

"Malawi, where we were also imprisoned."

"All four of you arrived together in Malawi?"

"And two of us were not allowed to leave."

"Why were they refused permission to leave?"

"They were raped in prison and detained."

"Again, you were spared. Why?"

"I was lucky."

James doesn't believe that luck spared him. But it is not surprising that Ahmed won't admit to being raped. James knows, from having interviewed former political prisoners, that they all deny the truth of the physical and sexual humiliation they suffered at the hands of prison wardens or political commissars.

"And then?"

"After Malawi, Mozambique and then South Africa."

"Your English is very good," James says.

"Thank you."

"Have you learned it since coming here?"

"No. I learned it in Somalia," Ahmed replies.

"I didn't think that would be possible."

"You mean because we have a civil war?"

"I understand that Arabic has been made the lingua franca there, and that even the use of Somali, a young tongue in terms of writing, has declined," James says.

Ahmed shakes his head and then explains, "My dad, he imported a teacher from Tanzania to teach us at home. He paid a good salary to the teacher—two hundred U.S. dollars a month. The teacher lived in our house. He was our family's teacher, eight of us school-going-age children in one class."

"And where is your home?"

"I come from Mogadishu," Ahmed says.

"I meant, where do you live now?"

Ahmed points at the floor. "Here!"

James is not shocked to hear that Ahmed lives, works, and sleeps in the store. He remembers how one morning he went to the restaurant unexpectedly early and found two of the North African waiters sleeping in the pantry, the sacks of onions, potatoes, and other items pushed into a corner to make space for one mattress that the two men shared. James has said nothing about it and continues to pretend that they live elsewhere. It did not occur to him that they might be homosexuals because they were sharing a single mattress; he thought, instead, that he should raise their salaries, even though he doubts that an increase would encourage them to rent an apartment—he knew that they were sending all their money back home. Anyhow, emboldened by his knowledge of what obtains among the migrants, James asks, "Here, where?"

Ahmed points to a hidden corner beyond the shelves, where a mattress stands against the wall.

James, needing to make himself taller for some reason, draws himself up, and then asks, "You are saying you work, live, and sleep here, and for food you collect the leftovers from my restaurant?"

Ahmed looks offended, but James is unable to fathom why. His lips are astir—James thinks that he is having difficulty matching the thoughts in his head with the language at his command, is hesitating for fear that he may not make sense. Finally, Ahmed manages to speak. "You say 'my restaurant'?"

"Who did you think the restaurant belonged to?"

"Yacine says the restaurant belongs to him."

"Oh, does he?"

So that is what is happening, James thinks. Ahmed isn't so much offended as surprised, having believed that the restaurant was owned by Yacine, thanks to whose generosity he was daily given the lunch leftovers. James remembers seeing a Senegalese film—he cannot recall the name of the filmmaker or the title—in which a young African in Paris, in the sixties, has a picture taken of himself leaning against a car parked in a street that he is sweeping. The young Senegalese sends the picture to his family, claiming the car as his own. No matter. The migrant is rich in imagination and, of course, the fact that Yacine claims to own the restaurant doesn't bother James in the least.

"You say he lying?"

Again, James notices the way Ahmed's control of English starts to slip, and he decides that it must happen whenever he becomes agitated or nervous.

"I own the restaurant, every brick of it," James now tells him.

"Why lie? He is a bad man, Yacine."

"You'll have to ask him yourself."

"I no like people lying," Ahmed says.

"Don't concern yourself about it."

"Lying is like killing—no good."

James says, "Still, it is O.K. for you to continue taking your lunch from the restaurant. You have no worries about that. In fact, I'll insist that they give you better food, healthier food."

"Thank you. Yes, I would like. Thank you."

But Ahmed still looks upset, and James cannot puzzle this out. James has to take care. The fellow is touchy. No Christian names and no questions pertaining to the lunch leftovers he takes away. Maybe it is time for James to go. He can come back, now that they have met, and perhaps they will arrange a convenient time to get to know each other better. No rush.

"Well, I'll tell you what, Ahmed," James says.

"What?"

"I'll see you another time. O.K.?"

"O.K."

"Bye."

"Goodbye. Till another time."

Back at his table in the restaurant, James is momentarily overjoyed to recall his youthful courtship of his late wife, Martha. (Her Portuguese parents, living in Lourenço Marques, had named her Marta, but she added an "h" to Anglicize it.) He paid court to Martha, a fellow-student at the University of Cape Town, by pampering her with gifts, including gorgeous bouquets of flowers from a Rondebosch florist, and a birthday card delivered express, direct to her hostel. She was wafer-thin, with hair cut close to the head. James's mother said that Martha wasn't her idea of a woman or, for that matter, a mother and she thought that her son needed his head examined. She said, "How can you? The woman is a Twiggy manqué. At least the other one is English, famous, and a talented artist. What is good about this one?" James had retorted, "Who says every marriage has to produce a child?" You could have floored his mother with the softest touch—and she was shocked to hear him speak of marriage. "But *I* do. I want a grandchild, who will continue our line. Remember, darling. You are an only child and so am I, and, with your father dead, that will be the end of us." He had shrugged off her comments, saying, "You make it sound as though this were a train, when you speak of the end of the line that way."

A number of things about Martha appealed to James: she had no local family to host her on weekends or holidays, and no one to worry about her if she didn't come home but spent a few days at his apartment, in Claremont. Moreover, she was willing to go to his digs whenever he invited her. He would cook candlelit dinners and offer her wine galore, the best and the most sought after in the Western Cape. It was a mystery to him, though, that she could gorge herself on boxes of imported chocolates nightly without gaining a single ounce. How did she manage it when all he had to do to become thick in the waist like a tree trunk was hold a sliver of chocolate in his hand? Looking back now on his and Martha's courtship, he finds that Ahmed's accent is similar in an uncanny way to Martha's. Her English was overlaid with Portuguese, which she never lost to her dying day, just as Ahmed's English is plastered with Somali inflections, a feature that seems quaint to James, terribly charming and sexy.

James is almost three times Ahmed's age. There is time yet for him to find out how recently Ahmed arrived in the country and whether his refugee application has been approved by Home Affairs. There is time to discuss Ahmed's plans for the future. And for James to consider his own. He lives all alone in a very big house, with only his dogs for company and a maid who comes during the day. There has been an eerie silence, ever since Martha died, two years ago. Of course there is room for Ahmed to join him. But not too fast—hey, not too fast, my man!

———————

First off, James alters Ahmed's status at the restaurant. He tells Yacine that, from today onward, Ahmed is not to be treated as a poor relation, given a sandwich made from leftovers and the heel of a loaf, but that he is to be offered a cooked meal twice a day, at lunchtime and in the evening. Yet, although Ahmed receives the new dispensation with joy, the instruction from on high without consultation riles the manager, who feels affronted, and those in the kitchen's lower order who had until then shown Ahmed only kindness are piqued into an unprecedented meanness, because they suspect him of having complained to their boss. On the second day of the new arrangement, the meal the chef cooked was too salty and almost inedible, and his tea had in it milk that was past its consumption date.

Ahmed takes ill the following day, his stomach runny. He spends a great deal of time going from the store to the shared outhouse toilet and back, and decides to close for the day. All the while, his vision is blurred. He rings his Somali friends, who suggest that he buy tablets for diarrhea and aspirin for his headache, which he does, but these are of no great help. So he leaves a handwritten message on the door that says "Bak tomoro!" and returns to bed.

Ahmed's no-show surprises James, for he has looked forward to seeing him and to hearing how delighted he is by the arrangement James has made for him. Early the following morning, on his way to his table at the restaurant, he stops in at the store to find Ahmed looking wan and withdrawn. He asks what is the matter, and Ahmed replies, "Food poison." James takes him to his own doctor in his car, wondering what to do about the chef and the kitchen staff, and wondering, too, if Yacine is in on this. He won't rush into anything; he is well aware that Yacine has a short temper, and that there is no point in confronting any of the kitchen staff unless it happens a second or a third time.

While waiting for the results from the clinic, James and Ahmed retreat to a café across the street. He asks Ahmed how long he has been in South Africa and what his current status is.

"Waiting for status," Ahmed says. "Applied and waiting, waiting for nine months, no answer." James notices, once again, that there is a shagginess to his language, as Ahmed continues, "There is no one to help me, don't know anyone who can help, don't know any officer in Home Affairs to assist me, or to bribe."

As they have breakfast, James watches Ahmed clumsily handling his fork and knife, unable at first to determine even how to cut off a slice of his chicken, or how to put jam on his toast. "Where did you apply, Joburg or Pretoria?"

"Joburg Home Affairs."

One of James's former students occupies a middle-ranking position at the Home Affairs office in Joburg, and he can put in a word to help expedite matters for Ahmed. However, it is too soon to promise to do that. Not yet. There is a proper occasion and a proper place for this sort of intervention, which requires a cautious approach on his part. In addition, he won't want to make everything appear so easy, as this may cheapen the favor that is on offer.

He asks, "So what papers do you have now?"

"I got a temporary permit to stay," Ahmed says, tripping over the word "temporary."

James has met people from the Middle East for whom the letter "p" is an ordeal to pronounce. Even Yacine, who has been here for almost a decade, often stumbles on it, in addition to mixing his verbs and misplacing his prepositional and adjectival phrases. James tells himself that a language like English has room enough for everyone from anywhere, which is why it has lately become everybody's second tongue.

He says, "How long have you been here now?"

"Two years and eight months."

"May I ask you a very personal question?"

"Go 'head and ask."

"Have you taken a loan to open the store?"

After a long silence, Ahmed says, "No."

"How did you get the money?"

"My father, he sent me money from Mogadishu."

"What business is your dad in nowadays?"

"He made plenty money in the early nineties." Ahmed gets to his feet, saying, "Sorry, toilet," and dashes off.

He is gone a long time, and when he comes back James asks how he is, and Ahmed says, "I feel better, much better."

James settles the bill, and they return to the clinic to collect the results of the tests. Neither is surprised to hear that they confirm Ahmed's self-diagnosis—food poisoning.

They stop at a pharmacy and James pays for the prescription, then they drive to James's house on the pretext that he needs to collect some documents from his study.

After parking the car in the two-car garage, James, out of thoughtfulness, says to Ahmed, "Please wait in the car for a moment. I know from previous associations with other Somalis that you may want me to put the dogs in the back yard, so they won't be a nuisance."

Ahmed says, "How many dogs do you have?"

"Three purebred," James says.

Ahmed speaks as if in awe: "Three dogs?"

Not that Ahmed is impressed by the fact that all three dogs are pure-blooded. For him, a dog is a dog; he is scared of them and won't go near one. So he sits in the car and does not relax until James comes out to tell him that the house is now clear.

He follows James in with the cautiousness of someone entering enemy territory. And when he hears a bang coming from the kitchen he stops in his tracks. He wants to know who is making the noise. "Dogs?" he inquires, ready to flee.

"It is the house help," James says.

"House help?"

"The maid in the kitchen, working."

And James calls to the maid, a large woman almost his size. The woman smiles and then curtsies and utters a few words of welcome. James asks for a glass of water so that Ahmed can take his medicine. The woman returns with a glass filled to the brim, waits and watches as the young Somali raises the glass to his lips.

After that, Ahmed moves about the house freely, unafraid. He goes from one room to another, opening the doors of the bathroom and, next to it, the toilet. James waits for him to return from his inspection, and when Ahmed comes back into the kitchen he sees that his eyes are open wide with wonder.

James says, "There is more upstairs."

Ahmed, obviously overwhelmed, goes up the stairs, James following, and passes through one bedroom after another. When he walks into the study and sees the number of books and the stacks of magazines, two desktop computers, and three laptops all in one room, he turns to James and asks, "How many people live here?"

"Only me," James replies.

He points at the laptops, asks, "Why three?"

"Would you like one of them?"

"As gift for me?"

"Yes, as a gift to you for our friendship."

"I am glad, yes, thank you."

James then explains that since the laptop contains some of his documents they will drop it off at a specialist's, who will save the documents and then wipe the computer clean for Ahmed's future use.

"You read all these books?" Ahmed asks.

James, modestly, says, "Most of them." Then, after a pause, he asks Ahmed, "Do you like reading yourself—and what type of books do you like?"

"My English bad—can't read books, only magazines."

"I can teach you to read. Would you like that?"

"Too old, maybe," Ahmed says.

James takes Ahmed's hand, and Ahmed doesn't pull it away and doesn't resist when he holds on to it. "You are young and intelligent, and you will learn fast when

I teach you. I am a good teacher; I've been a university professor for many years. It will make me happy to give you lessons here in this house."

And James leads him downstairs by the hand to the gym. Ahmed first gets on the bicycle and starts pedalling, then he steps onto the treadmill and, pressing the wrong buttons, almost falls off. James catches him in time and hugs him to himself, his heart beating at a faster rate. He is all memory, remembering the preteen, whom he never had. He thinks, This one is different. Here it will be consensual. Again, Ahmed doesn't resist or push James away.

Ahmed says, "We'll see. Our future is long."

Noticing a pile of books in the gym, almost all of them about Somalia, Ahmed asks if James has read these, too. To which James replies, "I borrowed them from the library of the university where I taught for many years, and I intend to read them. I want to have a better understanding of your country's history as I get to know you more. It is a fascinating country, where you come from."

Ahmed feels obligated to take a look at the books. He reads a few of the titles aloud, mispronouncing some of the words and massacring the names of the authors, except for the Somali ones.

"Can we go? I need to open store," Ahmed says finally.

"Of course."

In the car, Ahmed says, "I love everything in your house."

"Thank you."

"One day I would like house like this."

"Here or in Somalia?"

Ahmed says, "One big house like this here, another in Somalia. My father lives in house bigger than this, with more rooms, and near the ocean, two hundred metres from Lido, in Mogadishu."

"I cannot afford a house on the seafront."

"One day I'll take you to Mogadishu, if you want."

"I would love that. But is it safe?"

"My father will make sure you are safe."

James stops in front of the store to drop him off.

Curious about Ahmed's father and eager to know more, James seeks out a prominent Somali social-science professor who's visiting the University of Pretoria on a two-year stint.

Rashid and James meet at the university's main cafeteria. James plays up to Rashid, praising his scholarly acumen and describing his pieces as the most enlightening he has read on the phenomenon known as African warlordism. James adds, "No one writes about this as well as you do."

Rashid bubbles over with excitement and speaks at length about Somali warlordism as a scourge for which there is no cure, since it feeds on the dysfunctional nature of factionalism. James is thinking that he likes his liquors straight, but he doesn't like "isms" of any sort, because "isms" disempower you, when suddenly a familiar name—Mooryaan—catches his attention.

"'Mooryaan' means 'pillager,' you know, in Somali," Rashid says. "The man is a bloodthirsty criminal, a plunderer of the nation's wealth, accused of organizing the looting of the Central Bank, of dismantling working factories and selling the metal as scrap in the Arabian Gulf."

Rashid has a way of raising his voice a few decibels higher when he gets emotional, and of spraying anyone sitting close by with spittle. James wipes away the spit and then asks, "So, his wealth comes from these ill-gotten gains?"

"Ali-Mooryaan is one of the wealthiest men in Somalia," Rashid replies. "He 'owns' many villas on Mogadishu's seafront and has bought properties in Nairobi and in the Emirates. He has funded piracy, and he has made money out of exporting hard drugs via a small airstrip fifty kilometres outside Mogadishu."

"In other words, he is your typical warlord."

"He is one of the most wicked warlords."

James derives some pleasure from thinking that Ahmed is unlikely to return to Somalia for quite some time, given the precariousness of the politics there. And even though his father is powerful, Ahmed seems to lack that kind of ruthlessness. Perhaps he will be happy to stay out of his father's sphere of influence once James assures him of a firm foothold in South Africa from which he can further his own career. And, to this end, James decides to "invest" more in the young man in a way that will help him to gain his full trust and his eventual affection.

In an effort to achieve his aim and also to avoid upsetting the manager of the restaurant and the kitchen staff, he starts delivering Ahmed's lunch to him at the store and then picking him up in the car for an evening meal at his house, dropping him back at the store after coaching him in conversational English. That way, they meet at least once daily. In the store, if there are no customers around they chat longer; and, if there are, James hands over the package of food, and at times even adds a card with a brief message.

Nor is food the only gift that James gives. For he has bought Ahmed three pairs of trousers, three shirts, several pairs of underwear, and a pair of comfortable shoes. The way it goes is that James presents something as a gift, Ahmed, pretending, says, "I can't accept this," or "It is too much," or "You are spoiling me, my friend," and then finally he invariably says, "Thank you. You are most kind"—evidence that he appreciates what James is doing for him.

When, one evening after dinner, Ahmed complains of a toothache, James plays the dentist, making him open his mouth and holding down his tongue with a spoon. "Enough, I'll take you to my dentist first thing," he says, and sets up an emergency appointment very early the following morning. And he won't hear of Ahmed's protestations, saying, "You sleep in the downstairs room, because we need to get there by half past seven at the latest."

He lends Ahmed a pair of pajamas, his late wife's. Ahmed, afraid that the dogs may find their way into the house and, who knows, attack him, locks the door from the inside. In truth, it hasn't escaped James's notice that Ahmed is inclined to lock the bathroom door. Perhaps the fellow is just wary by nature. Anyway, at six in the morning James knocks on Ahmed's door to wake him. Ahmed has a shower, and after breakfast they go to the dentist together.

The dentist draws up a schedule after learning that he is the first dentist Ahmed has ever consulted, telling him that he must come back several times for the work on his teeth to be done.

Afterward, alone with James—Ahmed is now with the oral hygienist, having his teeth spruced up—the dentist asks, "Where did you find him?"

"He has a store near the restaurant."

The dentist says, "He strikes me as hand-carved, a young man made to order."

"He is, isn't he?"

"What is going on?" the dentist asks.

"Nothing yet."

"And where does he stay?"

"I won't tell you."

"You know he is not my type."

"As if I know what your type is."

"Anyhow, be careful. That is my advice."

James has been very cautious, the two hardly coming into bodily contact, except one day when James is in the gym and Ahmed, tired of watching TV, joins him. James proposes that he help stretch Ahmed's body and he sits on him, as personal trainers do. Then he touches him here and there, squeezing, massaging, and pressing his thighs, his groin—until he feels Ahmed's rising mound of manhood. James apologizes insincerely, even though he doesn't wish to stop, worried that continuing might upset Ahmed to the point where he will flee the nest that he has made his home.

———————

However, he makes no further move and nothing happens between them for another year and a half. And there comes a point where James suspects that the changes in Ahmed that are visible to the eye could match some changes that can't be seen. The store opens later and later in the morning and closes earlier. Ahmed's Somali friends see him infrequently and several come looking for him, wondering if he is O.K. And they notice the changes, not only because Ahmed is wearing freshly pressed trousers and sporting Ray-Bans or using the latest type of iPhone but also because he doesn't seem to have time to yammer with them. He is always in a hurry, mysteriously going somewhere, even though he won't explain where.

The Somalis aren't the only people who have noticed. One day, James eavesdrops on a conversation between Yacine and the Turkish chef—in which Yacine dismisses the Somali as a "toy boy," for the old man. James wishes that this *were* the case. He pretends not to have heard anything and collects the dinner for that night.

It is possible that others with an eye for more nefarious activities have observed Ahmed's frequent absences from the store, for it is broken into and everything of value taken, and the door left open until sunrise, when some of the passersby are said to have helped themselves to whatever they could lay their hands on.

With nowhere else to go, no store to mind, and nothing to do by way of a vocation, Ahmed moves full time into James's house. James, for his part, reduces his visits to the restaurant to a minimum and works from home, the house help cooking most of his and Ahmed's daytime meals, and the two of them either eating leftovers at night or rustling up light snacks. Ahmed spends more and more time in the family room watching TV. James joins him for the news and, sitting very close, they hold hands and talk.

One early morning, James sneaks into Ahmed's room and gets into bed and snuggles up to him. For a while, Ahmed pretends to be asleep and doesn't move at all. But when James, fully naked, nestles closer, his hand reaching out and making obvious what his intentions are, Ahmed says, "Please, not now," in the same tone of voice a woman uses when she says that she has her monthly. And the two of them sleep nude together, waiting for the appropriate day when they will consummate their union.

Presidential Portraits

Zachariah Rapola

Immediately after presenting his credentials to Dr. the Honourable Navinchandra Ramboolam, Prime Minister of Mauritius, South Africa's Ambassador designate, Matabane, retired to his sixth-floor luxury suite at the Labourdonnais Hotel. It was a temporary arrangement until suitable ambassadorial accommodation was found. The suite gave him an expansive view of the waterfront. Down below, his eye beheld a couple of naval boats. Their Coast Guard markings were distinctive. His gaze lingered on the red, blue, yellow and green flag of the island nation dancing to the wind.

He looked further away. The ocean beyond stretched as far as the eye could see. He was struck by its tranquil surface. A façade. Deadly and deceptive. Oceans and seas cannot profess honour. How can they, when during a clash of forces man is guaranteed to come off second best against nature?

Oceans and seas cannot claim innocence.

Ambassador Matabane retreated from the window. The embrace of his suite gave him assurance. Yet even at that height and distance he felt wary of the open sea. Tap water he could deal with, because it could be manipulated. Streams and rivers he tolerated, because they presented immediate sources of life. Not oceans and seas.

Oceans and seas cannot speak of incorruptibility
when genocide is in their psyche.

Hidden under that rippling mass were deadly agendas and conspiracies ready to explode without warning. Idle waves camouflage a deluge threatening to rise into tsunamis. Still fresh in his mind was the tsunami over Sumatra. So was the other westbound tsunami to Madagascar that toppled Ravalomanana, installing Rajoelina to power. Deadly and deceptive. The same caressing breezes conceal restless spirits of sailors, fishermen and pirates claimed by waves over the centuries.

Oceans and seas cannot proclaim their virtue.

Screams of Yao and Makua ex-slaves, Zanzibar-bound for South Africa, howled at him. Laments of indentured Indian labourers headed for the Natal sugar-cane fields haunted his soul. Skeletons of hundreds of slaves hurled overboard because they were surplus, leapt from the deep to gaze at him.

Oceans and seas bear silent witness to erased tribes and cultures.

Matabane turned away his gaze. Seeking solace, he found it in his jacket. It lay flung on a couch, colours of the South African flag emblazoned on the lapel pin staring at him. As he stood contemplating the green, gold and yellow colours, he allowed himself nostalgia. He couldn't begrudge nostalgia, given the many kilometres that separated him from his native land. A second later he experienced panic when loneliness hit him. A moment of reflection brought to his attention that it wasn't really loneliness clawing at his heart, but rather a sense of disorientation—a feeling of being lost.

This couldn't be jetlag. Not at all. Ambassador Matabane reassured himself. It certainly couldn't be. He had landed on the island a week ago. What he was experiencing was a temporary state of dizziness associated with being dislocated from the sacred ground where one's umbilical cord had been buried.

In a split of a second he chastised himself. Allowing homesickness to seduce him was a weakness and self-indulgence not befitting the representative of a foreign state and a power player on the African continent. He wished he were privy to the internal emotional experiences of other members of the diplomatic corps. Drumming on his BlackBerry keyboard, he quickly noted in his mental diary a need to visit his ancestral ground in Ga-Sekhukhune the next time he returned to South Africa.

Taking a step back to the window, he pressed his face against the window pane. His gaze randomly followed a dozen pedestrians, some walking in pairs and groups, and the odd individuals hurrying on their own here and there. From their hurried walk he could tell that they were in great discomfort at being single. There was, indeed, an oddness about solitary figures in Port Louis. It wasn't as though Port Louis was considered a romantic city, like, say, Paris, where natives and foreigners alike come searching for the mythical love bite. Yet in its own way, Port Louis seemed to embrace couples keen to explore the supposed romanticism offered by the island nation's tropical geography.

Ambassador Matabane's gaze fell on a couple sitting at the water's edge, their feet dangling above the dark water. From his vantage point on the sixth floor, he could not discern whether they were an old or young couple. Their postures nonetheless confirmed one certainty—they were lovers. In all likelihood, they were newlyweds on their honeymoon, or maybe recently betrothed, still flirting with matrimony. The probability of them being a couple with many years of marriage behind them seemed low. It was unfortunate how the distance between married couples seemed to widen with the duration of their years together.

As he strained to focus to interrogate their profiles closer, his vision blurred. In an instant he was shuttled back to the past. The illusion played itself before his eyes. He was a barefooted kid running alongside other boys on the banks of Tubatse River in Ga-Sekhukhune. Their loud chatter reverberated throughout the valley as they dived and splashed in the brooding waters. The waters were not unlike other waters that he would later come across in his adult life during his days in exile.

Unlike the Danube, which had pumped the acidity of bitter loneliness through his veins during his military training days in Yugoslavia, Tubatse River held fond memories of childhood innocence. In his consciousness he knew that not even the fabulous Thames or the romantic Seine would flow through his veins as did Tubatse.

Though not enamoured with foreign rivers, he found himself fascinated with the Mississippi. Not that its width and length had claim to great histories that could impress him nor any of the rivers the world over. He was certain, also, that no ancient civilizations had ever worshipped it or traced their ancestry to its hallowed depths. He was a bit prejudiced against this particular watercourse and tended to associate it with the greed of Wall Street hundreds of kilometres away in New York.

Like the seductress she is, Mississippi River had crossed Ambassador Matabane's path years ago. It was on the banks of this river that he had met Beth, his African-American wife. Though the marriage ended, the temporary merger of the two rivers, Mississippi and Tubatse, had resulted in a daughter.

That night Ambassador Matabane opted to forgo his habit of going to bed late. Tomorrow was going to be an eventful day. Two portraits that represented political power back home were going to be replaced. The exercise had been triggered by an official phone call from Pretoria. The call, dispatched personally by the Director General of the Department of International Affairs, had informed him of a regime change.

Was it a coup? Ambassador Matabane recalled wondering aloud. The Director General had, of course, found the question amusing. Though the telephone conversation did reassure the Ambassador otherwise, his initial reaction left him troubled. How could such a thought have entered his mind? A post-1994 South Africa was in safe hands, surely. From the revered Tata Mandela, the stewardship of the country had passed to Thabo Mbeki, a competent successor. But then, out of the blue, he was out. His passing of the baton without completing his leg of the relay signaled political disharmony.

During their conversation, the DG had further informed Ambassador Matabane that portraits of the new head of state, Kgalema Motlanthe, and his deputy, Baleka Mbete, would be dispatched the following morning by diplomatic bag. Having blank spots on the walls of the embassy reception hall was out of the question. What impression would that convey to the hosts? A coup would probably be their initial suspicion.

Which images to present in the interim, until the new portraits arrived? Time raced by as Ambassador Matabane sat pondering the question.

Was it a coup?

It was a valid and appropriate question, when taking political trends into perspective, especially for a native of Africa. Coups on the continent were as common as offshore bank accounts held by African heads of state. Undisputed poll results leading to peaceful regime changes were as rare as bumper crop harvests.

Whatever the cause of the regime change, Ambassador Matabane did not expect to be recalled for briefing. Whatever new regime came to power was likely to pursue the diplomatic path charted by his predecessor. The likelihood of his little piece of paradise on the Indian Ocean having a fallout with his new political masters was remote.

As far as he could recall, the only diplomatically thorny issue between the two countries arose from dealing with a dozen or so South African nationals serving prison terms for drug possession.

A coup? Could it be that his country was thumbing its nose at the world, saying, "What's been good for Africa is good for us as well"? There were no guarantees in politics, after all. He'd learned that through his travels and many years in the diplomatic service.

"The president has been recalled," the DG had elaborated. Vague as the words were, they had nonetheless eased the ambassador's trepidations. A recall was a demotion—"impeachment," as the fancy Americans pronounce it. In a matter of hours Mbeki had joined Richard Nixon amongst the few leaders ever to have been demoted.

Was it a disgrace to be impeached, or recalled? The phrase sounded more civil than having been "deposed." Being toppled, in some countries, carried the risk of not merely losing your state pension, but of a date with the firing squad or hangman's noose.

Recalled, impeached . . . two fancy verbs that convey the same thing—the sacking or firing of prominent figures from political office. Accused, indicted, arraigned, prosecuted, charged—now those carried a stigma!

So "The President's Recall" would be the official pronouncement on the matter. It was a politically bland communiqué that Ambassador Matabane and other South African diplomats around the world could convey to their host governments.

Ambassador Matabane's relief was boundless. His country was mature enough not to invoke another coup spectacle of the kind on which CNN and other international media vultures flourished. The limited nature of the change also meant that a crisis meeting with Prime Minister Navinchandra Ramgoolam was unlikely. A more probable scenario would be a relaxed meeting with the Minister of Foreign Affairs, Dr. the Honourable Arvin Boodell. Back home, the implications would include the state presses sending requisitions to the treasury for the printing of new professional seals and letterheads.

Thank heaven it was less dramatic than a coup. A coup in the traditional sense . . . tanks rolling towards parliament; the recently acquired Gripen jets bombarding Centurion Military Base, Waterkloof Air Force Base, and other military installations where loyal troops were holed up; renegade soldiers storming Mahlamba Mdlopu, the Presidential Palace, and frog-marching the dethroned President to Pretoria's C-Max Prison, unshaven and still in his shorts, pyjamas, or whatever current attire he was in; or pouncing while he was in front of television cameras, delivering his State of the Nation Address before a joint sitting of parliament, then frog-marching him away in front of international dignitaries and a shocked nation. Now, that would have been dramatic fare!

Just then a disconcerting thought crossed Ambassador Matabane's mind: what actions do coup plotters charged with arresting a president take when they find him engaged in carnal pleasures? With a mistress maybe, who serves as a Minister, or a Minister's wife? Do they let him finish the act or cuff him, permitting him to watch as they take turns in violating his companion? Do they record it on film to be broadcast as State Exhibit No. 1 during his trial for gross dereliction of duty and violation of executive powers?

Surely such an incident must have occurred somewhere. If he were to consider writing a book on the subject he might title it *Last Acts Deposed Leaders Were Found Engaged In*. With the world's appetite for kinky stuff, especially involving the rich, famous and prominent, surely the book would make its way to the bestseller list. He pushed the thoughts aside, but made a note to check with colleagues posted to countries that had experienced coups; countries like the DRC and others could be relevant case studies.

His mandate was reasonable compared with those of fellow diplomats in more troubled spots. His heart went out to his counterpart in Israel. To Israeli diplomats the world over. They, surely, were forever stressed by the frequent spin doctoring they had to do, and the daily threat of expulsion from their host nations each time Israel's dealing with its neighbours caused diplomatic tensions. One moment it would be over the aerial bombardment of Lebanon, the next over the blockade of Gaza, or the annexation of land for settlements on the West Bank. And diplomats had to clean up after the actions or words of their political masters.

Arriving at his office the next morning, Ambassador Matabane stood staring at portraits of Mbeki and his deputy, Phumzile Mlambo-Nqcuka. They hung side by side in the foyer. Still awaiting the arrival of portraits of the new leadership, he was not sure yet what action to take. Keeping Mbeki's and Mlambo-Nqcuka's portraits hanging could give the impression that they were still in power. Removing them without replacements could mean that his country was in political limbo. It was a perplexing moment, indeed.

His state of indecision would last until the diplomatic bag arrived around eleven in the morning. He finally gave the order for the removal of the Mbeki and Mlambo-Nqcuka portraits. He noticed that a couple of his staff shed a tear or two. It was a somber moment. Like a death. It was a permanent parting with a familiar uncle to be replaced by the unknown.

"My wish is that he is photogenic," a senior female staff member commented when the eagerly awaited diplomatic bag arrived. They'd better be, thought the Ambassador. They will be the face of South Africa's democracy until the next regime change. The faces of continuity and stability. Damn well better be.

The salesman in him assured him that the portraits of the new president and his deputy would do the country justice. Presidential portraits were key accessories in the marking of a country. It didn't surprise him that the packing was of the highest quality. How locals viewed their governments mattered, too. That was why portraits of ministers, their deputies and senior civil servants enjoyed the same artistic treatment.

In all his service and travels he didn't recall having come across an ugly—no, an un-photogenic—statesman in a photograph. Not because leaders of governments were endowed with better looks than others. Portraits and photographers of Idi Amin presented him as big and imposing, but never hideous. Portraits of Mugabe presented him as stern and dignified, but never ugly. Ugly heads of state didn't exist. Not even Adolf Hitler.

Ambassador Matabane knew the secret. As a career diplomat he knew that appearance mattered a great deal. Governments were extremely vigilant about who represented them in foreign states. They invested heavily in the protocol. The commissioning of official portraits was a highly specialised activity. Overseen by teams of designers, stylists, make-up artists, photographers, technicians, presidency and government spokespersons, their deputies and assistants. An entire bureaucracy presided over the shooting of those portraits. Days, weeks, months were spent in the consultations about the execution of portraits for presidents or prime ministers and their deputies. Such a bloated civil service was justified as necessary in the selling of leaders. Civil servants, like himself, after all, served as silent emissaries to both the populace and the international community.

Ambassador Matabane waited with bated breath as the faces of the new South African leadership were unwrapped. He sighed with relief after the last piece of bubble wrap had been removed from the photograph. There was Motlanthe, eyes staring straight ahead, well groomed, shiny black hair—admirable for someone his age. The new president looked dignified, confident and befitting the highest office in the land. As a former political prisoner, former unionist and deputy president of the ANC, he definitely enjoyed the support of the majority of the party.

His major credential was his stint on Robben Island. There was a code amongst cadres of the movement—never mess with anyone who has done time on the Island. There were other codes, of course, but over time they had been gradually shuttled into the background. Those included the following: never mess with Xhosas—they all have political connections; don't mess with former exiles, they might ascend to the presidency or evolve into BEE billionaires and remove you from the gravy train.

Ambassador Matabane watched as Motlanthe's and Mbete's portraits were mounted side by side on the wall. As dictated by protocol, Motlanthe's portrait stood a couple centimeters higher than Mbete's so that executive seniority was never in doubt. The last portrait to be hung was that of Minister of International Affairs Maite Nkoana-Mashabane.

Portrait-mounting duties done, Ambassador Matabane retired to his office. He had his day's allocation of reports to file and correspondence to respond to. One urgent matter was to respond to an invitation from the Mauritian Minister for Culture, Education and Human Resources, Dr. the Honourable Vasant Bunwaree. With so many former medical practitioners in the cabinet, he and any other visiting heads of state and dignitaries were guaranteed pre-eminent attention should they experience health complications. The entire cabinet could merely suspend heated budget, health and environmental debates and revert to the Hippocratic oath, with speech folders swapped for stethoscopes and scalpels.

His nation's daily affairs concluded, Ambassador Matabane decided to call it a day. As Dive, his young Mauritian chauffeur of Indian descent, guided the sleek black Mercedes down the streets of Cyber City's Ebene suburb, Port Louis–bound, Ambassador Matabane allowed himself a catnap. He looked forward to a well-deserved rest at the Labourdonnais.

A Private Experience

Chimamanda Ngozi Adichie

Chika climbs in through the store window first and then holds the shutter as the woman climbs in after her. The store looks as if it was deserted long before the riots started; the empty rows of wooden shelves are covered in yellow dust, as are the metal containers stacked in a corner. The store is small, smaller than Chika's walk-in closet back home. The woman climbs in and the window shutters squeak as Chika lets go of them. Chika's hands are trembling, her calves burning after the unsteady run from the market in her high-heeled sandals. She wants to thank the woman, for stopping her as she dashed past, for saying "No run that way!" and for leading her, instead, to this empty store where they could hide. But before she can say thank you, the woman says, reaching out to touch her bare neck, "My necklace lost when I'm running."

"I dropped everything," Chika says. "I was buying oranges and I dropped the oranges and my handbag." She does not add that the handbag was a Burberry, an original one that her mother had bought on a recent trip to London.

The woman sighs and Chika imagines that she is thinking of her necklace, probably plastic beads threaded on a piece of string. Even without the woman's strong Hausa accent, Chika can tell she is a Northerner, from the narrowness of her face, the unfamiliar rise of her cheekbones; and that she is Muslim, because of the scarf. It hangs around the woman's neck now, but it was probably wound loosely round her face before, covering her ears. A long, flimsy pink and black scarf, with the garish prettiness of cheap things. Chika wonders if the woman is looking at her as well, if the woman can tell, from her light complexion and the silver finger rosary her mother insists she wear, that she is Igbo and Christian. Later, Chika will learn that, as she and the woman are speaking, Hausa Muslims are hacking down Igbo Christians with machetes, clubbing them with stones. But now she says, "Thank you for calling me. Everything happened so fast and everybody ran and I was suddenly alone and I didn't know what I was doing. Thank you."

"This place safe," the woman says, in a voice that is so soft it sounds like a whisper. "Them not going to small-small shop, only big-big shop and market."

"Yes," Chika says. But she has no reason to agree or disagree, she knows nothing about riots: the closest she has come is the prodemocracy rally at the university a few weeks ago, where she had held a bright-green branch and joined in chanting "The military must go! Abacha must go! Democracy now!" Besides, she would not even have participated in that rally if her sister Nnedi had not been one of the organisers who had gone from hostel to hostel to hand out fliers and talk to students about the importance of "having our voices heard."

Chika's hands are still trembling. Just half an hour ago, she was in the market with Nnedi. She was buying oranges and Nnedi had walked farther down to buy groundnuts and then there was shouting in English, in pidgin, in Hausa, in Igbo. "Riot! Trouble is coming, oh! They have killed a man!" Then people around her were running, pushing against one another, overturning wheelbarrows full of yams, leaving behind bruised vegetables they had just bargained hard for. Chika smelled the sweat and fear and she ran, too, across wide streets, into this narrow one, which she feared—felt—was dangerous, until she saw the woman.

She and the woman stand silently in the store for a while, looking out of the window they have just climbed through, its squeaky wooden shutters swinging in the air. The street is quiet at first, and then they hear the sound of running feet. They both move away from the window, instinctively, although Chika can still see a man and a woman walking past, the woman holding her wrapper up above her knees, a baby tied to her back. The man is speaking swiftly in Igbo and all Chika hears is "She may have run to Uncle's house."

"Close window," the woman says.

Chika shuts the windows and without the air from the street flowing in, the dust in the room is suddenly so thick she can see it, billowing above her. The room is stuffy and smells nothing like the streets outside, which smell like the kind of sky-coloured smoke that wafts around during Christmas when people throw goat carcasses into fires to burn the hair off the skin. The streets where she ran blindly, not sure in which direction Nnedi had run, not sure if the man running beside her was a friend or an enemy, not sure if she should stop and pick up one of the bewildered-looking children separated from their mothers in the rush, not even sure who was who or who was killing whom.

Later she will see the hulks of burned cars, jagged holes in place of their windows and windshields, and she will imagine the burning cars dotting the city like picnic bonfires, silent witnesses to so much. She will find out it had all started at the motor park, when a man drove over a copy of the Holy Koran that had been dropped on the roadside, a man who happened to be Igbo and Christian. The men nearby, men who sat around all day playing draughts, men who happened to be Muslim, pulled him out of his pickup truck, cut his head off with one flash of a machete, and carried it to the market, asking others to join in; the infidel had desecrated the Holy Book. Chika will imagine the man's head, his skin ashen in death, and she will throw up and retch until her stomach is sore. But now, she asks the woman, "Can you still smell the smoke?"

"Yes," the woman says. She unties her green wrapper and spreads it on the dusty floor. She has on only a blouse and a shimmery black slip torn at the seams. "Come and sit."

Chika looks at the threadbare wrapper on the floor; it is probably one of the two the woman owns. She looks down at her own denim skirt and red T-shirt embossed with a picture of the Statue of Liberty, both of which she bought when she and Nnedi spent a few summer weeks with relatives in New York. "No, your wrapper will get dirty," she says.

"Sit," the woman says. "We are waiting here long time."

"Do you have an idea how long . . . ?"

"This night or tomorrow morning."

Chika raises her hand to her forehead, as though checking for a malaria fever.

The touch of her cool palm usually calms her, but this time her palm is moist and sweaty. "I left my sister buying groundnuts. I don't know where she is."

"She is going safe place."

"Nnedi."

"Eh?"

"My sister. Her name is Nnedi."

"Nnedi," the woman repeats, and her Hausa accent sheaths the Igbo name in a feathery gentleness.

Later, Chika will comb the hospital mortuaries looking for Nnedi; she will go to newspaper offices clutching the photo of herself and Nnedi taken at a wedding just the week before, the one where she has a stupid smile-yelp on her face because Nnedi pinched her just before the photo was taken, the two of them wearing matching off-the-shoulder Ankara gowns. She will tape photocopies of the photo on the walls of the market and the nearby stores. She will not find Nnedi. She will never find Nnedi. But now she says to the woman, "Nnedi and I came up here last week to visit our auntie. We are on vacation from school."

"Where you go school?" the woman asks.

"We are at the University of Lagos. I am reading medicine. Nnedi is in political science." Chika wonders if the woman even knows what going to university means. And she wonders, too, if she mentioned school only to feed herself the reality she needs now—that Nnedi is not lost in a riot, that Nnedi is safe somewhere, probably laughing in her easy, mouth-all-open way, probably making one of her political arguments. Like how the government of General Abacha was using its foreign policy to legitimise itself in the eyes of other African countries. Or how the huge popularity in blond hair attachments was a direct result of British colonialism.

"We have only spent a week here with our auntie, we have never even been to Kano before," Chika says, and she realises that what she feels is this: she and her sister should not be affected by the riot. Riots like this were what she read about in newspapers. Riots like this were what happened to other people.

"Your auntie is in market?" the woman asks.

"No, she's at work. She is the director at the secretariat." Chika raises her hand to her forehead again. She lowers herself and sits, much closer to the woman than she ordinarily would have, so as to rest her body entirely on the wrapper. She smells something on the woman, something harsh and clean like the bar soap their housegirl uses to wash the bed linen.

"Your auntie is going safe place."

"Yes," Chika says. The conversation seems surreal; she feels as if she is watching herself. "I still can't believe this is happening, this riot."

The woman is staring straight ahead. Everything about her is long and slender, her legs stretched out in front of her, her fingers with henna-stained nails, her feet. "It is work of evil," she says finally.

Chika wonders if that is all the woman thinks of the riots, if that is all she sees them as—evil. She wishes Nnedi were here. She imagines the cocoa brown of Nnedi's eyes lighting up, her lips moving quickly, explaining that riots do not happen in a vacuum, that religion and ethnicity are often politicised because the ruler is safe if the hungry ruled are killing one another. Then Chika feels a prick of guilt for wondering if this woman's mind is large enough to grasp any of that.

"In school you are seeing sick people now?" the woman asks.

Chika averts her gaze quickly so that the woman will not see the surprise. "My clinicals? Yes, we started last year. We see patients at the Teaching Hospital." She does not add that she often feels attacks of uncertainty, that she slouches at the back of the group of six or seven students, avoiding the senior registrar's eyes, hoping she will not be asked to examine a patient and give her differential diagnosis.

"I am trader," the woman says. "I'm selling onions."

Chika listens for sarcasm or reproach in the tone, but there is none. The voice is as steady and as low, a woman simply telling what she does.

"I hope they will not destroy market stalls," Chika replies; she does not know what else to say.

"Every time when they are rioting, they break market," the woman says.

Chika wants to ask the woman how many riots she has witnessed but she does not. She has read about the others in the past: Hausa Muslim zealots attacking Igbo Christians, and sometimes Igbo Christians going on murderous missions of revenge. She does not want a conversation of naming names.

"My nipple is burning like pepper," the woman says.

"What?"

"My nipple is burning like pepper."

Before Chika can swallow the bubble of surprise in her throat and say anything, the woman pulls up her blouse and unhooks the front clasp of a threadbare black bra. She brings out the money, ten- and twenty-naira notes, folded inside her bra, before freeing her full breasts.

"Burning-burning like pepper," she says, cupping her breasts and leaning toward

Chika, as though in an offering. Chika shifts. She remembers the pediatrics rotation only a week ago: the senior registrar, Dr. Olunloyo, wanted all the students to feel the stage 4 heart murmur of a little boy, who was watching them with curious eyes. The doctor asked her to go first and she became sweaty, her mind blank, no longer sure where the heart was. She had finally placed a shaky hand on the left side of the boy's nipple, and the brrr-brrr-brrr vibration of swishing blood going the wrong way, pulsing against her fingers, made her stutter and say "Sorry, sorry" to the boy, even though he was smiling at her.

The woman's nipples are nothing like that boy's. They are cracked, taut and dark brown, the areolas lighter-toned. Chika looks carefully at them, reaches out and feels them. "Do you have a baby?" she asks.

"Yes. One year."

"Your nipples are dry, but they don't look infected. After you feed the baby, you have to use some lotion. And while you are feeding, you have to make sure the nipple and also this other part, the areola, fit inside the baby's mouth."

The woman gives Chika a long look. "First time of this. I'm having five children."

"It was the same with my mother. Her nipples cracked when the sixth child came, and she didn't know what caused it, until a friend told her that she had to moisturise," Chika says. She hardly ever lies, but the few times she does, there is always a purpose behind the lie. She wonders what purpose this lie serves, this need to draw on a fictional past similar to the woman's; she and Nnedi are her mother's only children. Besides, her mother always had Dr. Igbokwe, with his British training and affectation, a phone call away.

"What is your mother rubbing on her nipple?" the woman asks.

"Cocoa butter. The cracks healed fast."

"Eh?" The woman watches Chika for a while, as if this disclosure has created a bond. "All right, I get it and use." She plays with her scarf for a moment and then says, "I am looking for my daughter. We go market together this morning. She is selling groundnut near bus stop, because there are many customers. Then riot begin and I am looking up and down market for her."

"The baby?" Chika asks, knowing how stupid she sounds even as she asks.

The woman shakes her head and there is a flash of impatience, even anger, in her eyes. "You have ear problem? You don't hear what I am saying?"

"Sorry," Chika says.

"Baby is at home! This one is first daughter. Halima." The woman starts to cry.

She cries quietly, her shoulders heaving up and down, not the kind of loud sobbing that the women Chika knows do, the kind that screams "Hold me and comfort me because I cannot deal with this alone." The woman's crying is private, as though she is carrying out a necessary ritual that involves no one else.

Later, when Chika will wish that she and Nnedi had not decided to take a taxi to the market just to see a little of the ancient city of Kano outside their aunt's neighborhood, she will wish also that the woman's daughter, Halima, had been sick or tired or lazy that morning, so that she would not have sold groundnuts that day.

The woman wipes her eyes with one end of her blouse. "Allah keep your sister and Halima in safe place," she says. And because Chika is not sure what Muslims say to show agreement—it cannot be "amen"—she simply nods.

The woman has discovered a rusted tap in a corner of the store, near the metal containers. Perhaps where the trader washed his or her hands, she says, telling Chika that the stores on this street were abandoned months ago, after the government declared them illegal structures to be demolished. The woman turns on the tap and they both watch—surprised—as water trickles out. Brownish, and so metallic Chika can smell it already. Still, it runs.

"I wash and pray," the woman says, her voice louder now, and she smiles for the first time to show even-sized teeth, the front ones stained brown. Her dimples sink into her cheeks, deep enough to swallow half a finger, and unusual in a face so lean. The woman clumsily washes her hands and face at the tap, then removes her scarf from her neck and places it down on the floor. Chika looks away. She knows the woman is on her knees, facing Mecca, but she does not look. It is like the woman's tears, a private experience, and she wishes that she could leave the store. Or that she, too, could pray, could believe in a God, see an omniscient presence in the stale air of the store. She cannot remember when her idea of God has not been cloudy, like the reflection from a steamy bathroom mirror, and she cannot remember ever trying to clean the mirror.

She touches the finger rosary that she still wears, sometimes on her pinky or her forefinger, to please her mother. Nnedi no longer wears hers, once saying with that throaty laugh, "Rosaries are really magical potions, and I don't need those, thank you."

Later, the family will offer Masses over and over for Nnedi to be found safe, though never for the repose of Nnedi's soul. And Chika will think about this woman, praying with her head to the dustfloor, and she will change her mind about telling her mother that offering Masses is a waste of money, that it is just fundraising for the church.

When the woman rises, Chika feels strangely energised. More than three hours have passed and she imagines that the riot is quieted, the rioters drifted away. She has to leave, she has to make her way home and make sure Nnedi and her auntie are fine.

"I must go," Chika says.

Again the look of impatience on the woman's face. "Outside is danger."

"I think they have gone. I can't even smell any more smoke."

The woman says nothing, seats herself back down on the wrapper. Chika watches her for a while, disappointed without knowing why. Maybe she wants a blessing from the woman, something. "How far away is your house?" she asks.

"Far. I'm taking two buses."

"Then I will come back with my auntie's driver and take you home," Chika says.

The woman looks away. Chika walks slowly to the window and opens it. She expects to hear the woman ask her to stop, to come back, not to be rash. But the woman says nothing and Chika feels the quiet eyes on her back as she climbs out of the window.

The streets are silent. The sun is falling, and in the evening dimness, Chika looks around, unsure which way to go. She prays that a taxi will appear, by magic, by luck, by God's hand. Then she prays that Nnedi will be inside the taxi, asking her where the hell she has been, they have been so worried about her. Chika has not reached the end of the second street, toward the market, when she sees the body. She almost doesn't see it, walks so close to it that she feels its heat. The body must have been very recently burned. The smell is sickening, of roasted flesh, unlike that of any she has ever smelled.

Later, when Chika and her aunt go searching throughout Kano, a policeman in the front seat of her aunt's air-conditioned car, she will see other bodies, many burned, lying lengthwise along the sides of the street, as though someone carefully pushed them there, straightening them. She will look at only one of the corpses, naked, stiff, facedown, and it will strike her that she cannot tell if the partially burned man is Igbo or Hausa, Christian or Muslim, from looking at that charred flesh. She will listen to BBC radio and hear the accounts of the deaths and the riots—"religious with undertones of ethnic tension," the voice will say. And she will fling the radio to the wall and a fierce red rage will run through her at how it has all been packaged and sanitised and made to fit into so few words, all those bodies. But now, the heat from the burned body is so close to her, so present and warm that she turns and dashes back toward the store. She feels a sharp pain along her lower leg as she runs. She gets to the store and raps on the window, and she keeps rapping until the woman opens it.

Chika sits on the floor and looks closely, in the failing light, at the line of blood crawling down her leg. Her eyes swim restlessly in her head. It looks alien, the blood, as though someone had squirted tomato paste on her.

"Your leg. There is blood," the woman says, a little wearily. She wets one end of her scarf at the tap and cleans the cut on Chika's leg, then ties the wet scarf around it, knotting it at the calf.

"Thank you," Chika says.

"You want toilet?"

"Toilet? No."

"The containers there, we are using for toilet," the woman says. She takes one of the containers to the back of the store, and soon the smell fills Chika's nose, mixes with the smells of dust and metallic water, makes her feel light-headed and queasy. She closes her eyes.

"Sorry, oh! My stomach is bad. Everything happening today," the woman says from behind her. Afterwards, the woman opens the window and places the container outside, then washes her hands at the tap. She comes back and she and Chika sit side by side in silence; after a while they hear raucous chanting in the distance, words Chika cannot make out. The store is almost completely dark when the woman stretches out on the floor, her upper body on the wrapper and the rest of her not.

Later, Chika will read in *The Guardian* that "the reactionary Hausa-speaking Muslims in the North have a history of violence against non-Muslims," and in the middle of her grief, she will stop to remember that she examined the nipples and experienced the gentleness of a woman who is Hausa and Muslim.

Chika hardly sleeps all night. The window is shut tight; the air is stuffy, and the dust, thick and gritty, crawls up her nose. She keeps seeing the blackened corpse floating in a halo by the window, pointing accusingly at her. Finally she hears the woman get up and open the window, letting in the dull blue of early dawn. The woman stands there for a while before climbing out. Chika can hear footsteps, people walking past. She hears the woman call out, voice raised in recognition, followed by rapid Hausa that Chika does not understand.

The woman climbs back into the store. "Danger is finished. It is Abu. He is selling provisions. He is going to see his store. Everywhere policeman with tear gas. Soldier-man is coming. I go now before soldier-man will begin to harass somebody."

Chika stands slowly and stretches; her joints ache. She will walk all the way back to her auntie's home in the gated estate, because there are no taxis on the street, there are only army Jeeps and battered police station wagons. She will find her auntie, wandering from one room to the next with a glass of water in her hand, muttering in Igbo, over and over, "Why did I ask you and Nnedi to visit? Why did my chi deceive me like this?" And Chika will grasp her auntie's shoulders tightly and lead her to a sofa.

Now, Chika unties the scarf from her leg, shakes it as though to shake the bloodstains out, and hands it to the woman.

"Thank you."

"Wash your leg well-well. Greet your sister, greet your people," the woman says, tightening her wrapper around her waist.

"Greet your people also. Greet your baby and Halima," Chika says. Later, as she walks home, she will pick up a stone stained the copper of dried blood and hold the ghoulish souvenir to her chest. And she will suspect right then, in a strange flash while clutching the stone, that she will never find Nnedi, that her sister is gone. But now, she turns to the woman and adds, "May I keep your scarf? The bleeding might start again." The woman looks for a moment as if she does not understand; then she nods. There is perhaps the beginning of future grief on her face, but she smiles a slight, distracted smile before she hands the scarf back to Chika and turns to climb out of the window.

Weight of Whispers

Yvonne Adhiambo Owuor

The collection of teeth on the man's face is a splendid brown. I have never seen such teeth before. Refusing all instruction, my eyes focus on dental contours and craters. Denuded of any superficial pretence; no braces, no fillings, no toothbrush, it is a place where small scavengers thrive.

"Evidence!" The man giggles.

A flash of green and my US$50 disappears into his pocket. His fingers prod: shirt, coat, trousers. He finds the worked snakeskin wallet. No money in it, just a picture of Agnethe-mama, Lune and Chi-Chi, elegant and unsmiling, diamonds in their ears, on their necks and wrists. The man tilts the picture this way and that, returns the picture into the wallet. The wallet disappears into another of his pockets. The man's teeth gleam.

"Souvenir." Afterwards, a hiccupping "Greeeheeereeehee" not unlike a *National Geographic* hyena, complete with a chorus from the pack.

"Please . . . it's . . . my mother . . . all I have."

His eyes become thin slits, head tilts and the veins on his right eye pulse. His nostrils flare, an indignant goat.

A thin sweat-trail runs down my spine, the backs of my knees tingle. I look around at the faceless others in the dank room. His hand grabs my goatee and twists. My eyes smart. I lift up my hand to wipe them. The man sees the gold insignia ring, glinting on my index finger.

The ring of the royal household. One of only three. The second belonged to my father. Agnethe-mama told me that when father appeared to her in a dream to tell her he was dead, he was still wearing it. The third . . . no one has ever spoken about.

The policeman's grin broadens. He pounces. Long fingers. A girl would cut her hair for fingers like his. He spits on my finger, and draws out the ring with his teeth; the ring I have worn for 18 years—from the day I was recognised by the priests as a man and a prince. It was supposed to have been passed on to the son I do not have. The policeman twists my hand this way and that, his tongue caught between his teeth; a study of concentrated avarice.

"Evidence!"

Gargoyles are petrified life-mockers, sentries at entry points, sentinels of sorrow, spitting at fate. I will try to protest.

"It is sacred ring . . . Please . . . please." To my shame, my voice breaks.

"Evidence!"

Cheek: nerve, gall, impertinence, brashness.

Cheek: the part of my face he chose to brand.

———————

Later on, much later on, I will wonder what makes it possible for one man to hit another for no reason other than the fact that he can. But now, I lower my head. The sum total of what resides in a very tall man who used to be a prince in a land eviscerated.

Two presidents died when a missile launched from land forced their plane down. A man of note, a prince, had said, on the first day, that the perpetrators must be hunted down. That evil must be purged from lives. That is all the prince had meant. It seems someone heard something else. It emerges later on, when it is too late, that an old servant took his obligation too far, in the name of his prince.

We had heard rumor of a holocaust, of a land hemorrhaging to death.

Everywhere, hoarse murmurs, eyes white and wide with an arcane fear. Is it possible that brothers would machete sisters-in-law to stew-meat-size chunks in front of nephews and nieces?

———————

It was on the fifth day after the presidents had disintegrated with their plane that I saw that the zenith of existence cannot be human.

In the seasons of my European sojourn, Brussels, Paris, Rome, Amsterdam— rarely London, a city I could, then, accommodate a loathing to—I wondered about the unsaid; hesitant signals and interminable reminders of "What They Did." Like a mnemonic device, the swastika would grace pages and screens, at least once a week, unto perpetuity. I wondered.

I remembered a conversation in Krakow with an academician, a man with primeval eyes. A pepper-colored, quill-beard obscured the man's mouth, and seemed to speak in its place. I was, suddenly, in the thrall of an irrational fear that the mobile barbs would shoot off his face and stab me.

I could not escape.

I had agreed to offer perspectives on his seminal work, a work in progress he called "A Mystagogy of Human Evil." I had asked, meaning nothing, a prelude to commentary:

"Are you a Jew?"

So silently, the top of his face fell, flowed towards his jaw, his formidable moustache-beard lank, his shoulders shaking, his eyes flooded with tears. But not a sound emerged from his throat. Unable to tolerate the tears of another man, I walked away.

Another gathering, another conversation, with another man. Mellowed by the well-being engendered by a goblet of Rémy Martin, I ventured an opinion about the sacrificial predilection of being: the necessity of oblation of men by men to men.

"War is the excuse," I said. I was playing with words, true, but, oddly the exchange petered into mumbles of "Never Again."

A year later, at a balcony party, when I asked the American Consul in Luxembourg to suggest a book which probed the slaughter of Germans during World War II, she said:

"By whom?"

Before I could answer, she had spun away, turning her back on me as if I had asked "Cain, where is your brother?"

What had been Cain's response?

To my amusement, I was, of course, never invited to another informal diplomatic gathering. Though I would eventually relinquish my European postings—in order to harness, to my advantage, European predilection for African gems—over après-diner Drambuie, now and again I pondered over what lay beneath the unstated.

Now, my world has tilted into a realm where other loaded silences lurk. And I can sense why some things must remain buried in silence, even if they resuscitate themselves at night in dreams where blood pours out of phantom mouths. In the empire of silence, the "turning away" act is a vain exorcism of a familiar daemon which invades the citadels we ever change, we constantly fortify. Dragging us back through old routes of anguish, it suggests: "Alas, human, your nature relishes fratricidal blood."

But to be human is to be intrinsically, totally, resolutely good. Is it not?

Nothing entertains the devil as much as this protestation.

———————

Roger, the major-domo, had served in our home since before my birth thirty-seven years ago. He reappeared at our door on the evening of the fifth day after the death of the two presidents. He had disappeared on the first day of the plane deaths. The day he resurfaced, we were celebrating the third anniversary of my engagement to Lune. I had thought a pungent whiff which entered the room with his presence was merely the Gorgonzola cheese Lune had been unwrapping.

Roger says:

"J'ai terminé. Tout a été nettoyé." It is done. All has been cleaned.

"What Roger?"

"The dirt." He smiles.

The bottle of Dom Pérignon Millésimé in my hand wavers. I observe that Roger is shirtless, his hair stands in nascent, accidental dreadlocks. The bottom half of his trousers are torn, and his shoeless left foot swollen. His fist is black and caked with what I think is tar. And in his wake, the smell of mouldering matter. Roger searches the ground, hangs his head, his mouth tremulous:

"They are coming . . . Sir."

Then Roger stoops. He picks up the crumbs of petit fours from the carpet; he is fastidious about cleanliness. The Dom Pérignon Millésimé drops from my hand, it does not break, though its precious contents soak into the carpet. Roger frowns, his mouth pursed. He also disapproves of waste.

In our party clothes and jewelry, with what we had in our wallets and two packed medium-size Chanel cases, we abandoned our life at home. We counted the money we had between us: US$3723. In the bank account, of course, there was more. There was always more. As President of the Banque Locale, I was one of three who held keys to the vault, so to say. Two weeks before the presidents died, I sold my Paris apartment. The money was to be used to expand our bank into Zaïre. We got the last four of the last eight seats on the last flight out of our city. We assumed then it was only right that it be so. We landed at the Jomo Kenyatta International Airport in Nairobi, Kenya, at ten p.m.

I wondered about Kenya. I knew the country as a transit lounge and a stopover base on my way to and out of Europe. It was only after we got a three months visitor's pass that I realized that Kenya was an Anglophone country. Fortunately, we were in transit. Soon, we would be in Europe, among friends.

I am Boniface Louis R. Kuseremane. It has been long since anyone called me by my full name. The "R" name cannot be spoken aloud. In the bustle and noises of the airport, I glance at Agnethe-mama, regal, graying, her diamond earrings dance, her nose is slightly raised, her forehead unlined. My mother, Agnethe, is a princess in transit. She leans lightly against Lune, who stands, one foot's heel touching the toes of the other, one arm raised and then drooping over her shoulder.

I met Lune on the funeral day of both her parents, royal diplomats who had died in an unfortunate road crash. She was then, as she is now, not of earth. Then, she seemed to be hovering atop her parents' grave, deciding whether to join them, fly away or stay. I asked her to leave the corps ballet in France where she was studying—to stay with me, forever. She agreed and I gained a sibylline fiancée.

"Chéri, que faisons-nous maintenant?" What do we do now?

Lune asks, clinging to my mother's hand. Her other arm curved into mine. Chi-Chi, my sister, looks up at me, expecting the right answer, her hand at her favorite spot, my waistband—a childhood affectation that has lingered into her twentieth year. Chi-Chi, in thought, still sucks on her two fingers.

"Bu-bu." Chi-Chi always calls me Bu-Bu. "Bu-Bu, dans quel pays sommes nous?"

"Kenya," I tell her.

Chi-Chi is an instinctive contemplative. I once found her weeping and laughing, awed, as it turns out, by the wings of a monarch butterfly.

Low voiced, almost a whisper, the hint of a melody, my mother's voice. "Bonbon, je me sens très fatiguée, où dormons-nous cette nuit?"

Agnethe-mama was used to things falling into place before her feet touched the ground. Now she was tired. Now she wanted her bed immediately. Without thinking about it, we checked into a suite of the Nairobi Hilton. We were, after all, going to be in this country for just a few days.

"Mama, such ugliness of style!" Lune's summation of Kenyan fashion, of Kenyan hotel architecture. Mama smiles and says nothing. She twists her sapphire bracelet, the signal that she agrees.

"Why do I not see the soul of these people? Bonbon . . . are you sleeping?" Chi-Chi asks.

"Shh," I say.

Two days later, Agnethe-mama visited the jewelry shop downstairs. Not finding anything to suit her tastes, she concluded:

"Their language and manner are not as sweet and gentle as ours."

She straightens her robes, eyes wide with the innocence of an unsubtle put-down.

"Mama!" I scold. The women giggle as do females who have received affirmation of their particular and unassailable advantage over other women.

A week has passed already. In the beginning of the second one, I am awakened by the feeling I had when I found my country embassy gates here locked and blocked. The feeling of a floor shifting beneath one's feet. There is no one in authority. The ambassador is in exile. Only a guard. Who should I speak to? A blank stare. I need to arrange our papers to go to Europe. A blank stare. A flag flutters in the courtyard. I do not recognize it. Then I do. It is my country's flag, someone installed it upside down. It flies at half-mast. An inadvertent act, I believe. Shifting sands: I am lost in this sea of English and I suspect that at five thousand Kenya shillings I have spent too much for a thirty-kilometer taxi ride. Old friends have not returned phone calls.

The lines here are not reliable.

Lune is watching me, her long neck propped up by her hands. Her hair covers half her face. It is always a temptation to sweep it away from her eyes, a warm silk. When the tips of my fingers stroke her hair, the palms of my hands skim her face. Lune becomes still, drinking, feeling and tasting the stroking.

Soon, we will leave.

But now, I need to borrow a little money: US$5000. It will be returned to the lender, of course, after things settle down. Agnethe, being a princess, knows that time solves all problems. Nevertheless, she has ordered me to dispatch a telegram to sovereigns in exile, those who would be familiar with our quandary and could be depended on for empathy, cash assistance and even accommodation. The gratitude felt would extend generation unto generation.

Eight days later, Agnethe-mama sighs; a hiss through the gap of her front teeth. She asks, her French rolling off her tongue like an old scroll.

"When are we leaving, Bonbon?" A mother's ambush. I know what she really wants to know.

"Soon," I reply.

"Incidentally," she adds, folding Lune's lace scarf, "What of the response of our friends in exile . . . ah! Not yet . . . a matter of time" she says, answering herself.

"Agnethe-mama," I should have said, "we must leave this hotel . . . to save money."

It is simpler to be silent.

———————

A guard with red-rimmed eyes in a dark blue uniform watches me counting out fifteen 1000 Kenya shilling notes. The eyes of the president on the notes blink with every sweep of my finger. The Indian lady in a pink sari with gold trim, the paint flaking off, leans over the counter, her eyes empty. My gold bracelet has already disappeared. Two days from this moment, while standing with Celeste on Kenyatta Avenue, where many of my people stand and seek news of home, or just stand and talk the language of home or hope that soon we will return home, I discover that fifteen thousand Kenya shillings is insufficient compensation for a 24 carat, customized gold and sapphire bracelet. Celeste knew of another jeweler who would pay me a hundred thousand for the bracelet.

I return to confront the Indian lady; she tells me to leave before I can speak.

She dials a number and shouts, high-voiced, clear; "Police." I do not want trouble so I leave the jewelry shop, unable to speak, but not before I see her smile. Not before I hear her scold the guard with the red-rimmed eyes.

"Why you let takataka to come in, nee?"

Outside the shop, my hands are shaking. I have to remind myself to take the next step and the next step and the next step. My knees are light. I am unable to look into the eyes of those on the streets. What is my mind doing getting around the intricacies of a foreign currency? I have to get out with my family.

Soon.

The newspaper on the streets, a vendor flywhisks dust fragments away. A small headline reads: "Refugees: Registration commences at the UNHCR."

The Kuseremanes are not refugees. They are visitors, tourists, people in transit, universal citizens with an affinity . . . well . . . to Europe.

"Kuseremane, Kuseremane, Kuseremane" . . . unbeknown to me, one whisper had started gathering other whispers around it.

———————

The Netherlanders, the Belgians, the French, the British are processing visa applications. They have been processing them for three, four, five . . . nine days. At least they smile with their teeth as they process the visa applications. They process them until I see that they will be processed unto eternity, if only Agnethe, Chi-Chi, Lune and I could wait that long. There are other countries in the world.

Chi-Chi's ramblings yield an array of useless trivia:

"In Nairobi, a woman can be called Auntí or chilé, a president called Moi, pronounced Moyi, a national anthem that is a prayer and twenty shillings is a pao."

"But Bu-Bu . . . So many faces . . ."

So many spirits gather here . . .

We must leave soon.

———————

The American embassy visa section woman has purple hair. Her voice evokes the grumbling of a he-toad which once lived in the marsh behind our family house in the country. One night, in the middle of its anthem, I had said:

"Ça suffit!"

Enough!

Roger led the gardeners in the hunt which choked the croak out of the toad. At dawn, Roger brought the severed head to me, encased in an old, cigar case which he had wiped clean.

I cannot believe what this purple hair woman has asked of me.

"What?"

"Bank details . . . bank statement . . . how much money."

My eyes blink, lashes entangle. Could it be possible another human being can simply ask over the counter, casually and with certainty of response, for intimate details of another person's life?

I look around the room. Is it to someone else she addresses this question?

"And title deed. Proof of domicile in country of origin . . . And letter from employer."

Has she not looked at my passport in her hands?

"I'm not Kenyan."

She folds her papers, bangs them on the table and frowns as if I have wasted her time. She tosses my passport out of her little window into my hands that are outstretched, a supplication on an altar of disbelief.

"All applications made at source country . . . next!"

"Madame . . . my country . . . is . . ."

"Next!"

Woven into the seams of my exit are the faces in the line winding from the woman's desk into the street. Children, women and men, faces lined with . . . hope? I must look at that woman again, that purveyor of hope. So I turn. I see a stately man, his beard grey. His face as dark as mine. He stoops over the desk—a posture of abnegation. So that is what I looked like to the people in the line. I want to shout to the woman: I am Boniface Kuseremane, a prince, a diplomat.

I stumble because it is here, in this embassy, that the fire-streaking specter of the guns which brought down two presidents find their mark in my soul. Like the eminent-looking man in a pin-striped suit, I am now a beggar.

———————

We have US$520 left. My head hurts. When night falls, my mind rolls and rings. I cannot sleep.

The pharmacist is appealing in her way, but wears an unfortunate weave that sits on her head like a mature thorn bush. Eeeh! The women of this land! I frown. The frown makes the girl jump when she sees me. She covers her mouth with both her hands and gasps. I smile. She recovers:

"Sema!"

"Yes, sank you. I not sleep for sree nights and I feel . . ."

I plane my hands, rocking them against my head. She says nothing, turns around, counts out ten piritons and seals the envelope: "Three, twice a day, 200 shillings."

These Kenyans and their shillings!

It is possible that tonight I will sleep. The thought makes me laugh. A thin woman wearing a red and black choker glances up at me, half-smiling. I smile back.

I cannot sleep. I have taken five of the white pills. Lune, beside me, in the large bed, is also awake.

"Qu'est-ce que c'est?" What is it?

"Rien." Nothing.

Silence. Her voice, tiny. "I am afraid."

I turn away from her, to my side. I raise my feet, curling them beneath my body. I, too, am afraid. In the morning, the white Hilton pillow beneath my head is wet with tears. They cannot be mine.

The sun in Nairobi in May is brutal in its rising. A rude glory. My heart longs to be eased into life with the clarion call of an African rooster. Our gentle sunrises, rolling hills. Two months have passed. A month ago, we left the hotel. I am ashamed to say we did not pay our bill. All we had with us was transferred into and carried out in laundry bags. We left the hotel at intervals of three hours. We also packed the hotel towels and sheets. It was Lune's idea. We had not brought our own. We left our suitcases behind. They are good for at least US$1500. Agnethe-mama is sure the hotel will understand.

We moved into a single roomed place with an outside toilet in River Road. I have told Agnethe-mama, Lune and Chi-Chi not to leave the rooms unless I am with them. Especially Chi-Chi.

"Bu-Bu, when are we leaving?"

Soon Agnethe-mama. Soon Lune. Soon Chi-Chi.

Chi-Chi has learned to say "Tafadhali, naomba maji." She asks for water this way, there are shortages.

We must leave soon.

Every afternoon, a sudden wind runs up this street, lifting dust and garbage and plastic bags and whispers.

Kuseremane, Kuseremane, Kuseremane.

I turn to see if anyone else hears my name.

Sometimes, I leave the room to walk the streets, for the sake of having a destination. I walk, therefore I am. I walk, therefore I cannot see six expectant eyes waiting for me to pull out an aeroplane from my pocket.

Ah! But tonight! Tonight, Club Balafon. I am meeting a compatriot and friend, René Katilibana. We met as I stood on the edge of Kenyatta Avenue, reading a newspaper I had rented from the vendor for five Kenya shillings. Four years ago, René needed help with a sugar deal. I facilitated a meeting which proved lucrative for him. René made a million francs. He offered me fifty thousand in gratitude. I declined. I had enjoyed humoring a friend. I am wearing the Hugo Boss mauves and the Hervé handkerchief. I am hopeful, a good feeling to invoke.

"Où vas-tu, chéri ?" Where are you going? A ubiquitous question I live with.

I stretch out my arms, Lune flies into them as she always does. She wraps her arms around me. Her arms barely span my waist.

I tell her, "I am hopeful today. Very hopeful."

I still have not heard from the friends I have called. Every night, their silence whispers something my ears cannot take hold of. Deceptive murmurings. This country of leering masses—all eyes, hands and mouths, grasping and feeding off graciousness—invokes paranoia.

My friends will call as soon as they are able to. They will.

I realize this must be one of those places I have heard about; where international phone calls are intercepted and deals struck before the intended, initial recipient is reached.

A contact, Félicien, who always knows even what he does not know, tells me that a list of génocidaires has been compiled and it is possible a name has been included. Kuseremane. Spelled out by a demure man, an aide he had said he was.

Soon we will be gone. To Europe, where the wind's weight of whispers does not matter; where wind and all its suggestions have been obliterated.

Even as she stays in the room, Chi-Chi leaves us more often than ever, a forefinger in her mouth. She has no filters. I worry that the soul of this place is soaking into her.

The city clock clicks above my head into the two a.m. position. Rain has seeped into my bones and becomes ice. My knees burn. The rain water squelches in my feet. My Hugo Boss suit is ruined now, but I squeeze the water from the edges.

Club Balafon was a microcosm of home and the Zaïroise band was nostalgic and superior. The band slipped into a song called "Chez Mama." The hearth of home. The women were beautiful and our laughter loud. It was good to taste good French cognac served in proper glasses. We lamented the fact that Kenyans are, on the whole, so unchic.

And then René asked me where I was and what I was doing. I told him I needed his help, a loan. US$5000, to be returned when things settle down back home. He listened and nodded and ordered for me a Kenyan beer named after an elephant. He turned to speak to Pierre who introduced him to Jean-Luc. I touched his shoulder to remind him of my request. He said in French: I will call you. He forgot to introduce me to Pierre and Jean-Luc. Two hours later he said in front of Pierre, Jean-Luc and Michel:

"Refresh my memory, who are you?"

My heart threatens to pound a way out of my chest. Then the band dredges up an old anthem of anguish, which, once upon a time, had encapsulated all of our desires. Ingénues Francophones in Paris, giddy with hope. This unexpected evocation of fragile, fleeting longings drives me into an abyss of remembering.

"L'indépendance, ils l'ont obtenue / La table ronde, ils l'ont gagnée . . ."

Indépendance Cha-Cha, the voice of Joseph Kabasellé.

Then, we were, vicariously, members of Kabasellé's "Les Grand Kalle." All of us, for we were bursting with dreams encapsulated in a song.

Now, at Balafon, the exiles were silent to accommodate the ghosts of saints: Bolikango . . . Kasavubu . . . Lumumba . . . Kalondji . . . Tshombe . . .

I remember heady days in Paris; hair parted, like the statement we had become, horn-rimmed glasses worn solely for aesthetic purposes, dark suited, black tied, dark skinned radicals moving in a cloud of enigmatic French colognes. In our minds and footsteps, always, the slow, slow, quick, quick, slow, mambo to rumba, of Kabasellé's Indépendance Cha-Cha.

"L'indépendance, ils l'ont obtenu . . .

La table ronde, ils l'ont gagnée . . ."

I dance at Club Balafon, my arms around a short girl who wears yellow braids. She is from Kenya and is of the opinion that "Centro African" men are soooo good. And then the music stops. There can be no other footnote, so the band packs their musical tools, as quietly as we leave the small dance floor.

When I looked, René, Pierre, Jean-Luc, Michel and Emanuel were gone. Perhaps this was not their song.

"Which way did they go?" I ask the guard in black with red stripes on his shoulder. He shrugs. He says they entered into a blue Mercedes. Their driver had been waiting for them. He thinks they went to the Carnivore. It is raining as I walk back to River Road. Three fledglings are waiting for me, trusting that I shall return with regurgitated good news.

I am Boniface Kuseremane. Refresh my memory, who are you? There are places within, where a sigh can hide. It is cold and hard and smells of fear. In my throat something cries, "hrgghghg." I cannot breathe. And then I can. So I hum:

"Mhhhh . . ."

"L'indépendance, ils l'ont obtenue . . ."

It is odd, the sounds that make a grown man weep.

———————

I sleep and dream of whispers. They have crossed the borders and arrived in Nairobi. Like many passing snakes. Kuseremane. Kuseremane. Kuseremane. Kuseremane. Kuseremane.

But we left on the fifth day!

Now whenever I approach Kenyatta Avenue, they, my people, disperse. Or disappear into shops. Or avert their eyes. If I open a conversation, there is always a meeting that one is late for. Once, on the street, a woman started wailing like an old and tired train when she saw me. Her fingers extended, like the tip of a sure spear, finding its mark.

Kuseremane. Kuseremane. Kuseremane. Kuseremane. Kuseremane.

The whispers have found a human voice.

I can tell neither Agnethe-mama nor Chi-Chi nor Lune. I tell them to stay where they are, that the city is not safe.

Agnethe wants to know if the brother-monarchs-in-exile have sent their reply. "Soon," I say.

One morning, in which the sun shone pink, I found that a certain sorrow had become a tenant of my body and weighed it down on the small blue safari bed, at the end of which my feet hung. The sun has come into the room but it hovers above my body and cannot pierce the shadow covering my life. A loud knock on the door, so loud the door shakes. I do not move so Lune glides to the door.

"Reo ni Reo, ni siku ya maripo. Sixi hundred ant sevente shirrings." Kenyans and their shillings! The proprietor scratches his distended belly. His fly is undone and the net briefs he wears peek through. I want to smile.

Lune floats to my side, looks down at me. I shut my eyes. From the door a strangely gentle, "I donti af all dey."

I open my eyes. Lune slips her hand into my coat pocket. How did she know where to look? She gives him the money, smiling as only she can. The proprietor thaws. He counts shillings. Then he smiles, a beatific grin.

I have shut my eyes again.

And then a hand, large, soft, warm strokes my face, my forehead. Silence, except for the buzzing of a blue fly. Agnethe-mama is humming "Sur le Pont d'Avignon." I used to fall asleep wondering how it was possible to dance on the Avignon bridge. Soon, we will know. When we leave.

I slept so deeply that when I woke up I thought I was at home in my bed and for a full minute I wondered why Roger had not come in with fresh orange juice, eggs and bacon, croissants and coffee. I wondered why mama was staring down at me, hands folded. Lune looks as if she has been crying. Her eyes are red rimmed. She has become thin, the bones of her neck jut out. Her fingers are no longer manicured. There! Chi-Chi. Her face has disappeared into her eyes which are large and black and deep. I look back at Agnethe-mama and see then that her entire hair front is grey. When did this happen?

"We must register. As refugees. Tell UNHCR we are here."

Now I remember that we are in Kenya; we are leaving Kenya soon. Am I a refugee?

"You slept the sleep of the dead, mon fils."

Agnethe said, lowering the veil from her head. If only she knew how prophetic her words were. Being a princess once married to her prince, she should have been more circumspect. I have woken up to find the world has shifted, moved, aged and I with it. Today I will try to obtain work. There cannot be too many here who have a PhD in Diplomacy or a Masters in Geophysics. The immigration offices will advise me. In four days we will have been here three and a half months.

The sun is gentle and warm. The rain has washed the ground. Kenyans are rushing in all directions. A street child accosts me. I frown. He runs away and pounces on an Indian lady. Everybody avoids the child and the lady, rushing to secret fates. Destiny. Who should I meet at the immigration office but Yves Fontaine, a former college mate. We had been at the Sorbonne together. He was studying art but dropped out in the third year. We were drawn together by one of life's ironies. He was so white, so short, and so high voiced. I was so tall, so black and deep voiced. We became acquainted rather than friendly because it was a popular event to have the two of us pose for photographs together. It did not bother me. It did not bother him.

"Yves!"

"Boni-papa." His name for me. Boni-papa. We kiss each other three times on either cheek.

"It is inevitable we meet again?"

"It is inevitable."

"What are you doing here?"

"A visa renewal . . . I am chief technician for the dam in the valley."

"Ah, you did engineering?"

Yves shrugs, "Pfff. Non. It is not necessary here."

The sound of a stamp hitting the desk unnecessarily hard. A voice.

"Whyves Fontana."

Yves changes his posture, his nose rises, he whose nose was always in the ground avoiding eyes so he would not be carried off by campus clowns.

"Ouais?" It is an arrogant Oui. The type of Oui Yves would never have tried at the Sorbonne.

"Your resident visa."

Yves grabs his passport, swivels on his feet and exits. But first he winks at me.

"Next!" The voice shouts. I am next.

———————

From outside the window of a travel agency, on Kaunda street, a poster proclaims:

"Welcome to your own private wilderness."

At the bottom of the poster, Nature close at hand: Walking safaris available. The picture in the foreground is that of a horse, a mountain and a tall, slender man wrapped in a red blanket, beads in his ears. It is all set within a watermark of the map of Kenya. I keep walking.

Beneath the steeple where the midday Angelus bells clang, I sit and watch the lunchtime prayer crowds dribble into the Minor Basilica. The crowds shimmer and weave behind my eyelids.

The immigration officer demanded papers. He would not listen to me. I told him about my PhD and he laughed out loud. He said:

"Ati PhD. PhD gani? Wewe refugee, bwana!"

He whispers that he is compelled by Section 3(f) of the immigration charter to report my illegal presence. He cracks his knuckles. "Creak. Crack." He smiles quickly. Fortunately, all things are possible. The cost of silence is US$500. I have 3000 shillings.

He took it all. But he returned 50 shillings for "Bus fare."

"Eh, your family . . . where are they?"

"Gone" I say.

"Si I'll see you next week? Bring all your documents . . . eh write your address here." A black book. Under "name" I write René Katilibana. Address, Club Balafon. He watches every stroke of my pen.

A resumption of knuckle cracking. His eyes deaden into a slant.

"To not return . . . is to ask for the police to find you." He turns his head away. He calls:

"Next!"

I have used 5 shillings to buy small round green sweets from a mute street vendor. Good green sweets which calm hunger grumbles. A few more days and we will be leaving. I have resolved not to bother compiling a curriculum vitae.

I join the flow into the church, sitting at the back. Rhythm of prayer, intonation of priests; I sleep sitting before the altar of a God whose name I do not know.

Chi-Chi says:

"They laugh at themselves . . ."

"They are shy . . . they hide in noise . . . but they are shy."

"Who?"

"Kenya people."

We must leave soon.

We woke up early, Agnethe, Chi-Chi, Lune and I. Walked to Westlands, forty-five-minute walk away from our room just before River Road. We reached the gates of the UNHCR bureau at 10:00 a.m. We were much too late because the lists of those who would be allowed entry that day had been compiled. The rest of us would have to return the next day. We did, at 7:00 a.m. We were still too late because the lists of those who would be allowed entry had already been compiled. We returned at 4:00 a.m. But at 2:00 p.m. we discovered we were too late because the lists of those who would be allowed in had already been compiled. I decided to ask the guard at the gate, with long, black hair and an earring, a genuine sapphire.

"How can list be compiled? We are here for sree days."

"New arrivals?" he asks.

"Yes?"

"A facilitation fee is needed to help those who are compiling the list."

"Facilitation fee?"

"Yes. That's all."

"And what is zis facilitation fee?"

"US$200 per person."

"And if one . . . he does not have US$200?"

"Then unfortunately, the list is full."

"But the UN . . . Sir?"

He raises his brow.

I told Lune and Chi-Chi. They told Agnethe. Agnethe covered her face and wailed. It is fortunate she wailed when a television crew arrived. The guard saw the television crew and realized that the list was not full. Five UN staffers wearing large blue badges appeared from behind the gate and arranged us into orderly lines, shouting commands here and commands there. Three desks materialized at the head of the queue as did three people who transferred our names and addresses into a large black book. After stamping our wrists we were sent to another table to collect our Refugee Registration Numbers. Chi-Chi returned briefly from her spirit realm to say:

"Is it not magical how so full a list becomes so empty in so short a time?"

"Toa Kitambulisho!" I know this to be a request for identification. A policeman, one of three, grunted to me. I shivered. I was standing outside the hotel building watching street vendors fight over plastic casings left behind by an inebriated hawker. I was smoking my fifth Sportsman cigarette in two hours.

"Sina." I don't have an identity card.

"Aya! Toa kitu kidogo." I did not understand the code. Something small, what could it be? A cigarette. One each. It was a chilly evening. The cigarettes were slapped out of my hand. I placed my hand up and the second policeman said:

"Resisting arrest."

A fourth one appeared and the second policeman said:

"Illegal alien . . . resisting arrest."

They twisted my arm behind my back and holding me by my waistband, the trouser crotch cutting into me, I was frog-marched across town. Some people on the street laughed loudly, pointing at the tall man with his trouser lines stuck between the cracks of his bottom.

"Please . . . please chief . . . I'll walk quietly" My hand is raised, palm up. "Please." Someone, the third one I think, swipes my head with a club. In a sibilant growl.

"Attempted escape."

A litany of crimes.

"What's your name?"

"I . . . I . . ." Silence. Again, I try. "I . . . I . . . I . . ."

"Aaaaaaa . . . aaaaii . . . eee." It amuses them.

What is my name? I frown. What is my name?

I was once drinking a good espresso in a café in Breda in the Netherlands with three European business contacts. Gem dealers. We were sipping coffee at the end of a well-concluded deal. A squat African man wearing spectacles danced into the café. He wore a black suit, around his neck a grey scarf, in his hand a colorful and large bag, like a carpet bag. Outside it was cold. So easy to recall the feeling of well-being a hot espresso evokes in a small café where the light is muted and the music a gentle jazz and there is a knowing that outside it is cold and grey and windy.

The squat African man grinned like an ingratiating hound, twisting and distorting his face, raising his lips and from his throat a thin high sound emerged:

"Heee heee heee, heh heh heh."

Most of the café turned back to their coffees and conversations. One man in a group of three put out his foot. The squat African man stumbled, grabbed the man's back, rearranged himself and said to the man:

"Heee heee heee, heh heh heh." He flapped his arm up and down. I wondered why, and then it dawned on me. He was simulating a monkey. He flapped his way to where I was, my acquaintances and I.

Sweat trickled down my spine. I think it was the heat in the café.

"What is your country of origin?" I ask him. Actually, I snarl the question at him and I am surprised by the rage in my voice.

He mumbles, his face staring at the floor. He lowers his bag, unzips it and pulls out ladies' intimate apparel designed and coloured in the manner of various African animals. Zebra, leopard, giraffe and colobus. There is a crocodile skin belt designed for the pleasure of particular sadomasochists. At the bottom of the bag a stack of posters and sealed magazines. Nature magazines? I think I see a mountain on one. I put out my free hand for one. It is not a mountain, it is an impressive arrangement of an equally impressive array of Black male genitalia. I let the magazine slide from my hand and he stoops to pick it up, wiping it against the sleeve of his black coat.

"Where are you from?" I ask in Dutch.

"Rotterdam."

"No, man . . . your origin?"

"Sierra Leone."

"Have you no shame?"

His head jerks up, his mouth opens and closes, his eyes meet mine for the first time. His eyes are wet. It is grating that a man should cry.

"Broda." He savors the word. "Broda . . . it's fine to see de eyes of anoda man . . . it is fine to see de eyes."

Though his Dutch is crude, he read sociology in Leeds and mastered it. He is quick to tell me this. He has six children. His wife, Gemma, is a beautiful woman. On a good day he makes 200 guilders; it is enough to supplement the Dutch state income and it helps sustain the illusions of good living for remnants of his family back home. He refuses to be a janitor, he tells me. To wear a uniform to clean a European toilet? No way. This is why he is running his own enterprise.

"I be a business mon."

"Have you no shame?"

"Wha do ma childs go?"

"You have a master's degree from a good university. Use it!"

Business man picks up his bags. He is laughing, so deeply, so low, a different voice. He laughs until he cries. He wipes his eyes.

"Oh mah broda . . . tank you for de laughing . . . tank you . . . you know . . . Africans we be overeducated fools. Dem papers are for to wipe our bottom. No one sees your knowing when you has no feets to stand in."

He laughs again, patting his bag, smiling in reminiscence.

"My broda for real him also in Italy. Bone doctor. Specialist. Best in class. Wha he do now? Him bring Nigeria woman for de prostitute."

Business man chortles.

"Maybe he fix de bone when dem break."

I gave him 20 guilders.

"For the children."

It was when Joop van Vuuren, the gem dealer, idly, conversationally asked me what the business man's name was that I remembered I had not asked and he had not told me.

In exile we lower our heads so that we do not see in the mirror of another's eyes what we suspect: that our precarious existence rests entirely on the whim of another's tolerance of our presence. A phrase crawls into my mind: "Psychic Oblation." But what does it mean?

———————

"What is your name?"

I can smell my name. It is the smell of salt and the musk of sweat. It is . . . surprise . . . surprise . . . remembered laughter and a woman calling me "Chéri . . ." I want to say . . . I want to say Yves Fontaine. As Yves Fontaine I would not be a vagrant immigrant, a pariah. As Yves Fontaine I would be "expatriate" and therefore desirable. As Yves Fontaine I do not need an identity card.

"I . . . I . . . My . . . I . . ." Silence.

The sibilant hoarseness of the Superintendent:

"Unco-oparatif. Prejudising infestigesons."

Agnethe-mama saw it happen. She had just raised her shawl to uncover her face so that she could shout at me to bring her some paracetamol for her headache. At first she thought she was reliving an old tale. Three men had arrived for her husband. She crawled up the stairs, lying low lest she be seen. Lune told me mama had sat on the bed rocking to and fro and moaning a song and whispering incantations she alone knew words to. In the four days I was away, making an unscheduled call on the Kenya Government, my mother's hair deepened from grey to white. We did not know that her blood pressure began its ascent that first day. Time, as she had always believed, would accomplish the rest.

It was at their station that the policemen found all manner of evidence in my pocket. All of which they liked and kept. After three days I was charged with "loitering with intent." At the crucial moment the proprietor turned up with my refugee registration card. My case was dismissed and I was charged to keep the peace.

Lune paid the proprietor with her engagement ring. Whatever he had obtained from the sale of the ring caused him to put an arm around me, call me brother and drag me into a bar where he bought me three beers. He said, "Pole." Sorry.

He said we did not need to pay rent for three months. He wanted to know if we had any more jewelry to sell. I said no. He bought me another beer. He slides a note into my pocket before he leaves. A thousand shillings.

The UNCHR are shifting people out of Kenya, resettlement in third countries. Soon, it will be us. Agnethe-mama now wakes up in the night, tiptoes to my bed. When she sees it is me, she whispers:

"Mwami." My Lord.

Sunday is a day in which we breathe a little easier in this place. There are fewer policemen and the diffident laughter hiding in hearts surfaces. It is simpler on Sunday to find our kind, my people in an African exile. We visit churches. Agnethe, Chi-Chi always go in. Lune sometimes joins them and sometimes joins me. I am usually seated beneath a tree, on a stone bench, walking the perimeter wall or, if it is raining, seated at the back of the church watching people struggling for words and rituals indicating allegiance to a God whose face they do not know. The hope peddlers become rich in a short while, singing, "Cheeeeessus!" Even the destitute will tithe to commodified gods, sure in the theatrics of frothing messengers. Hope is being doled out. Investing in an eternal future? I do not have a coin to spare. Not now, maybe later, when all is quiet and normal, I will evaluate the idea of a Banker God created in the fearful image of man.

After church, to Agnethe's delight, she found Maria. Maria and Agnethe used to shop in Paris together. Once, they bypassed France and landed in Haiti. Maria's brother was an associate of Baby Doc's wife. They returned home unrepentant to their husbands and children; they treated their daring with the insouciance it deserved. It was fortunate Agnethe met Maria here because it was from Maria we learned that the Canadian government had opened its doors to those of us in Kenya.

Chi-Chi emerged from her sanctuary to say, "Bu-Bu . . . patterns of life . . . somewhere lines meet, non?"

A statement of fact. I am hopeful.

Maria was living well. Her brother had settled in Kenya years ago. His wife was from Kenya. Maria was with them.

"Is Alphonse with you?"

Agnethe, being a princess, had been unaware that after the two presidents had died, one never asked one's compatriots where so and so was. If one did not see so and so, one did not ask until the party spoken to volunteered the information of whereabouts. Alphonse was not with Maria. That was all Maria said. Even if Agnethe was a princess, because she was a princess in exile, she read nuances. She kept her mouth shut, and looked at the ground.

Maria's brother, Professor George, and his wife and his two children were going to the Nairobi Animal Orphanage. Did we want to visit animals with them?

"Oh yes. Unfortunately . . . as you imagine . . . money is . . ."

"Don't worry, it is my pleasure," Professor George said.

So we went to meet animals. We met Langata the leopard who did not want people staring at him while he slept. Langata felt the intimacy of sleep is sacred and should be recognized as such. Apparently, he told Chi-Chi this. So Chi-Chi told us. Professor George glared at her. Chi-Chi refused to look at the animals.

Lune said animals lived behind fences to protect them from humans. Agnethe-mama was surprised to find that her dead prince did indeed look like a lion.

She and Maria stared at Simba, who stared back at them as if he knew he was being compared to a prince and the prince was increasingly found to be lacking.

"Why the name 'Professor George'?" I said to Professor George.

"They find it hard to say Georges Nsibiriwa."

"They" were his wife's people. I sensed the "and" so I said:

"And?"

Professor George walked on without replying, pointing out the difference between a Thomson's gazelle and a Grant's gazelle. Something about white posteriors. At a putrid pool, in which sluggish algae brewed a gross green soup, in between withered reeds and a hapless hyacinth, Professor George sighed and smiled. A dead branch, half-submerged, floated on the surface of the pool.

"Ah. Here we are . . . look . . . in the place you find yourself . . . in the time . . . camouflage!" A glorious pronouncement.

Surreptitious glance. Professor George then picks up a twig and throws it into the pond. From within the depths, what had been the dead branch twisted up with a surge of power. Its jaws snapped the twig in two; a white underbelly displayed before transforming itself once again into a dead branch, half-submerged, floating on the surface of the pool.

"Ah! See! Camouflage . . . place dictates form, mon ami. Always."

I start to tell him about the police.

Professor George nods: "Yes . . . yes . . . it is the time." And he asks if I have heard word from Augustine, a mutual friend who lives in Copenhagen.

"Augustine has changed address, it seems."

Professor George says: "Yes . . . it is the time."

I need to ask something. "You have heard about the list?" He looks up at me, his face a question.

"Les génocidaires?"

"Ah yes . . . but I pay no attention."

The relief of affirmation. A name's good can be invoked again. So I tell him, "Ah! It's difficult, mon ami, and . . . Agnethe-mama doesn't know."

"Know what?"

"Our name is on the list."

With the same agility that the crocodile used to become a log again, Professor George pulls away from the fence. He wipes his hand, the one I had shaken, against his shirt. He steps away, one step at a time, then he turns around and trots, like a donkey, shouting, looking over his shoulder at me:

"Maria! We leave . . . now!"

The first lesson of exile—camouflage. When is a log . . . not a log? When a name is not a name.

On Monday we were outside the UNHCR at 4:30 a.m. We hope that the list is not full. It is not. Instead there is a handwritten sign leading to an office of many windows which says "Relocations, Resettlement." At the front, behind the glass, are three men and two women with blue badges which say UNHCR. They have papers in front of them. Behind them, four men, a distance away. They watch us all, their bodies still. I straighten my coat and stand a little taller.

We are divided into two groups, men and women. The women are at the front. The women are divided into three groups: Young Girls, Young Women, Old Women.

At the desks, where there is a desk sign which says "Records Clerk" they write out names and ages, previous occupation and country of origin and, of course, the RRN—refugee registration number. Those who do not have an RRN must leave, obtain one in room 2004 and return after two weeks.

Later, flash! And a little pop. Our faces are engraved on a piece of paper. Passport photograph. Movement signified, we are leaving.

"Next," the photographer says. Defiance of absence. Photographer, do you see us at all? Inarticulation as defense. Let it pass. Soon, we will be gone from this place.

The Young Women are commanded to hand over babies to the Old Women. Young Girls and Young Women are taken into another room. A medical examination, we are informed. We are told to wait outside the office block, the gate. Perhaps we will be examined another day.

Agnethe-mama and I are sitting on a grassy patch opposite a petrol station. Agnethe bites at her lips. Then she tugs my sleeve.

"Bonbon . . . do other monarchs in exile live in Canada?

"Perhaps."

Chi-Chi and Lune emerge, holding hands. It is two hours later and the sun hovers, ready to sink into darkness. They do not look at either of us. We walk back, silently. Chi-hi has hooked her hand into my waistband. Lune glides ahead of us all, her stride is high, the balance of her body undisturbed. A purple matatu, its music "thump thumping" slows down and a tout points north with a hand gesture. I decline. It speeds off in a series of "thump thumps." Agnethe frowns. We walk in silence. Long after the matatu has gone, Agnethe says, her face serene again:

"The reason they are like that . . . these Kenyans . . . is because they do not know the cow dance."

———————

When Lune dipped her hand into my coat pocket while I slept and took out eight hundred shillings, returning in an hour with a long mirror, I should have listened to the signal from the landscape.

Chi-Chi used Lune's mirror to cut her hair. She cut it as if she were hacking a dress. She stepped on and kicked her shorn locks. Agnethe-mama covered her mouth, she said nothing as if she understood something. For Lune, the mirror evokes memories of ballet technique. She executes all her movements with her legs rotated outward. Agnethe-mama looks to the mirror so she can turn away and not look.

Two weeks later, I kick the mirror down. I smash it with my fists. They bleed. Agnethe screams once, covering her mouth. Silence enters our room. Silence smells of the Jevanjee Garden roasted Kenchic chicken; one pack feeds a frugal family of four for three days.

On the third day, I find Lune looking down at me.

"It was mine. It was mine." She smiles suddenly and I am afraid.

From across the room, Agnethe-mama, "Ah Bonbon . . . still . . . no word from the kings in exile?"

The anger with which the rain launches itself upon this land, the thunder which causes floors to creak sparks a strange foreboding in me. That night, while we were eating cold beans and maize for dinner, Lune pushed her plate aside, looked at me, a gentle, graceful crane, her hands fluttering closed, a smile in her eyes.

"Chéri, we can leave soon, but it depends on a certain . . . cooperation."

"Cooperation?"

"A condition from the medical examination."

Agnethe looks away. Chi-Chi clutches her body, staving off in her way something she is afraid of.

"How do we cooperate?" I am afraid to know.

"By agreeing to be examined," she laughs, high, dry, cough-laugh, " . . . examined by the officials at their homes for a night."

"I see."

I don't. Silence. Agnethe is rocking herself to and fro. She is moaning a song. I know the tune. It is from the song new widows sing when the body of their dead spouse is laid on a bier.

Annals of war decree that conquest of landscapes is incomplete unless the vanquisher's women are "taken." Where war is crudest, the women are discarded afterwards for their men to find. Living etchings of emasculation. Lune has not finished yet. I sense I am being taunted for my ineffectuality by this woman who would be my wife.

"Now . . . it has been discussed with family, it is not a question of being forced."

A recitation. I lower my head. The incongruity of tears. A persistent mosquito buzzes near my ear. The food on my plate is old. Lune leaves the table, pushing back her chair, she places her feet in a parallel arrangement, one in front of the other, the heel of a foot in line with the toes of the other. Her right arm extends in front of her body, and the left is slightly bent and raised. She moves the weight of her body over the left foot and bends the left knee. She raises her right heel, pointing the toe. Her body is bent toward the extended knee. She holds the pose and says:

"Pointe tendue!"

Conscious now, I read the gesture. She will perform as she must, on this stage. I can only watch.

"No."

Now Chi-Chi raises her head, like a beautiful cat. I know the look; tentative hope, tendrils reaching out and into life. Lune closes her feet, the heel of one now touching the toes of the other; she pushes up from the floor and jumps, her legs straight, feet together and pointed. She lands and bows before me. Then she cracks and cries, crumbling on the floor.

Outside the window, the drone of traffic which never stops and the cackle of drunkards. Creeping up the window a man's voice singing:

"Chupa na debe. Mbili kwa shilling tano. Chupa na debe."

Bottle and tin, two for five shillings, bottle and tin, Kenyans and their shillings.

I stood on the balcony staring at the traffic, counting every red car I could see. Nine so far. Behind me, Agnethe approached. In front of my face she dangled her wedding ring.

"Sell it."

"No."

She let it fall at my feet.

We used the money to leave the room on River Road. We went to a one-roomed cottage with a separate kitchen and an outside toilet. It was in Hurlingham, the property of a former Government secretary, Mr. Wamathi, a drinking acquaintance of the proprietor. I observed that his gardening manners were undeveloped; he had subdivided his quarter acre plot, cutting down old African olive trees and uprooting the largest bougainvillea I had ever seen, on the day we arrived. He was going to put up a block of flats. Mr. Wamathi was delirious with glee about selling the trees to the "City Canjo" for fifteen thousand shillings. His laughter was deep, rounded and certain with happiness.

He laughed and I felt hope joining us.

Agnethe started tending a small vegetable patch. Her eyes gleamed when the carrot tops showed. Lune made forays into a nearby mall, an eye-fest of possibilities satiating her heart, extending her wants. Chi-Chi, over the fence, befriended an Ethiopian resident who introduced her to his handsome brother, Matteo.

The day Chi-Chi met Matteo she slipped her hand into my waistband, looking up at me she said:

"He ... can ... see ..."

Every day I tried to contact home, seeking cash for four air tickets on a refugee pass. Word appeared in dribs and drabs. Detail gleaned from conversations heard, strangers approached and newspapers slyly read.

The bank? Burned down. The money? Missing from the safes. And once, the sound of a name accused, accursed:

Kuseremane.

But hadn't we left on the fifth day?

The day flows on. I sit in different cafés, telling the waiters that I am waiting for a friend. Thirty minutes in some cafes. In the more confident ones, the ones which are sure of their identity, I can wait for a full hour before I make a face, glance at my non-existent watch, frown as if tardy friends are a source of annoyance and I exit.

Whispers had floated over the land of hills and nestled in valleys and refused to leave, had in fact given birth to volleys of sound. Now tales had been added of a most zealous servant instructed by an heir to sluice stains.

"Ah! Roger. Mon oncle ..."

Excoriating women's wombs, crushing fetal skulls, following the instructions of a prince.

They said.

Today I woke up as early as the ones who walk to work maneuvering the shadows of dawn, crochet covered radios against ears, in pockets, or tied to bicycle saddles. Sometimes music, Rumba. And in the dawn dark I can forget where I am and let others' footsteps show me the way. I hear Franklin Bukaka's plea, pouring out of so many radios, tenderly carried in so many ways.

"Aye! Afrika, O! Afrika . . ."

I return from so many journeys like this and one day, I find Agnethe-mama lying on her back in her vegetable patch. At first I think she is soaking up the sun. Then I remember Agnethe-mama never let the sun touch her skin. An African princess, melanin management was an important event of toilette. I lean over her body. Then, head against her chest, I cannot hear a heartbeat.

I carry my mother and run along the road. The evening traffic courses past. Nairobi accommodates. Room for idiosyncrasies. So to those passing by, it is not strange that a tall, tall man should carry a slender woman in his arms.

At the first hospital. "My mother . . . she is not heart beating . . . help."

"Kshs 12,000 deposit, Sir."

"But my mother . . ."

"Try Kenyatta."

At Kenyatta, they want a four-thousand shilling deposit and I will still have to wait, one of about three hundred people waiting for two doctors to see them. I do not have four thousand shillings.

"Where can I go?"

"Enda Coptic." Go to the Copts.

"Tafadhali . . . please, where are they?"

"Ngong Rd."

"How far?"

"Next!"

———————

Agnethe sighs, opens her eyes and asks:

"Have the monarchs-in-exile sent our reply yet, Bonbon?"

"Soon . . . mama."

She has suffered a mild stroke.

I return to the cottage to pack a bag for mama. Exile blurs lines. So a son, such as I, can handle a mother's underwear. Agnethe-mama told Chi-Chi once, in my hearing, that all in a woman may fall apart, may become unmatched, but never her underwear. I place sets of underwear for Agnethe; black, brown and lacy purple.

Kuseremane, Kuseremane, Kuseremane.

It seems that the whispers have infringed upon the place where my tears hide. I cannot stop bawling, sniveling like a lost ghoul. My shoulders bounce with a life of their own. Lune watches me, her eyes veiled in a red, feral glow.

At six p.m. I rejoin a river of workers returning to so many homes. To be one of many, is to be, anyway, if only for a moment. The sun is setting and has seared into the sky a golden trail; it has the look of a machete wound bleeding yellow light. It is an incongruous time to remember Roger's blackened hands.

Agnethe has taken to sitting in the garden rocking her body, to and fro, to and fro. She does not hum. But sometimes, in between the fro and to, she asks:

"Have the brother sovereigns sent a letter?"

"Soon."

At night, Chi-Chi shakes me awake, again. My pillow is soaked, my face wet. Not my tears.

The next morning, I left the cottage before sunrise. I have learned of hidden places; covered spaces which the invisible inhabit. The Nairobi Arboretum. The monkeys claim my attention as does the frenzied moaning of emptied people calling out to frightened gods for succor. Now, it starts to rain. I walk rapidly, then start to jog, the mud splattering my already stained coat. The other hidden place is through the open doors of a Catholic Church. Hard wooden benches, pews upon which a man may kneel, cover his eyes and sleep or cry unheeded before the presence that is also an absence.

My return coincides with Mr. Wamathi's winding his way into the house. He rocks on his feet:

"Habe new yearghh." "Year" ends with a burp and belch.

"Happy New Year." It is July and cold and time is relative.

Agnethe outside, uncovered. Rocking to and fro. She clutches thin arms about herself, shivering.

"Aiiee, mama!" I lean down to lift her up.

"Bonbon, il fait froid, oui?" It is cold.

"Lune? Chi-Chi? Lune?" Why is mama sitting out in the night alone.

"Oú est Lune . . . Chi-Chi, mama?"

Agnethe stares up at the sky from my arms.

"Bonbon . . . il fait froid." Two anorexic streams glide down, past high cheekbones and nestle at the corner of her mouth. She looks up and into my eyes. The resolute eyes of an ancient crone. Now . . . now the cold's tendrils insinuate themselves, searing horror in my heart.

Chi-Chi returned first. She stumbled through the door, her body shuddering. She is wiping her hand up and down her body, ferociously, as if wiping away something foul only she can sense.

"Everything has a pattern . . . Bu-Bu, non?" She gives me the folded papers.

Three laissez-passers. Tickets to rapture. Let them pass. It favors Agnethe, Boniface and Chi-Chi Kuseremane.

I am not there.

I watch from afar, the ceiling, I think, as the tall man tears the papers to shreds. I am curious about the weeping woman with shorn hair crawling on the ground gathering the fragments to her chest. I frown when I see the tall, dark man lift his hand up, right up and bring it crashing into the back of the girl who falls to the floor, lies flat on her belly and stops crying. She is staring into herself where no one else can reach her. A sound at the door. The tall, tall man walks up to his fiancée, who bows low, the end of a performance. She too has a clutch of papers in her hand. The tall man sniffs the girl, Lune, as if he were a dog and he bites her on the cheek, the one upon which another man's cologne lingers. Where the teeth marks are, the skin has broken. Drops of blood. Lune laughs.

"We can leave anytime now."

"Putaine!"

She giggles.

"But I shall live, Chéri . . . we shall live . . . we shall live well."

Agnethe-mama heaves herself up from the bed and brushes her long white hair. I return to the body of the tall, black man whose arms are hanging against his side, his head bowed. He sees that Lune's feet are close, the heel of one touching the toes of the other. She slowly raises her hands over her head, paper clutched in the right, she rounds her arms slightly, en couronne—in a crown.

Paper fragments, a mosaic on the floor. I stoop, the better to stare at them. I pick up my sister. She is so still. But then she asks, eyes wide with wanting to know: "Bu-Bu . . . there's a pattern in everything. Oui?"

"Oui, Ché-Ché." A childhood name, slips easily out of my mouth. Now when she smiles, it reaches her eyes. She touches my face with her hand.

———————

That night, or more accurately, the next morning—it was three a.m.—Agnethe went to the bathroom outside. Returning to the room she had stepped into and slid in a puddle. She stepped out again to clean her feet and then she screamed and screamed and screamed.

"Ahh! Ahh! Ahhhee!"

She points at the rag upon which she has wiped her feet. It is covered in fresh blood. She points into the room, at the floor. I return to look. Lune is now awake. Lights in the main house are switched on and Mr. Wamathi appears in the doorway, a knobkerrie in his hand.

"Where, where?" He shouts.

The neighbourhood dogs have started to howl. The sky is clear and lit up by a crescent moon. I remember all this because I looked up as I carried my bleeding sister, my Chi-Chi-Ché-Ché into Mr. Wamathi's car, cushioned by towels and blankets while her blood poured out.

At the hospital emergency wing where we had been admitted quickly, a tribute to Mr. Wamathi's threats, I watched the splayed legs of my sister, raised and stripped. My sister, led to and stripped bare in the wilderness of lives altered when two presidents were shot to the ground from the sky. I remember a blow bestowed on a back by a defenseless brother-prince.

How can a blow be unsung?

A doctor and a nurse struggle to bring to premature birth a child we did not know existed. Chi-Chi's eyes are closed. Her face still. When she left us, the moment she went, I felt a tug on my waistband as in days of life, and her body lost its shimmer, as if a light within had gone off for good. She left with her baby.

The child's head was in between her legs. A boy or girl, only the head was visible and one arm, small fists slightly open as if beckoning. Skin like cream coffee. The offspring of African exiles. An enigma solved. The Ethiopians had abruptly disappeared from the radar of our lives and Chi-Chi had said nothing. The dying child of African exiles in an African land. I stroked the baby's wet head. Did baby come to lure Chi-Chi away? A word shimmers into my heart: fratricide. I douse it with the coldness of my blood. I am shivering. A distant voice . . . mine.

"Leave them . . . leave the children." Keep them together . . . the way they are.

Landscape speaks. The gesture of an incomplete birth. Of what have we to be afraid? Metamorphoses of being. There must be another way to live.

"Is there a priest?" Even the faithless need a ritual to purge them of the unassailable scent of mystery.

"What shall we do with the body?"

A body . . . my sister. When did a pool of blood become this . . . absence? They let me cover her face after I have kissed her eyes shut.

Vain gesture.

Agnethe and Lune are outside, waiting. Islands in their hope. I open the door to let them in, gesturing with my hand. They step into the room and I step out. I let the door close behind me and try to block out the screams emanating from within. Staccato screams. Screams in a crescendo and then a crushing moan.

A nurse offers forms to be filled in.

"Nairobi City Mortuary."

It will cost eight thousand Kenya shillings to rent space for Chi-Chi. I do not have eight thousand shillings. It's OK, the nurse says. I can pay it tomorrow at the mortuary.

Eeeh! Kenyans and their shillings.

Nurse turns: "Pole." Sorry.

But Mr. Wamathi makes an arrangement with his wives, and they find 35,000 shillings for Agnethe.

Is this it?

Later. After all the bluster of being . . . this? A body in a box, commended to the soil.

A brother's gesture: 12 torches alight in a sister's cheap coffin. Chi-Chi and her Nameless One will see in the dark.

It is a challenge to match paper fragments so that they match just right. It is fortunate there are words on the paper, it makes it easier. Three laissez-passers. Chi-Chi's is complete, almost new.

Lune returned to my bed. Agnethe resumed her rocking which accelerated in both speed and volume. Her eyes are brown and a ceaseless rivulet of tears drips onto her open palm. But she smiles at us, Lune and I, and does not utter a word. Sometimes her eyes have a film of white over them as if she had become a medium, in constant communion with the dead. Sometimes I imagine that they look at me with reproach. I look to the ground, the quest for patterns.

I have lost the feeling of sleep. I will not touch Lune nor can I let her touch me.

It is the ghost of another man's cologne which lingers in my dreams and haunts my heart. I am bleeding in new places. But we are leaving.

"Bu-Bu, everything has a pattern, non?"

We will be leaving for Canada on Saturday night.

Agnethe shocked us by dying on Friday morning in my arms as I entered the gates of the Coptic hospital. On the streets, as before, no one found it strange, the idea of a tall, tall man carrying a slender woman in his arms. A pattern had been established, a specific madness accommodated.

When Agnethe-mama left, the energy of her exit made me stumble.

"Ah! Bonbon! Ah!" she says.

At the Coptic gate, "Mwami!"

She leaves with such force, her head is thrown back against my arms.

Agnethe-mama.

The Copts cannot wrench her from my arms. They let me sit in their office and rock my mother to and fro, to and fro. I am humming a song. It is the melody of "Sur le Pont d'Avignon" where we shall dance.

At the cottage, old bags with few belongings are packed. On the bed, a manila bag with Agnethe's clothes, the bag she was packing when her body crumbled to the ground.

"Où est maman?" Lune asks. Where is mama?

I stretch out my arms and she lifts her hand to her long silk hair and draws it away from her face. She rushes into my arms and burrows her face into my shoulder.

"Forgive me."

We do what we can to live. Even the man whose cologne stayed on her face. I have no absolution to give. So I tell her, instead, that Agnethe has just died. And when Lune drops to the ground like a shattered rock, I slap her awake, harder than necessary on the cheek upon which another man's cologne had strayed and stayed. She does not move, but her eyes are open. Arms above her head, hair over her face.

She smirks. "I'm leaving. I am living."

She grabs my arm, a woman haunted by the desire for tomorrow where all good is possible. "I am leaving."

"Ma mère . . . Lune-chérie."

Lune covers her ears, shuts her eyes.

For the most fleeting of moments, I enter into her choice. To slough the skin of the past off. To become another life form. I look around the room. Agnethe-mama's slippers by the bed. What traces have they left on the surface of the earth? The gossip of landscape. It is getting clear. I stoop low and kiss Lune on her forehead. In the pattern of things, there is a place in which the body of a princess may rest. Isn't there?

A Coptic priest, a Coptic doctor, Lune and I, Mr. and Mrs. Wamathi—the sum total of those gathered around Agnethe-mama's grave. Lune's airplane bags are over her shoulders, her plane ticket in her purse. In four hours' time she will be in a plane taking her to the Canada of her dreams. We forgot grave-diggers must be paid, their spades attached to Kenya shillings. So I will cover my mother's grave myself, when the others are gone.

A plane departs from Nairobi. Kenya Airways to London. From London, Air Canada to Ottawa.

I have been laughing for an hour now. True, the laughter is interspersed with hot, sour, incessant streams of tears. Squatting on my mother's grave. The unseen now obvious.

Life peering out of lives. Life calling life to dance. Life, the voyeur.

I will start dancing now.

"L'indépendance, ils l'ont obtenue / La table ronde, ils l'ont gagnée . . ."

"Mhhhh . . . Mhhhh . . . Mhh . . . Mhh . . . Mhhhh"

"L'indépendance, ils l'ont obtenue . . ."

Kabasellé laughs.

Who can allay the summon of life to life? The inexorable attraction for fire. The soul knows its keeper. Inexorable place, space and pace. I see. I see.

There!

Life aflame in a fire-gold sun. And dust restoring matter to ash. The ceaseless ardour for life now requited:

"Mhhhh . . . Mhhhh . . . Mhh . . . Mhh . . . Mhhhh."

"L'indépendance, ils l'ont obtenue . . ."

"La table ronde, ils l'ont gagnée . . ."

"Cha-cha-cha!"

Thus began the first day of my second life.

Murambi

Boris Boubacar Diop

The young woman in the green blouse was sitting alone on a bench in the hallway.

As soon as she saw the visitor come through the door of the Polytechnic, she pulled on her rubber gloves and slipped into a spacious room.

When he got close to her, Cornelius realized that she was busy arranging human remains. She picked up a tibia and placed it next to others of the same length; she set on a pile of remains a skull that had been left in the middle of the way and sprinkled it all with a white powder with an awful smell. These frighteningly banal gestures and this need for order must be part of the routine of her existence, thought Cornelius. Important people would sometimes come in delegations from far off countries to visit the Murambi Polytechnic. She did her best to receive them properly.

Cornelius had prepared himself for the worst. But his glimpse of the first skeletons behind a window had an unexpected effect on him: he immediately wanted to turn around and go back. These dead people laid out on the ground struck him as very different from the ones he had already seen. In Nyamata and Ntarama time had put the finishing touches to the work of the Interahamwe: skulls, arms, and legs had become detached from their torsos and the different types of remains found there had had to be organized separately. In Murambi, the bodies, which were covered with a fine layer of mud, were almost all intact. Without his being able to say why, the remains in Murambi gave him the impression of still being alive. He took fright. Instead of going into the classrooms, he started pacing up and down the hallway, glancing indecisively in every direction, as if looking for a place to flee. Saliva was collecting in his throat and he swallowed it to conceal his disgust. Even from the outside the stench of the cadavers was intolerable.

A bearded man of about forty, tall and thin in gray trousers and a white shirt, appeared at the back of the courtyard and came toward him:

"May I help you, sir?"

Cornelius looked at him without seeing him.

"I came home from abroad about ten days ago," he said. "My relatives were killed here."

After a moment's hesitation he added:

"My name is Cornelius Uvimana. I am the son of Doctor Karekezi."

He had nothing to hide. Everyone must know what infamous person he was the son of.

But the man seemed not to have heard him. Cornelius followed him, not without noticing that the man hadn't introduced himself.

The Murambi Polytechnic School was composed of seven or eight buildings arranged without any apparent order on a vast lot of several hectares.

The man gave Cornelius detailed explanations. The World Bank had given a grant, he told him, for the construction of the school, but work had been interrupted by the events. The rooms in the back were supposed to serve as apprentices' workshops for the high school students. A bit further, behind the trees, a football field had been planned. He pointed out the buildings and turned toward Cornelius:

"You see, of course, that they didn't have the time to paint the buildings."

And, in fact, the walls were all a sinister gray color.

The man started talking about the massacre:

"During the genocide, a prominent Murambi man gathered thousands of Tutsis here, promising to protect them. Then, when there were enough of them, the Interahamwe arrived and the carnage started."

Cornelius said calmly:

"It's my father who did that."

"I know," said the man, without showing the slightest emotion.

Cornelius wanted to tell the man that what happened was his fault but thought that such a declaration wouldn't make any sense.

"How many people died here?"

"Between forty-five and fifty thousand."

At the entrance to each room the man turned to Cornelius and said:

"There are sixty-four doors like this one. . . ."

And each time Cornelius thought to himself: "The doors of Hell." Was the man expressing himself in such a strange way on purpose?

In this place, amid sorrow and shame, his own life and the tragic history of his country met. Nothing spoke to him of himself as much as these remains scattered on the naked ground. Siméon's words came back to him. He had told him, a few days earlier: "Cornelius, don't regret leaving, because you deserved to live more than anyone." He had asked him why and Siméon had answered: "Because your mother, Nathalie, brought you into this world running, to escape from the people who wanted to kill her." And that was where his destiny had come full circle: a young woman in labor hiding from bush to bush in Bugesera, and now him, Cornelius Uvimana, standing in the middle of these remains in Murambi. Presently, he could add: "After all, she ended up being killed. By my father. And her body is here. Lost among thousands of others." Nathalie Kayumba. Julienne. François. Pathetic little bits of bone. Yes, he had been right to smile during his discussion with Jessica. In a way, all of this was comical.

But why did these rooms piled with corpses make him think of life rather than of death? Perhaps because of the way their arms were stretched out toward the Interahamwe in a last absurd plea? A forest of arms still murmuring with the cries of terror and despair. He stopped next to a corpse: a man or a woman whose left foot had been cut off at the ankle. What remained of the leg was stiff like a real crutch. He was surprised not to be thinking of anything in particular. He was satisfied to look, silent, horrified.

"Do you want to go on, sir?"

The man must have noticed Cornelius's efforts to brave the nauseating stench of decomposing bodies.

"Yes. I want to see everything."

"You'll see the same bodies everywhere."

"No," said Cornelius dryly, "I don't think so."

He was so furious with the unknown man that he almost asked him to leave him alone. This sudden bout of rage revealed to him his own suffering, much more profound than he had thought.

The man said:

"Yes, you're right. I'm sorry."

Of course he was right. Each one of these corpses had had a life that was different from that of all the others, each one had dreamed and navigated between doubt and hope, between love and hate.

Cornelius understood better now the authorities' decision not to bury the victims of the genocide after the controversy that came up about it in the country. Some people said that they had to be given a decent burial, that it isn't good to exhibit cadavers like that. Cornelius didn't agree with that point of view. Rwanda was the only place in the world that these victims could call their home. They still wanted its sun. It was too soon to throw them into the darkness of the earth. Besides, every Rwandan should have the courage to look reality in the eye. The strong odor of the remains proved that the genocide had taken place only four years earlier and not in ancient times. As they were perishing under the blows, the victims had shouted out. No one had wanted to hear them. The echo of those cries should be allowed to reverberate for as long as possible.

Cornelius sometimes lingered on the faces of very young children. They seemed peaceful, as if they were simply asleep.

They continued the visit. On one body he saw bits of braids; on another, a piece of green cloth; a skeleton was curled up like a fetus: someone who must have resigned himself to death without daring to look it in the face. A skull, lying solitary in a corner, particularly struck him. The victim—surely a giant when he was alive—had had his nose severed before being decapitated. Faint black spots were still visible on his right cheek. A dark line, lightly curved, represented his mouth. It was like a death mask, forgotten in the middle of the other corpses. Or—Cornelius, however, didn't dare let this vaguely indecent idea linger in his mind—a clown with a moon face. It was as if fate had carefully sculpted, according to some mysterious design, this massive and slightly sullen face.

In another room his guide showed him the weapons used by the Interahamwe: sticks, clubs studded with rusty nails, axes and, of course, machetes.

As they were crossing the courtyard in the direction of other buildings, Cornelius suddenly raised his head toward the man:

"How do you know who I am?"

"Everyone in Murambi knows that Doctor Karekezi's son is in town."

Cornelius was silent. That was another story, that. For the moment, he had to concentrate on the dead.

"It seems that there were ten or so survivors. . . ."

"I'm one of them," declared the man.

Cornelius, shocked, turned quickly toward him.

"You didn't say anything to me about it. . . ."

"You didn't ask me anything. My name is Gérard Nayinzira. It's the old man who asked me to get here before you."

"The old man?"

"Siméon Habineza."

"I thought you were the caretaker. I'm sorry."

"You still don't see who I am?" said the man, in turn.

Cornelius understood immediately.

Skipper.

"They call you the Skipper, don't they? We saw each other one night in Kigali."

"Yes, at the Café des Grands Lacs."

"I'm really sorry, Gérard. Please don't hold it against me."

"I understand very well what must be going on in your head right now."

The man showed him an enormous crater in the center of some wild grass:

"There are several of these in this school. These holes served as mass graves."

"I was told that in Murambi the victims were buried, then exhumed," said Cornelius.

"That's correct. The bodies are intact because there's clay in the soil here. Besides, you've noticed that the skeletons are all a bit red."

It was still possible to see, at the edges of the graves, part of the sand that had been loosed when the bodies had been exhumed after the victory of the RPF.

"But who had had them buried?"

"Some French officers with Operation Turquoise."

"Oh, really?"

"Yes. Come with me, I'm going to show you something."

He led Cornelius behind some other, bigger rooms, and had him touch a flagpole put up on top of a little pile of brown pebbles:

"This is where they hoisted their flag. As soon as they arrived in the zone, they saw that this school was just what they needed. But there were cadavers all over the place. A certain Colonel Étienne Perrin asked the authorities to find a solution."

"You mean that he went to my father?"

"Yes. Doctor Karekezi ordered the Interahamwe to place the bodies in these common graves. At that time, the militia weren't taking orders from anyone anymore, but they still had a lot of respect for the doctor, whom they called 'Papa.'"

"I see," said Cornelius.

"The French soldiers lent them the equipment, and when the cadavers were collected in the graves, they set up camp on top of them."

Cornelius, fascinated, speechless with amazement, took a long time to leave the Murambi Polytechnic. He took the tour of the classrooms again. He waited for the bodies to divulge their secret to him. Which one? There was only one, of which, confusedly, he had a premonition.

On the way back Gérard swore to him:

"The other evening, in the Café des Grands Lacs, I was just about to do something really stupid."

"You were holding it against me. It's normal."

"I wanted you dead. It's your father who did it. And you, you weren't there when we were suffering."

"That's what lots of people think, I'm sure, but there's nothing I can do about it. In any case, I appreciate your talking to me so frankly, Gérard."

"I had come to call you, publicly, the son of a murderer. But at the last minute, I remembered Siméon Habineza. He is such a good man. I couldn't do that to him."

Cornelius thought that Gérard would never fully forgive or forget what had happened. For himself, everything had been so easy: he felt that he would never be able to understand the pain that had not been his. His return was almost becoming another exile.

Homeland

Extract from Book I

Véronique Tadjo

I feel so close to you, and yet so much separates us.

I.

Impossible to sleep.

Nina had thought that sunset would bring her a bit of peace. Yet after sending streaks of purple and gold across the sky, the orb had begun to melt away, sinking below the horizon. Now, it was over. Nothing remained but darkness, dense and troubling. She turned away from the dark hole, pulled down the window shade, reclined her seat, and tried to fall asleep. The plane's wings cut through the night.

Anguish rose brutally in her. In just a few hours she would be there, at the house. But without him, without his presence, what would remain? Walls, objects, what else? She would need to reconsider everything she had taken for granted.

"What makes a homeland?" she had asked Frédéric the evening before she left.

Excerpt from *Far from My Father*, translated from the French by Amy B. Reid.

"I don't know," he admitted, looking a little confused. "Memories, I guess."

Yes, memories . . . the feel of the sky, the taste of the water, the color of the earth. Faces. Moments of love and loss. A homeland was all of that. A rainbow of sensations stored up as the days passed by.

But how can one be sure of memories? The country was no longer the same. War had scarred it, left it disfigured, wounded. To live there now one had to deny those outdated memories, ideas from another time.

She had been gone for too long. How could they not hold it against her? She had thought that she could travel freely over hill and dale until she needed to return. Come back? Everything would be just as it had been, each thing in its place. All she'd have to do is to drop her bags and pick up her life, right where she had left it. Welcomed with open arms, the traveler would return, all the richer for her travels.

But that was before the war, before the rebellion.

Everything had been turned upside down, had crumbled away. The full force of her exile hit her like a whip and sent her reeling.

Voices began to shout in her head: "Just who do you think you are? You are nothing. Your house was destroyed. Your parents are dead and gone. No one wants you here. Get out!"

Nina woke with a start. She must have dozed off. Her heart was pounding. Where was she? Her feet were swollen, her body ached. I have to get up, stretch my legs, she thought. She got out of her seat.

Careful not to bump into the sleeping passengers. Some were curled into balls, their mouth open or their nose buried in their neighbor's shoulder, others with arms sticking out from under blankets, like the stiffened limbs of badly wrapped corpses. She wobbled as she walked, her eyes fixed on the light at the end of the passageway. A stewardess was organizing trays of food.

She tried a few relaxation exercises in the back of the cabin, but was unable to overcome the stiffness that had invaded her. She felt like the flight would never end. It wasn't only her body that was abandoning her, but her spirit as well. A black sea as thick as the night. She felt herself beginning to sink. "Have I really lost my home?"

And what if this was really her fault, if she had deliberately set herself apart from the others? Now she was going to find herself face to face with everyone she had left behind years before. How would they look at her?

When her father fell sick, Nina wanted to be at his side.

"I'll come right home, papa. No question."

"Wait a little longer, the war isn't over yet," he had replied firmly. "You won't find any work here. Your aunts are taking very good care of me. Don't you worry, just stay put."

She had thought: "This isn't how life should be. Why am I so far from him?"

"No one knows what direction we're headed. The tone has grown harsh, people are becoming more radical, more rigid. Everyone is talking at once and no one is listening. Faces are closed. We distrust one another."

After a moment of silence that had made Nina think the line had been cut, he finally added, "My child, now everyone has to take a stance, choose sides. It's become impossible to remain neutral. The country is split in two."

She had felt a great tiredness in him, his anger squelched by so many dashed hopes. Not fear, just the feeling of having failed in what he set out to do.

Nina's head began to nod. She thought she would finally drop off into a deep and healing sleep, but she was roused by the harsh glare of her neighbor's overhead light. The man was looking at a film she had already seen, the story of a ferry sinking at sea, a little like *The Titanic*. A handful of passengers decide to set out, leaving the remaining thirty or so who were gathered in a watertight room to look for a way up to the surface. That's how the story begins. Nina wondered why they so often showed disaster films on planes. Was it to exorcise people's fear of flying?

Her head was spinning from lack of sleep and the incoherence of her own thoughts when the image of what awaited her in Abidjan suddenly appeared. She wished with all her might for the return of daylight. To be done with this torture. To feel solid ground beneath her feet, even if there was no joy in her heart.

The sun had just reappeared when the plane landed. The heavy door opened and, despite the early morning hour, the passengers were suddenly engulfed in a wave of heat that rushed into the cabin: the country's burning breath.

While she waited in the immigration line, Nina wondered who would be there to greet her. In the plane she had been careful to avoid catching the eyes of the other passengers, for fear of being recognized by someone, something not unlikely on a flight to Côte d'Ivoire.

"How are you? So, what are you up to these days? Where do you live? And your dad, he's well?"

Anything not to have to pronounce the words that told of his death. Not now. Not yet.

From behind the window, the officer questioned her in a detached voice:

"How many days will you stay?"

Nina hesitated.

"I'm from here. Does it matter how long?"

"I asked you a question."

"I'm not sure, about a month . . ."

Suddenly the man's face lit up.

"You're Doctor Kouadio Yao's daughter?" he asked, holding the passport open in front of him.

"Yes," Nina replied hesitantly, because she wasn't quite sure where he was heading with all his questions.

"Oh, I know your father well! We're from the same place. You'll have to say hello to him for me. I'm Corporal N'Guessan."

He stamped her passport and handed it back with a wide smile, one meant to suggest their complicity, then added quickly, "Welcome home!"

Nina picked up her suitcase and headed toward the customs officers, who were chatting among themselves, for once apparently unconcerned by what was going on around them. She opened and closed her bag quickly, before any of them could change their mind. She was sweating heavily. Her clothes were sticking to her skin. She regretted having put on a long-sleeved top.

Ahead of her, the exit: the point of no return.

A tightly packed crowd was waiting in the arrival hall. She looked all around. No familiar faces.

Disoriented, she moved mechanically toward the exit. Suddenly someone appeared at her side.

"Hey, auntie, want a taxi?"

Without waiting for an answer, the young man grabbed her suitcase.

That's when she heard Hervé's voice.

"No, put it down. I've come to get her, I'll take care of the bag myself."

"No trouble, I've already got it," answered the guy, clearly unwilling to let go.

A bit of a scuffle followed. Hervé pulled the suitcase in one direction, the guy in the other. Nina didn't know what to do. She hadn't even had a chance to say hello to her cousin. She tried to intervene. "It's no big deal. He can carry my bag . . ." But the other members of her family had just appeared. Seeing himself surrounded, the guy finally gave up his prize, but not without first asking, "Got some change for me?"

They turned their backs on him. Nina hugged everyone. Their faces were somber and they were dressed in black. Chantal, the youngest of the group, began to cry.

As soon as she was settled in the car, Nina asked, "How are things at the house?"

"Don't worry," answered Hervé, without taking his eyes off the road. "It'll all work out. Your aunts are there. Everything's being taken care of."

"That's good," she murmured, before returning to her own thoughts.

No one was speaking, for fear of disturbing her. Only Chantal's muffled sobs broke the silence. Nina couldn't help but feel irritated by it. Deep inside, she still harbored hopes that this was all just a bad dream.

The city passed by before them. Nothing seemed to have changed. The same crowded streets, the same noises, the same buildings. Everything was still in place, even though for her nothing would ever really be the same. How was it possible that the two people who mattered most to her were now gone, just like that? The city had known them. It bore their traces. It had listened to their joys and sorrows, reserved them a place in the chaos of daily life. Why abandon them now?

"How will I ever be able to live in the face of such indifference?" She thought she had landed on a stage where the main actors had vanished and the scenery now seemed unreal.

The sun was already burning the necks of the workers who marched along, single file. Some of them stopped briefly to grab some breakfast on the side of the road. Huddled close together, they ate at a table under a tree, their faces still bearing the marks of a night cut short. They dipped their pieces of bread into cups of steaming coffee, as the man serving them added more water to the enormous kettle, poked the fire, and washed the plastic bowls and plates. The workers had been on their way since dawn, leaving their families still asleep in narrow little rooms with tiny windows.

At the bus stops civil servants were waiting patiently in their clean clothes. School-children were there too, chatting and gesturing wildly. The girls wore white blouses and dark blue skirts, the boys khaki uniforms.

As they came up to the Houphouët-Boigny Bridge, Hervé started to slow down. In front of them, a line of cars had stopped dead. Soldiers were coming through and checking papers.

"Your papers, please," ordered a soldier with the face of a kid and a machine gun slung over his shoulder. Everyone in the car handed over their ID cards. Nina gave him her passport.

"Don't you have an ID card?" the soldier asked suspiciously. "A passport isn't a valid form of ID."

Hervé jumped in immediately. "Boss, we're coming from the airport. She's not a resident here."

The soldier seemed to hesitate for a moment. He looked toward his superior who was a bit further along in the line. Seeing that he was busy, he came back to Nina and stared her straight in the eyes.

"Ok, I'll let you go this time, but you have to get your papers in order."

Then turning toward the driver, with a nod of his head, "Show me the car's registration and open the trunk."

"Boss, is there a problem?"

"No, just a routine check," he replied as he continued his inspection. "Where's the owner of the car? These papers aren't in your name."

Hervé got out of the car quickly and leaned toward him, whispering confidentially, "He's dead. That's his daughter right there. She came for the funeral."

The soldier looked in the car again and stared at Nina. Then he stepped back and waved his arm. "All right, just go ahead!"

Behind them, drivers were growing impatient. Most were headed to work, or were taking their kids to school. The bridge now looked like a bus station. Several people had gotten out and were standing by their cars, with crossed arms and grim faces. Others were waiting patiently for their turn. Mothers tried to comfort their children, who were sitting in the back seat and bawling. Several taxis were blocking the way.

When Hervé had finally negotiated a path off the bridge, Nina asked him a question that had been troubling her: "Are their weapons loaded?"

"Nobody knows . . . But they say they are."

Nina couldn't believe what she'd heard. Was this really happening in Abidjan, the city where she had always felt so safe?

She turned her eyes toward the lagoon, so calm, so beautiful. The tall buildings of downtown rose, majestic, their silhouettes reflected in the mirror of the water.

They went via Le Plateau. Most of the banks were still closed, but some shops had begun to open their doors. How many times when she was younger had she wandered through these streets window-shopping? She and her friends had made the public garden their headquarters. It was there that she had her first kiss. What was his name . . . ? Roger, yes, that was it, Roger. She tried to remember his face, but the image was blurry.

Two men wearing ties and carrying black briefcases hurried into a building.

An elegantly dressed woman, her hair finely braided, emerged nonchalantly from a car as a young kid approached, obviously going to ask for some change. A taxi appeared from the left and, after fishtailing in front of them, stopped for a client standing on the sidewalk. A group of bleary-eyed street kids crossed at the light.

———————

Then the car headed by the sky blue cathedral. The immense marble statue that guarded its entrance was still imploring the Eternal One. When they reached the main boulevard, Nina realized that the house wasn't much further. She would have liked Hervé to do a U-turn and whisk her off to someplace far away from the terrible truth she would have to confront.

———————

Her cousin, however, just kept going. After a few minutes, they came into the neighborhood. She saw their street, a thin strip of tar, bordered by low-slung houses and trees with tufts of green leaves.

———————

Two horn blasts. The guard opened the gate and the car parked inside the yard, just where it always did. Her aunts were there, standing in the doorway. They hugged her tight, one after the other.

"My daughter, be strong," murmured Aunt Affoué.

"Take heart . . . ," added Aunt Aya.

Feeling the warmth of their embrace, Nina couldn't hold back her tears any longer. She let herself go in their arms.

Slowly, the two women led her into the house.

———————

The house had been invaded. People were coming out from all of the rooms. Some familiar faces, some not. Nina hugged her relatives and shook the hands of the others. Tall candles had been placed in the four corners of the living room. This was no longer the home where she had lived. Her father's absence was too much for her to bear.

———————

After greeting everyone, she asked to go to the master bedroom. The door was locked. Aunt Affoué opened it and then left her alone. The curtains had been drawn, but everything was in its proper place. The bed had been made. Clothes were still hanging on the back of the chair. His glasses, his watch and his wallet were on the bedside table. The room still smelled of her father, that scent she had known all of her life.

She lay down on the bed, her head buried in the pillow. The mattress still bore the imprint made over the years by her father's body. She tried to get ahold of her emotions.

Memories kept bubbling up to the surface. She remembered the last time she had spoken to him. She was in an airport, waiting for her plane, heading off on another of her many trips. She had called him on her cell phone. The connection had been so clear she felt like she was right there next to him.

"What's going on there now? Is the peace treaty really going to be signed soon?"

Trying not to show her fear. The last news she'd heard on the French radio wasn't good.

"Nothing's certain yet, my child. The government is insisting on unilateral disarmament as a precondition. The rebels have to turn in their weapons."

She thought his voice sounded weaker than usual.

"Papa, what's wrong? You're not feeling well?"

"Oh, it's nothing, just a little tired. I'm already in bed. There's a wedding party at the house today, but I had to go to bed early. It's your cousin, Hortense, you remember her, don't you? Uncle Jacob's daughter. I was the god-father for the ceremony."

Voices and bits of music filtered in through the phone.

"And you, haven't you found a new wife to take mom's place yet?" she asked, trying to sound lighthearted.

He laughed on the other end of the line.

"Oh, you know me, women . . . I'm just too old now . . ."

"You'll never be too old!" she just had time to exclaim when the loudspeakers cut her off, loudly announcing her flight.

A line of passengers was already forming at the gate.

"Hugs and kisses, papa. I'll call you when I get back. Take good care of yourself."

It was typical. Typical of her life. Of the whirlpool her life had become. Her last conversation with her father had taken place in a soulless public place, where people were heading off to the four corners of the earth. How could she ever have believed, even for an instant, that the telephone would make up for her absence at his side?

Abdar and Terhas

Abu Bakr Hamid Khaal

Terhas woke early the following morning and I lay listening as she rinsed her body with water in the bathroom beside our bedroom. Our hosts had brought us a stove, some coals and two small jars—one half-filled with sugar and the other with a large handful of red tea leaves. When Terhas returned from the bathroom, she immediately went to light the stove.

"Morning," I greeted her.

"Morning," she answered softly, "I just washed a small mountain of sand from my hair."

"I think I'll do the same," I murmured, heading to the bathroom.

One by one, our companions stirred from their slumber as the fragrant aroma of freshly brewed tea wafted through the room. By the time I came out of the bathroom Terhas had handed steaming cups to everyone who had stumbled from bed and we sat around, pressing them to our foreheads and struggling against fatigue. Terhas remained beside the stove, her cup lying untouched next to her. I could plainly see the pain and misery in her eyes.

From Abu Bakr Khaal, *African Titanics*, Trans. Charis Bredin, London, UK, Darf Publishers, 2014, 39–47, Chapter 4.

Eventually, the room emptied and we were left alone. The others had gone outside to smoke and discuss the next stages of our journey in anxious, hushed tones. It was only then that Terhas began to sob, weeping for all those who had died on the journey, for Assgedom, whom she had nursed for so long and who had struggled so desperately against death, even as he thrashed around and tried to throw himself out of the car. I drew close and pulled her to my chest, trying to calm her violent sobs. But she could not stem her tears and wept bitterly all morning.

When we had buried Assgedom, most of our companions had not found the courage to approach his grave, but Terhas had remained close as we covered his body. In silence, she had made the sign of the cross, her eyes wide with grief as she struggled to comprehend the tragedy before her.

That afternoon most of our companions went to investigate the various routes to Tripoli and little by little we were released from the despair that had gripped us and the terrible certainty of death. Thus, life unfolds with utter simplicity. One moment, there seems no way forward, and the next everything is within our grasp. One moment, we are lost in a snake-infested desert, and the next we are wandering the city streets. Either we travel on or we are taken forever from our intended paths. All beginnings and all ending are in the hands of the great unknown, whose merciless ways remain an eternal mystery.

––––––––––

After three days of rest and recuperation we bade Naji farewell, following his directions to the nearest car station as he inspected the damage to his own vehicle.

"You were a good companion," Naji smiled, shaking my hand.

"Will you continue with these trips?"

"I've no choice," he said softly, "It's all I'm fit for."

––––––––––

In Tripoli, Terhas and I went to live with a group of friends who had arrived before us. I immediately began to suss out the reputations of all the local smugglers, remaining in a state of anxious indecision as to which of them I should do business with. There was "Fatty," known for his reliability and the care he took of those who travelled aboard his Titanics. His reputation extended all over Africa and travellers from Eritrea, Sudan, Somalia, Ghana and Liberia would hunt him down as soon as they arrived in the city. Other smugglers were known for how swiftly they could arrange crossings. Every week, one of their Titanics would leave for the far shore, completely devoid of safety precautions, and likely to sink a few miles out to sea. The city was also swarming with fraudsters who would disappear as soon as they'd conned their unlucky victims out of every last coin. Our final decision to leave came by chance one evening—not even Terhas had planned for it—as we spotted a crowd of men and women clambering into an Iveco truck parked outside our building.

"Are you leaving?" I asked.

"Yes," one of them replied brusquely, hurrying through the door. I assessed the situation swiftly and knew we must leave. If I remained in my lodgings for one more week, my savings would run dangerously low and I would risk falling short of the thousand dollars required for passage aboard a Titanic. If I was even a dollar short I might never leave.

I hastily grabbed my sack of belongings and Terhas fetched her small shoulder bag, and then we were hauled into the truck, which had already left the main street and was wending its way down a narrow side alley, leading eventually out of the city to cut across several plantations. A black BMW was waiting for us at a junction, and it pulled off as we approached. After a short distance, the truck slid to the left, following a dirt track bordered by dry and meagre vegetation. The truck was old and slow, skidding and swerving along the road, before eventually pulling up next to the BMW in front of a low-walled building.

Two men emerged from the car. The first was short and stout, with a bristling bunch of keys hanging from the belt of his jeans, and large sunglasses covering his eyes. The other man was twice his age, tall and gangly, with sharp features and suspicious eyes. The short one pulled open the truck door and ordered us to walk in silence towards the building. I found myself at the front of the line, my fingers damp with sweat and clenched around the bag I had shoved all my earthly possessions into: trousers, trainers, a shirt bought at the last minute in Tripoli, shaving kit, and a pocket English dictionary.

I hesitated at the door and the tall man gestured impatiently for me to enter. I gently pushed it open and slipped through, followed in single file by the rest of the group. We found ourselves in a large courtyard with eight rooms leading off it, their doors standing open. There was a bathroom to the right and a kitchen on the left. Piles of clothes were strewn across the floor alongside heaps of bags of all shapes and sizes, some half empty and others full, some threadbare and others apparently brand new. A jumble of iron bedsteads leaned against the walls.

The rooms were in a state of chaos too, filled with even more garments and shoes. There were precarious piles of tea cups, kettles and bottles. Broken watches, socks, wigs and used sanitary towels lay here and there.

Bulging bags of sugar stood amidst a mess of shaving equipment, fake jewelry, makeup, dirty underwear and empty, foreign-looking cigarette packets. Blankets had been thrown carelessly on the floor, and clothes hung from nails on the wall. I couldn't understand why anyone would have wanted to hammer so many in, but in the days to come, whenever I grew particularly bored, I would amuse myself by counting their small heads, imagining them to be little flies.

"Look at all this. They must have been left by previous travellers," Terhas whispered, sticking close to my side.

"We'll have to leave things behind too." I replied, taking great comfort in her presence beside me.

The two men ordered us to gather in the courtyard. We left the rooms and congregated before them as a white-haired man strode through the door, acknowledging us with a cursory wave before going to mutter with his men, making arrangements for the next load of travellers and the boat that would carry us onwards. Wielding a pen and paper, the short man began recording our names, while his gangly colleague collected a thousand dollars from each of us, under the watchful eyes of his boss. In total, we were twenty-five Eritreans and a handful of other nationalities.

As the smugglers moved down the line, I couldn't help but notice the strange behaviour of one of my companions: his hands were trembling uncontrollably and his nose was streaming as he handed over his fare. These symptoms were particularly perplexing given how hot the day was. The mystery, however, was soon solved as the smuggler handed back more than half his cash.

"Fake," he announced.

The man was shaking like a leaf and looked to be on the verge of tears, and even more so as the smuggler held the notes under the tap and the colours ran slowly from them until they were no more than soggy white paper. He must have known his money was forged, I was convinced of it. Those shaking hands had betrayed him. When the rest of us had paid, the short man folded up his list.

"You're not leaving this building. We're locking the door from the outside. Keep your voices down. No one will come here but us three."

They left. It was midday. Everyone headed to the rooms, taking shelter from the August heat. I closed my eyes, trying to fight off my nagging fear that we had fallen victim to an elaborate scam. In such circumstances, questions always attack from every side, making sleep impossible. Could the smugglers be trusted—or would they disappear with our money? When would our journey finally end? Would the boat prove watertight, or be no more than a leaky sieve? Would the police discover us, storming the building and leading us away in handcuffs, our money lost? And what of the sea? Was it impatiently awaiting us, ready to offer us up in sacrifice to its god? My eyes closed beneath the weight of these questions and when I opened them after nearly an hour, the heat had not diminished.

I left the room and put my head under the tap for several minutes to cool off. Then I wandered through the courtyard, picking through the scattered objects and trying to imagine their owners. What fate had they suffered? Had they crossed safely, or become fish fodder? Had they even left? Or had they retraced their steps to their homeland? I picked a magazine up from the floor and an envelope fell from it. It was open, and contained a love letter, several pages long and written in English, dated 12 March, 1998. It was addressed to a woman named Malfanita. After several expressions of longing and well-wishing, it began: "If this letter reaches you, I beg you will not feel sad or fearful for me. Please do not shed any of your precious tears on my account as I tell of my journey from Nigeria to the shores of North Africa."

"My beloved," I read in another section, "I can keep nothing from you. The mere thought that you might share my journeys gives me the strength to continue."

I took the letter to Terhas, who was tidying up one of the bedrooms, ready to spread out some blankets. Together we cleared the debris from about half the space, and then I handed her the letter. She began to read:

I experienced death for the first time in the desert. I was travelling with a group of men who spoke a language I couldn't understand. Suddenly, their voices rose and they began to quarrel and occasionally even to struggle. We had no idea what to do. The men spoke angrily amongst themselves and I guessed they were arguing about money because they kept repeating words like "dollar" and "franc." Sometimes one of them would gesture towards us and violently disagree with whatever the other was saying. Eventually, I realised they must be fighting over who would take our money after they had robbed us.

I waited for a chance to jump from the car as it moved slowly over the sand. I heard their voices suddenly grow louder. Then one of them pulled a rifle from his bag and emptied it into the other's head. After that, I had no choice but to jump. I flung myself from the car with three other men and ran for my life as the car pulled to a stop. We heard gunshots behind us. They fired several volleys. But all of them missed.

"My God, what a journey!" Terhas shook her head, folding up the letter.

The afternoon went slowly by, and eventually it was sunset. No one came to visit, despite the men's promises of bringing food. When it was completely dark, we discovered that the fuses had blown in several of the rooms. The kitchen was still illuminated, however, and I went in to find Terhas staring in astonishment at the walls and fighting back her tears once again. I assumed it must be the memory of her family, and went to comfort her, but she simply mopped the tears from her cheeks and pointed to the wall in front of us.

"Read it."

"My God," I murmured, my gaze travelling over the many messages written by migrants over the years as they awaited their departure. The scribbled words testified to their fears and doubts as well as their particular personalities and life philosophies. Most evident was the candour with which they had expressed themselves as they faced the most crucial juncture in their lives. The writing entirely covered the four walls in a mixture of languages: some we didn't recognize at all, and some we could understand, or at least identify, such as Arabic, French, English, Amharic and Tigré. Like me, Terhas spoke the latter three fluently. I also knew Arabic.

"Where will you take me, oh fleeting hours?" read one beautifully written message in Tigré, dated 1 May, 1999, and signed "Anonymous."

"How can the journey from shore to shore be so very difficult? It seems so simple on the maps," a French hand had written just a few days earlier.

"Forgive me, my dear Hamouddi," came another message in Arabic, which looked to be the work of a woman. When I translated it to Terhas, fresh tears welled in her eyes.

"Perhaps Hamouddi was her husband," I suggested, "or a lover? Or a friend?"

"Or maybe it was her son. Maybe it was a little baby she left behind because she thought the journey would be too difficult. I know mothers from Eritrea and Somalia who did that. What agony their lives must be!"

Alongside the many melancholy messages there was also the odd amusing one. "The date of his Majesty's sea voyage will shortly be announced!" read one of them in French, translated for us by one of the travellers from Morocco.

Memoirs | 3

Photography Is Like Hunting

Emmanuel Iduma

Photography is like hunting, Malick Sidibé says.

When we visit, he is wearing a fitted white jalabiya, sitting outside a house, part of a cluster of buildings, each coated in reddish brown. His eyesight is failing. I cover his hands in mine, in greeting. A woman and a man prepare him for the public eye. The woman brings a towel and spreads it across his lap; the man brings sunglasses. I am overwhelmed. I feel as though his entire oeuvre is compressed into a moment in time, this.

Before we talk, we are shown into a room with his negatives, old equipment, and stacks of photo albums. Things are in bad shape, worn by time, layered with dust. Some of the dust will leave with us. There's a bed in the room. Perhaps he lies here when exhausted, to remember photographs without looking at them.

We sit and he talks. Igo Diarra of Medina Gallery, our host and guide, translates the conversation from French. Sidibé tells us he started drawing in 1945, using charcoal. He drew because he wanted to imitate natural forms.

First published in *A Stranger's Pose*, Cassava Republic Press, 2018. Copyright © Emmanuel Iduma 2018. Reprinted by permission of Cassava Republic Press. Photograph, *Untitled 2014*, copyright Tom Saater.

Because he has never used a digital camera, he conceives photography as an act of deliberation. He learnt what he knew about photography by observing closely. To observe is to be alert, to find precision, balance.

Now that he is losing his eyesight, Sidibé cannot continue working. I suppose that not even impaired eyesight can take away his ability to perceive images. Every nerve in his body seems to respond to light and movement. Time has slowed him down, but he is here, still.

Sidibé asks the young man to bring us a photograph from 1963. It is his favourite and known around the world as one of his most iconic: a young man and woman dancing during a Christmas party. It had to be about dancing, I think, remembering something about dance being the fulcrum of desire. Photography is a charismatic medium. Sometimes it takes five decades for a photograph to unravel itself.

In the photograph, the girl was barefoot, the boy was wearing a suit and tie, and their knees could touch, it seemed, at any minute. What interested me were the smiles on their faces, and the girl's arm, which held her gown in place; a dance of such zest threatened to reveal her underwear. I wonder what he thought when he took that photograph. It strikes me that the pose is similar to that of Amiri Baraka dancing with Maya Angelou in Harlem, in the 1991 photograph by Chester Higgins Jr.

People come to him from around the world, he says. He's responding to a question about his children. The question has been lost in translation. Yet the image is perfect: a man whose way of seeing has stirred the hearts of thousands, indisputable as father.

When asked about photography going digital, the democratization of the photo-making process, he says, It's okay sometimes. Everyone has a right to have their image taken, but people can also transform the image into something else. He seems ambivalent about this. I guess he's still fascinated with the old ways of working. He tried to catch up with digital cameras, he says, but it just seemed overwhelming.

He jokes that these days you don't need your eyes to make photographs, you just shoot. We laugh.

The other time we laugh is when he talks about being in Mauritania. It had been difficult to put his subjects in good positions because men didn't want him to touch their wives. A photographer is like a doctor, he tells us. If you don't touch, you do nothing.

UNTITLED 2014, PHOTOGRAPH BY MALICK SIDIBE, USED WITH PERMISSION OF TOM SAATER.

He adds that he had been a composer of images, favouring the studio over the street. The contours of his subjects' bodies form poses like in a drawing, line added to line.

Someone asks if he has questions for us. No. Any advice? None, he says, but it is good to travel, you understand many things.

I am very happy, he says at the end.

While Sidibé spoke I mulled over a sentence with which he opened the conversation: Photography is like hunting.

Unknown to a sprinting deer, the hunter's hand was steadied on the trigger, and combining precision with an element of indeterminacy, he shot. The animal was shot in motion, its movement truncated.

I am reminded of an encounter with Idrissa. The meeting took place in Diéma, a thoroughfare town on the road out of Mali, 1,000 kilometres before Dakar. Idrissa—he seemed in his early twenties—managed a station where I stopped to buy petrol. His voice was full of laughter and great knowledge. At first he spoke French to me, then he saw the plate number of my van.

Oh, he said, I have been to Nigeria.

In Lagos, he sold ice cream, hawked on the streets. He chose Nigeria because English was spoken everywhere—you didn't have to go too far, or even to school, he said, people spoke English on the street. I followed lorries, he continued, which could mean he had to squat on the back of trucks, a co-passenger with cows being transported for sale and slaughter.

Then he confirmed he had been elsewhere. After six months in Nigeria, he spent eighteen months in Cameroon, and two in Gabon. Diéma was his birthplace, where his family lived, but if he had the opportunity, and once he had saved enough money, he'd return to Nigeria.

His life, as he narrated it, consisted of many truncated movements: the pause, for instance, between saving money, and buying his way of out Diéma. His time in Diéma was transitory, a placeholder for subsequent movement. Idrissa did not describe his movement in linear terms, but as a circular journey. He spent time in Cameroon and Gabon, returned to his hometown, but kept a final destination in view.

The route I travelled—across Mali, Senegal, then Mauritania—was punctured with stories of women, men, and children transiting towards Europe. Often they met bureaucratic brick walls, stiff immigration policies imposed by the governments of North African countries in collaboration with the European Union (Mauritania is 800 kilometres south of the Spanish Canary Islands). And meeting these brick walls, they stopped to regroup. They found new ways to outmanoeuvre the omnipresence of the Spanish civil guard, to keep moving towards an imagined better life.

Hargeisa Snapshots

Doreen Baingana

The best coffee in town is at Sinow's. He's a tall, elegant, grey-haired man who wears all white, every day, topped by a brown kaffiyeh. Sinow makes the coffee himself, behind a huge red contraption that looks like it belongs to a museum. After I am served, he comes over and asks, "E buono?" I had told him I speak Italian, which I don't really, but we stagger along until he has to ask my guide, in Somali, what on earth I am saying. Once Sinow takes your order, he won't ever forget it. I keep changing mine, though, from caffe latte to espresso to macchiato and back again. Still, always, he comes over to ask, do I like it?

On election day, I ask Sinow if he has voted. He whispers in my ear that he is from Mogadishu. He smiles, half-shy, half-sly. But everyone knows this. He had a coffee shop there for years, first working for Italians, then on his own. He escaped the war and came up north to Hargeisa. His family, wife and kids, are still there. He sends all his money back to them.

Somalia, the festering wound. Somaliland, a wound healing, though the scars are huge: rubble from bombed-down buildings; rusting tankers along the highway sinking into sand; veterans on crutches; everyone's story that begins, *When I came back to Hargeisa*... And, of course, the city's central monument: one of the fighter jets that bombed Hargeisa to dust in the 1988–91 civil war against the south. It is raised high as if to be worshipped, balancing atop an ugly pedestal roughly painted with a battle scene showing bloody bodies with heads and limbs chopped off. No wonder everyone tells me again and again: "All we want is peace."

We take our coffee in the car when all we need is a quick refuelling of energy. When there's more time, we sit outside the café on plastic chairs on the sandy pavement, shaded by two trees, close to the road that is bustling with people and lumbering 4x4s (I'm told Hargeisa has the highest number of four-wheel drives per capita in the world. My guess is it rates just as high for its number of goats), donkeys dragging carts, lorries and buses painted in carnival colours, and always, everywhere, the flowing, swaying black, or every other possible colour and pattern, of the women's clothing. I haven't seen women sitting outside the café, though a woman owns it.

One afternoon I have coffee with Abdihakim Mohamed Dirir, a painter who sells his work in a store opposite the café. He paints pastoral scenes of majestic camels and chubby sheep and goats against golden-yellow desert backgrounds, or traditional milk gourds, thumb pianos and hair combs arranged into group portraits. He says these paintings sell well, especially when diaspora Somalis are back for the summer. He says of course he paints anything else he wants, and is inspired by what he sees on the internet, but he won't display those in the shop.

As we talk on in the still midafternoon heat, a couple of baboons, with heart-shaped cheeky faces, long grey hair, and flared pink bottoms, join us. One of them is given an almost empty bottle of Sprite, which it drinks from like a child. The wind rises, whips our faces with sand.

Next to the art shop is a stall selling *khat*, the leafy intoxicant sold all over Hargeisa. On election day, I ask the stall owner, "How is business?" She says, "Same as usual." She is wide with success and self-satisfaction, glowing in a white and blue flowered hijab. A boy of about ten sits next to her drinking tea out of a tin cup. He stares at me, curious, open-faced.

"What about Fridays, is it business as usual?" I ask.

"*Khat* chewers don't take holidays," she says. "They don't even fall sick." She adds, laughing, "They grow fat."

I laugh with her. She reaches between her widespread feet and throws back a brown sack to reveal *khat* stems tied in large bunches that she says go for US$30 (which everywhere are used just as often as Somali shillings).

I am in awe of her self-assured matter-of-factness; I no longer want to ask her, but what about all the men who do nothing but chew? What about all that money not used for school fees or saved? What about the ethical issues? Shouldn't her customers "Just Say No"? Was it just the same as selling coffee, only more lucrative? She would have a sassy comeback, for sure.

———————

Ryszard Kapucinski once wrote that political rallies in Africa are celebrations. We all know such sweeping statements should be swept into the dustbin, and we are more familiar with political bloodbaths than celebrations, but in late June 2010, in Hargeisa, a celebration it was. In the last week leading up to the vote, when each party was given a day for its final campaign, the roads were full of cheering crowds by seven in the morning. I joined the crowd supporting the main opposition party, Kulmiye, as it chanted and danced its way to Liberty Park. Everyone was wearing green and yellow headscarves or bands or waving green and yellow cuts of cloth way above their head. In the park, groups of women formed circles and danced, stamping feet, raising dust and drawing sweat as one woman beat a goatskin-covered drum vehemently.

The scene was repeated the next day, except the colour that covered the city now was the dark avocado green of the other opposition party, UCID, pronounced more like a gurgle than a word. Hundreds of cars raced by with men and women hanging from the windows, sitting on the boots of the cars, clambering on the tops, crowded in lorries, shouting, singing, delirious with excitement. The scene was repeated yet again, at an even higher pitch, a few nights later when the winner, Kulmiye, was announced.

Why the fuss? This was my reaction as an observer bred to be cynical about politics. Why expend, expel such passion? Yes, a party is good fun, of course. And a good excuse to publicly dance and sing, in a country that boasts not a single disco. Public theatre, public catharsis, and so on.

———————

Somalilanders have fought hard and paid much to reject a joint destiny with Somalia, and were continuing to do so with this dance and this vote. They were in the streets and campaign halls and in long lines at voting centres all over country, knowing full well that the al-Shabaab terrorist group had called the elections "the work of the devil." Anything awfully bloody could happen. But they celebrated the sheer audacity of holding a national election, a peaceful and organised one at that, whether the world recognised Somaliland or not. They danced in the streets, knowing how precious this was, because down south, their fellow Somalis in Mogadishu were dying in the streets. As my guide on election day said, all that their political leaders asked of them was their vote, while in Somalia people were asked for their lives.

The bullet or the ballot? This wasn't a hypothetical question, not for Somalis. So how could they not, as Somalilanders, celebrate the choice they were making? Whatever the election outcome, it was already a victory. It was time to party.

Zanzibar, circa 1996

Heidi Grunebaum

long-forgotten book in the cluttered library of my mind. I stumble across it as I repack the book shelves, releasing memories pungent with sea salt, boat fumes, pots cooking slowly. Cinnamon, jeera, clove, coffee, softened cardamom pods waft between fuel lines and fishing nets. Stone Town rushes back: grasses pushing between the ancient veins of quarried blocks along the fort walls.

The orange blossom flowers, frangipani, and jasmine: pungent, they seeped through the skies above courtyards sequestered behind immense carved teak and brass-embossed doors. All competed with their fragrance for my drowsy attention. Weary—I was there and not there. My mind was dragged by the scents back to the place I had left. The tip of the continent whose name, for all its high drama and epic history, is but a tepid reference to its geography: South Africa.

The weight of my backpack: it was rather empty except for the books. Light cotton dresses, mosquito coils, and silky shawls. Instead of a travel guide or one of those *Lonely Planet* books, I brought verse with me to Zanzibar. A Swahili poetry anthology with English translations found in a secondhand shop in Cape Town.

A heavy tome that translated the traces of poetic creation across ten centuries to the place of its writing. There was Kader and Louise Asmal and Ronald Suresh Robert's book, *Reconciliation through Truth: Reckoning with Apartheid's Criminal Governance*. Elias Canetti's *Auto-da-Fé* was there too, which, on reflection, suggested a long-standing tendency to self-punish. The Swahili/English anthology of poems, long given away to a Palestinian friend with a passion for Swahili and Arabic verse from the Indian Ocean, added elegant heft.

There were some loose sheets of poems by Angifi Dladla. He had given them to me at a poetry festival in Cape Town. After a poetry reading we had found common cause in wine and complaint. Huddled in a corner, we had quaffed and fretted about the refusal of our country to better wrestle with its poisonous bequest. As if apartheid, a small word, had not been some monstrous experiment in the mutilation of the human psyche. Instead, everyone seemed to pretend that we had merely lived through a political disagreement that had been taken too far. And that a state commission was proper for us to measure the shadows of our dispute. A stanza in one of his poems held a jar with a hand. Tucked quietly away in one of its lines, the hand accused the dismemberer from a shelf in a police station. But wine went a good way to numb the cut and slash which gave lie to the story everyone so fiercely wished to believe. That bygones could be set to rest. Perhaps because what was damaged was not visible, and what was visible did not seem so damaged. Perhaps that was why we had become a country of serious drinkers rather than poets. Seeking the spirits of oblivion, we drank to forget that which we could not forget.

The air was humid and heavy: the lightly packed bag, the weight of books mocking all paradise, Stone Town and Cape Town blurred until both became confused in a single obsession with my inability to quiet the noise in my head. No, I kept lugging it everywhere with me. In my head. Like Canetti's protagonist, cruel and unlikeable, who heaved his infinite Chinese library around inside his cranium. From Cape Town to Johannesburg, from Nairobi to Dar Es Salaam to Stone Town, echoes of phrases from 230-something days of public storytelling, South Africa's newest experiment, kept leaking into my mind. Louder than the unfamiliar bouquet of scents at the Stone Town harbor, the peculiar grief of strangers spilled over the retelling of prison statements and torture reports and death notices. Grief that cracked words open with sledgehammers of loss too long unspoken. Grief that ripped the world apart again and again so that the tissue of what remained could be neither identified nor repaired.

Chefs at open-air food stalls by the harbor: before sunset they set up portable cooking stations and conjured feasts of grilled spices and seafood. Families came down from narrow Stone Town roads to take their evening meal in the open dusk. History was all that, there and now. The sunset at the bustling water's edge that bathed walls streaked with rust by weather and time. People gathered in debate and gossip sat on low benches beside doorways, along verandas. The cobbled paths between lawn, old fort, and the promenade jutting into the ocean. Yesterday's footsteps retreaded and erased those made the day before. And the day before.

The golden bodies of European tourists: they would travel to Stone Town from the private beach resorts that sealed off the island coastline from the rest of its residents. Resorts that sold package holidays peddling Africa-meets-the-Orient in a fantasy of tropical print hijabs and cocktails in coconuts. An Indian Ocean paradise glistening in an eternal present. I remember my envy of their ease, their play, their lightness. My anger, though, was sharpest towards the many white South Africans in Zanzibar who had come to snorkel and cavort. How dare they take a holiday from the mangled mess of atrocities unspooled into words each day all through that trembling year? How dare they frolic when they should have been holding their heads low with shame and self-reproach, close to the ground, in search of their conscience? How dare they not prostrate themselves in humility and apology? In ashes to disrobe the gods and monsters of their deception. In sackcloth to join the mourning. At a time when the dead demanded names and the living called for justice, I declared myself prosecutor, judge, and jailer of those golden ones at play. I wanted them to be punished, not pampered.

The boat ride to the prison island in the archipelago: the ocean, calm, dazzled the sun. Giant tortoises eating mangoes. It reminded me of Robben Island; its archaeology of burials and *kramats* recalling lepers shunned and learned men stolen from distant lands. Sent to rot under the torture of static time, a torture reserved for prisoners, exiles, rebels, and runaway slaves. Perhaps that is why empires and despots have long chosen prison islands to smash rebellions. If an island cannot quarantine the desire to be free, stopping time in an eternal present might.

In Stone Town, I visited the Anglican church. I listened to the tour guide's history—how redemption followed conquest, freedom followed slavery, grace followed enlightenment. Slowly, I circled the altar built atop the amputated trunk of the old slave tree. Perhaps there was some sanctuary in the fiction promised by the sacred altar, some refuge in the story of the inexhaustible battles of the unfree. Sometimes my ignorance is a better shelter than wine or fiction.

Banished far beyond "the edges of the imagination," the great massacres in Zanzibar that followed the post-independence revolution were mute. Besides its inventions, history is a terrific pact of silence, like the contours of stories whose edges are marked by war yet still not textured into words. While words are always there they come in ways given a more careful regard after the percussive shocks of war have ended, after the wars of propaganda and denial have ended and the words rise from the memory of ruin and off the tongues of survivors. Those are the words that come after time has broken the great silence that fall the smashing of days and nights. After discontent and grievance have been stirred by the political ambitions of charismatic leaders looking for their scapegoat. Long after their scapegoats have been named, given the attributes of "enemies." Long after the time the enemies have been "dealt with." Neither justice nor redemption are found in those shadows, nor in the words that rise from beyond the edges of frozen time.

Cape Town and Stone Town kept blurring. Like the grief that weighed my brain, pulled my backpack.

The high glamour of a Ta'arab concert: Compositions in the hands of a full orchestra stretched the night into the crisp lilac of near-dawn. Sections of oud, guitar, and percussion braided the vocalist's notes along a snaking path, deepening slowly and then lifting, carrying her voice down their twists and turns. The skein of sound connected the musicians' fingers, then slowly, slowly, imperceptibly at first, the instruments faded as one, and the singer's voice rose to fill the space of their absence until her voice soared above the orchestra, high above our heads. Moved to dance, women came to the stage from the audience to hand her notes of gratitude. Fronds of palm trees quivered in piety, bowed in prayer.

The Athaan at dawn on the first day of Ramadan: the bustle of the port town was replaced by a more solemn and slow comportment, encouraged by the humidity and relentlessness of an equatorial sun. The rhythms of prayer, like the swaying palms, punctuated the passage of night and daylight, of day and twilight. In that monthlong chastity, the devout are squeezed by a hunger that releases the body into the beautiful defiance of timelessness. A release offered too by the sound of the muezzin's voice stirring us to wakefulness. Just as the reverberations of the ancient ram's horn rouse the soul's shadows from slumber and forgetfulness in the other Abrahamic faith.

The book becomes as still as the faded fragrance of a memory. I stack it with others side by side on the shelf. Words at rest. What do they do when they march along the page and into my mind? Can they provide a measure of justice for the dead in naming what cannot be measured? Or is it but the needs of the living that words appease? We, who think the dead need us to do their bidding.

Fugee

Hawa Jande Golakai

There's a saying that goes, "You can't go home again." It offers no direction on where you're supposed to go. It's meant to be poignant: some manner of existential examination of how things once lost can't be retrieved, relived—at least, not from the same perspective. I think. I've always been a little too literal for deep sayings.

16–22 MARCH 2014

DURBAN, SOUTH AFRICA

"Ja, but where are you from originally?" the journalist presses me.

Ah. This again. I'm one of the featured authors at Durban's seventeenth *Time of the Writer* arts festival and, at these events, being grilled about "otherness" is a train that's never late. "You can't be unoriginally from somewhere. I don't think that's a thing."

Hawa Jande Golakai for "Fugee" originally appeared in *Safe House*, (Dundurn Press, 2016), by permission of Dundurn Press Limited.

She waves her hand. "But you know what I mean. You're quite accomplished, considering." She catches herself and flinches at "considering." I let it slide. "You've lived in South Africa for years, right? You've gotten most of your education here?"

I smile. She's doing that cherry-picking thing people feel obliged to do with foreigners, timelining the best of your attributes so their country can take credit for them. "Postgrad education," I correct. But I'm tired and cranky, not exactly shipshape for interviews. It's not going to matter anyway. No one reads articles about writers, and we don't much care—just buy the book.

"So. West Africa. There's that virus scare starting up at the moment."

I sit up. "It's across the border. In Guinea." Is she putting this in the piece? Why do I keep clarifying where the reported cases are from whenever I'm asked? It's not like viruses need visas to travel.

"You mentioned you moved home two years ago. Why'd you decide to go back?"

I want to say it was less a deliberate decision and more a quest for closure, a need to tie up a loose end that had dangled, frayed and fraught, for too long. But I've stopped saying this. I morph into a mumbling cretin when I do, as if afraid that the *real*-real reasons will seem ridiculous. People then feel the need to tilt their heads and nod, like it's noble and they get it, or they don't but won't be rude enough to admit it.

Instead, I beauty-queen my reply: it was time to move on, to help my recovering country. To fully revert to my native state, which, aside from the odd visit, I haven't done in over two decades. To see how much it's changed, the land in which small me took for granted she'd grow up, get a job, marry, have piccaninnies, likely grow old and die. Life has taken me down brighter, more meandering lanes, for which I'm very grateful. The journalist nods to my words, scribbling away.

When the article comes out, it says I went home because it's where I'd always wanted to get married and have children, as if finally I can stop being a loser and make it happen. My best friend calls me to laugh; she's just learnt something new about me. I sigh. No one reads articles about writers anyway.

23 MARCH–12 APRIL

JOHANNESBURG, SOUTH AFRICA

My friend Fran laughs like a bawdy barmaid in a Chaucer tale, a comforting sound. I've decided to round my stay up to a month, so I'm staying at her flat, plotting insidious ways of never leaving. Our mouths run all day, about shoes and sex, politics and career changes, original versus fusion curry recipes, TV content—the meaningful mindlessness that any red-blooded woman who lives in a male-dominated household doesn't know she is missing until the tap is turned back on. Her spare bedroom is a cloud of amenities. Superspar is five minutes away, full of strawberries, peaches and other edible exotica that I never see or can't afford in Monrovia. The guy behind the counter at the Clicks pharmacy is so delicious he's practically a food group. I trawl the malls, stoked to be back in Jozi, home of posh cars and cinched-waist lovelies with awesome hair. Feeling uncouth, I get a Zimbabwean hairdresser to braid me; her price is a blip on my radar. I'm balling in dollars.

On rare occasions, Fran gets serious. "Ebola's making the news online. You know it's getting serious when it makes the news." She glances at me. I stay quiet. "Are you considering going back to your job?"

"I'm at my job," I answer tersely. "National health coordinator at Ministry of Health" is a title I've buried, along with career dissatisfaction. After all those years studying to be, then working as, a medical immunologist, I'm now an author, a career switcher, trying to fade out the former as I find my feet in the latter. The irony is that I left a tough profession involving assays and articles that few understood to do "what anyone who knows the alphabet could manage," as my critics say. Writing isn't respectable—not in Africa, anyway. I'm considered a sufferer of Me Disease, an unrepentant member of the selfish generation, we who shirk duty to follow pipe dreams. There's little consideration for how hard it's been to let go—which I still haven't done fully—for how much I question myself.

"Do you think they'll be able to contain it?" Fran asks.

"No." Snip. Snarl. I cringe at my tone. She means well. We drop it, switch back to safe terrain. A guy back home has thrown his hat into the ring for my affection. I don't know. Men are dicks . . . but then again, men *have* dicks. So. I'm vacillating between uncertainty and blushes. We've spent more time talking and texting now that I'm on the other side of the continent than we did when I was home; social media makes Bravehearts out of us all. Fran does her laugh: please give Contender a whirl. Hmm.

At night, though, on my laptop, I'm stealth-surfing the web. Numbers are climbing in Guinea, and now Sierra Leone, but I know the true figures are understated. Through the grapevine at my old job, I hear they're not really doing anything or mobilising forces to stop it leaking through the borders. Immobile. Do we even have forces? The Neglected Tropical Diseases Unit—they contend with elephantiasis and yellow fever, last of the unicorn afflictions. Is Ebola contemporary enough and, if not, will it get an upgrade quickly enough to make us take it seriously? Because haemorrhagic viruses are the last word in seriousness. And we don't have testing centres. We won't know which measures to take. We don't have anywhere near enough doctors. On a normal day, our one major hospital, John F. Kennedy Medical, is heaving with humanity, all waiting for hours on end for treatment.

"But it's across the border mostly," says my ex-colleague. "And we weren't really *infectious*-infectious. You were one of the few real disease scientists we had. And you left." Pause. "Anyway, you know our government. These old guys move slow. Let's see."

Guilt bites a chunk out of me. I kick it in the teeth. It goes away. Well, retreats. Into a dark corner, where it squats, eyeing me, gnawing on something I didn't give it permission to eat. I don't lock it up or put it on a leash. I want it to come back and harass me. We have a weird relationship.

13 APRIL

10:00 P.M.

O.R. TAMBO INTERNATIONAL AIRPORT, JOHANNESBURG, SOUTH AFRICA

The airport is cold. Winter should be winding down, but Joburg tends to be clingy when it comes to its seasons. I'm double-layered, jacket in carry-on just in case. I don't mind airports; they're like hospitals—you do your time and get out. Mostly. I do hate this particular red-eye, though. Departure: one-frickin'-thirty in the morning. The airline assured me the flight would leave an hour earlier than usual, but it seems they didn't take into account that the plane needed things like cleaning and refuelling before they made their wayward promises, so it looks like we're taking off at the same time. I can't wait to leave. Airports get seriously wrong, creepy, after all the shops close. Like abandoned warehouses. Unlucky stragglers huddle by the gates, bleary-eyed, giving each other grim stares. And there are always a few gratingly cheerful chipmunks who want to story-of-my-life you until the boarding call sounds. I walk around to avoid them, Viber-flirting with Contender as I pace.

14 APRIL

12:00 A.M.

O.R. TAMBO INTERNATIONAL AIRPORT: LAST ROUND OF IMMIGRATION

The official asks me why I don't have a national ID book since I'm a permanent resident. I explain: I applied, and it took over a year for it to be processed, by which time, when I went to collect it, Home Affairs told me the ID had been misplaced and I needed to reapply. They assured me it would be no problem, and in the three years I've travelled on my permit stamp it's never been one. The official and I snicker over a Home Affairs joke. He raises his hand to stamp the exit permit, pauses for too long. (*Stamp it!*) He doesn't. He calls over a colleague; they confer at length out of earshot.

"Are you from Zimbabwe?" Official Two asks.

"No!" Immediately I twinge at my vehemence. I had good times in Zim. Jacaranda days.

They take my passport and other papers and disappear. On the other side of the glass partition passengers get on their feet, many throwing me worried glances. Boarding has begun. My skin prickles and my temper blooms; I suck the storm back in. I'm going home, dammit. They can throw me out if I want to stay; they can't hold me if I'm trying to leave. I'm going home.

The two officials in grey return and escort me upstairs, neither of them answering my questions. They leave me in an office with a new lot in navy uniforms. Ambient IQ drops fifty points. Office navies look more jaded, less equable. No, actually they just look shittier. Their job is to clear out the filth, and once you're dragged upstairs you've qualified, no negotiation. They begin filling out forms and throwing instructions at each other in isiZulu, or Sesotho, or isiXhosa. Shaking, I remind them they're supposed to speak in a language I understand and explain what's going on. They shout that this doesn't concern me (*How the hell do you figure that?!*); what's concerning is a passport stating I'm Nigerian (*Liberian! Oh my God, can you read?!*), yet their system has me down as Zimbabwean. I shout back. Behind the desk, Navy Bitch, the most abusive and least helpful, decides to settle it. After a short phone call to their boss, who's clearly too big of a shot to be here fielding crises of this kind, she informs me at her leisure, "We're arresting you." (Later I realise they meant "detaining," but at that point, nuance).

"For what?!"

Impersonating a resident. Carrying fake documents. Maybe they'll think of more infractions, but that's enough to be getting on with for now. One of the flight attendants, who followed me upstairs and is miraculously still outside, is deeply apologetic as she says my baggage will be offloaded from the plane and put in holding. They have to go.

"I get to make calls," I quail, already dialling. I wake Contender in Monrovia. He's a lawyer; he'll know what to do. He immediately realises this is not a practical joke and switches to disaster response mode. He'll call my mother and the ambassador in Pretoria. I hang up, thinking if ever I've owed a man my firstborn, this is it. Drinks. We'll start with drinks.

Nothing else can be done. It's well past one in the morning. I didn't even hear the plane take off.

14 APRIL

2:00 A.M.–3:00 A.M.

JOHANNESBURG, SOUTH AFRICA: THE STATIONS

At the first station they put me in a cell alone, the sole insurgent of the evening. It's unbelievably cold. I'm totally blank on how so many greats have produced good pieces of literature from lock-up. The place is a buzzkill, even for a crime writer. I wait for stirrings of productive angst and all I get are claws of hunger raking up and down my stomach; I haven't eaten in about five hours.

The next station is Kempton Park. This is lock-up, proper. The cops fill out paperwork, not asking for my story. I don't bother giving it to them. I expect monstrously vile mistreatment, shouts in my face, and the contents of my carry-on emptied onto the floor and lit into a pyre to warm their hands. They all look bored; this isn't Robben Island. This time around the cells are appalling, and I've seen a lot. Filthy, freezing and cramped, the walls practically marinated in human effluent. I perch on an outcrop of the wall and try to sleep.

14 APRIL

5:00 A.M.–7:00 P.M.

JOHANNESBURG, SOUTH AFRICA: KEMPTON PARK STATION . . . STILL

The situation moves, in the wrong direction at first. I wake up in a cloud of my own stench. The officer in charge has updates: I'm to be deported, my permit revoked.

For the first time I feel real fear, and rage. I earned that permit through hard work, mounds of application documents, and countless bile-inducing visits to Home Affairs. Now I am to be hustled onto a flight, a disgraced imposter.

The threats fizzle to nothing at dusk. An official from Airport Immigration swoops in, barks orders at the cops, who gather me and my belongings together, and drives me to the airport. He tells me he assisted the Liberian ambassador in proving my permit's validity. At head office I receive profuse apologies and pleas for forgiveness, from none other than the dickhead boss who couldn't have been bothered to leave his bed and put a stop to my arrest. In the interest of security, they have to make certain assumptions, and sometimes innocent people get caught in the crossfire. They are incredibly sorry . . . oh, and by the way, they cannot foot the cost of the forfeited air ticket. Collateral damage, unfortunately . . . again, so sorry. I shout and cuss and deflate, tearful and exhausted. The ambassador squeezes my hand—let it go, the embassy will carry the cost.

15 APRIL

10:30 P.M.

O.R. TAMBO INTERNATIONAL AIRPORT, JOHANNESBURG, SOUTH AFRICA

I'm finally going home.

MID-MAY TO MID-JUNE

MONROVIA, LIBERIA

Ebola is here. It's been at our back door since March, waiting like a wolf, the big bad wolf. The atmosphere I met when I touched down in April didn't indicate that there was a huge threat looming, which is reckless for a country that can't withstand its straw house being blown down. I wanted to look around the airport and be pleasantly surprised, see some hand-washing stations and men in protective gear checking for ailing passengers, see signs screaming about what to look for, see something. I was disappointed at my disappointment; I know better. Monrovia is the Liberia that matters most, and this has always been so, shamefully elitist as that is; until something unsettles our tiny capital, it will never cause a stir.

Now Ebola has crept out of the deeply forested villages and truly permeated the psyche of Monrovia. "Real" is the buzzword for its takeover—*the huge reality, the horrifying realness!*—as if when it was across the border it was an underfed, coquettish slip of a thing, and now it's gorging itself to a respectable maturity within our borders. Hipco songs on the radio make light of it; others tell the populace to pull up their socks or die. For every believer that the threat is real, there's a naysayer guffawing at a mystery virus that skulks out of the jungle, riding bush meat as a host. Officials argue on the radio: the offensive strikers want the borders closed immediately; the more mercenary counter that it's already through the gates, what would isolation solve? Debate rages about "the responsibility of the international community"—how many aid agencies have come, will there be more, which measures would they advise us to put in place in the meantime? It's the usual distress code of all African countries to the West to bring the fury, the Bat-Signal in the sky to summon the superhero, the underhanded "we're not asking but . . . okay, we're asking for your help." Things have gotten out of hand. In truth, there had never really been a hand for it to be in in the first place.

"We've never had a health crisis like this before," shrills every radio and TV announcer.

LATE JUNE

News comes thick and fast from different communities about the steadily climbing death toll. It sounds movie-script-bizarre and melodramatic—*bodies piling up!*—but unless there's an undercover and seriously twisted Hollywood crew micromanaging the debacle for ratings, it really is happening. Facebook is electric with commentary. Liberians in the diaspora flare up, playing crisis managers: corruption has once again let us down in the worst way, how could the citizenry allow this to happen? Liberians at home fire back with righteous outrage: people are dying! We on ground and y'all don't know what's going on, step up or shut up! My own posts start off level-headed and descend into flatulent rants. Everyone on the outside feels they know what those of us in the mix should be doing, and it enrages me. Friends on social media aim and fire only two questions at me now: *Are you okay?* and *Are you doing something to help?* I lash out, but underneath the anger, my guilt creature taunts me. I'm trained to handle every substance that can ooze or squirt out of a human being and, in doing so, have rarely felt afraid. Now, fear taints everything. Ebola kills heroes, too. Helplessness is unfamiliar and, in typical me style, that which I can't solve or soothe makes me livid.

We are all on edge. Our tiny country has been through enough.

Every day, every newspaper, everybody adds a new tale to the fray. There's the one about the household that lost both parents (or the aunt, or uncle, or grandparents), leaving the kids to fend for themselves. There's the household where everyone died saved one, and the neighbourhood barricaded the lone survivor inside to stop the spread to other homes. There's the pregnant woman who ruptures like an overripe mango at a community clinic, her dead body dragged into a corner of the ward for the emergency response team to pick up because the nurses were too afraid to treat her.

Driving alone, I often stop to give lifts to hopefuls at the roadside, waiting for public transport. We drive to town in silence, everyone but me drenched, thanks to rainy season. I put the radio on—prevention ads and songs abound now, warning us that the crisis is no joke, listing symptoms to watch out for. A young nurse breaks the lull at last. She intimates in a leaden voice that she's stopped going to work and found a desk job doing data entry with an NGO (non-governmental organisation). She's trained to help the sick, but this isn't what she signed up for, the possibility of bleeding out and liquefying to death. She looks like she'll never forgive herself. I want to tell her how much I get it, feeling like a coward, a deserter. I want to, but I don't. Something about this particular emotional tumult feels like it should be borne alone, unalleviated by sharing and understanding. When the car empties out I drive on, realising I ought to stop giving rides to strangers, because you never know. Another dick move added to my list.

EARLY TO LATE JULY

The life we know is fractured. By month-end the border will be closed, for God knows how long. We are advised of our civic duty to report via hotline anyone who looks vaguely zombie-like, or neighbours who are harbouring Anne Frankensteins in the back room. Physical friendliness is over. All unnecessary touching must stop: handshaking, kissing, hugging, humping, all of it. The embargo on frivolous sex seems to hit the hardest. Men across the spectrum of virility laugh uproariously: "Dah whetin you say—no eatin' sumtin' because of Ebola?!" Women crow and flash superior smirks. Mother Nature is a girl after their own heart, cracking the whip so they don't have to. Now their significant others are forced, in theory at least, to come home to them and only them. Significantly othered myself, I am unfussed—Contender and I are now in a relationship, though it's more a polite passing of time, the only cool, composed thing going on in a frenzied hot zone.

Buckets filled with bleach water for sanitising hands and in-ear thermometers have become *du jour* outside places of business. Conspiracy theories flow thick and fast. The United States designed Ebola and released it on us as a form of population control. Pharmaceutical companies wanted to run a massive trial of a new vaccine, but they needed to create an epidemic to test its legs. The cure-all remedies are not far behind. Bathing in hot water mixed with raw pepper or bouillon cubes will stop the virus from infecting you. Churches hold prayer vigils for the infected and pronounce them cured after all-night hallelujahs. Calamity breeds a tragic form of hilarity.

The three little ruffians from the house next door no longer run to anyone for hugs. They scamper away and peep from behind the mango tree in their yard, giggling and slow-waving at me whenever I pass. Their mother's face is grave as she shoots me an apologetic smile: *Don't take it personally.* They've been warned. We all have.

The inevitable media pile-on is in full swing. The worst has happened, in the worst way possible. After a sluggish debut, the outbreak is now headlining internationally. It has also acquired its first poster boy in the form of Patrick Sawyer. The government official travelled on business and singlehandedly turned Lagos International Airport into a biohazardous area, becoming the patient who drew Nigeria into the epidemic. His case leaves nineteen infected and eight dead in total. Online, the Naijas spew pure vitriol: how could the Liberian government allow their people to travel willy-nilly, without getting tested for exposure? Where was the regard for protocol, for citizens of other nations, for international security?! All flights from affected countries must be monitored or stopped!

Clubbing and partying has petered out. Gatherings are furtive and sombre, and we can't help but pontificate and piss-contest. Everyone is an expert now; the situation demands it. It makes us feel useful somehow, especially since the international health agencies have taken over, rendering the natives superfluous. We smelt questions into fiery debates: Was it ever a serious consideration to ground flights to and from affected countries when SARS broke out, or was the medical community simply put on high alert? In fact, didn't SARS spread even faster because air traffic to Asia was so busy? Come to think of it, this virus has never been known to spread this fast over so short a period—what's changed all of a sudden?

A friend drops by one afternoon. My father has banned all casual visitors, so she drops in for only a couple of hours while he's at work. Patrick Sawyer was employed at the Finance Ministry where she works, she says, partly horrified, partly amused, partly thrilled. Of course, she only had dealings with him in a very peripheral way, and only saw him once from afar before he travelled (oh, he really didn't look sick ... you're only infectious when you look sick), but still. My sister and I are wild-eyed, practically levitating in disbelief. A possible contact of a celebrity index case is in our house. We all make light of it, scooching away and forcing her to sit at the far end of the living room and not touch anything, *ha ha ha this is so hilarious, right!* But she stays long enough for ...

Three days later I have a headache that morphs into a mild fever. Our jolliness rises to screeching hysterics. "HA HA HA, SLEEP IN THE OTHER ROOM!!" my sister says, face clenched in a rictus smile that she thinks is reassuring. I know it's malaria. My pulse has always been a siren song to mosquitoes, my blood their elixir. Of course it's malaria. No one goes full-blown in thirty-six hours. I start the three-day treatment course.

At night, insomniac with fever, I strip down to nothing and examine my entire body for sores, lesions, any signs of bleeding or necrosis. None ... but my eyes look like marinara meatballs. (*This is how I go ... this is how I end ... and I won't be a hero, I'll be that fucking moron who should've known better, the infectious disease scientist that blundered into the worst infectious disease ever ... I didn't finish writing my book, my latest draft is tripe, no publisher will care to publish it posthumously ...*)

In two days, the malaria's melted off.

EARLY AUGUST

My neighbourhood, Duport Road, is now steadily reporting cases. We're not as badly hit as other high-densities like New Kru Town, for instance; so far, we tiptoe rather than sprint. Our watchman revels in regaling us with new developments. One morning, he has an alarming update: at the marketplace up the road there's an uproar over a man's body. Nearly two days dead; the clean-up ambulances have been alerted, but none have shown up. Enraged, the market women have dragged the body from the vendors' compound and dumped it in the middle of the road.

Out loud I say it's rubbish, but make a mental note to keep an eye out on my way to the supermarket. I board a pehn-pehn motorbike. As we zip down the road, I see nothing. Just before the supermarket, we pass a blockade of sorts in the middle of the street. As the pehn-pehn driver slows and manoeuvres around it, I catch a glimpse of a human face. Or what looks like a human face, had it been whizzed in a blender. I tap the driver's shoulder till he stops, and I jump down. The misshapen heap of debris is indeed mostly human, the body of a man surrounded and partly covered by rocks and wooden planks. I tell the pehn-pehn guy to wait because I want to take a picture. He laughs and tells me kindly, matter-of-factly, to go fuck myself. He's not taking me anywhere after I've gone within selfie distance of an Ebola corpse. Chewing my lip at the side of the road, I think long and hard. I hear my parents' roars in my head, think of the household of trusting individuals who swarm around me day in and out. Think of what I'm contemplating, and the reason behind my compulsion to make up for one thing by doing an even stupider one. I trudge back and climb onto the bike. Pehn-pehn guy nods sagely before pushing off, as if proud of my sound decision. This time, regret boxes with my conscience. I feel horrible, but I wanted to take that photo.

He could have died of anything, I keep telling myself. Any old thing. (*But you've never seen someone's eyes caked with blood like that, their flesh turn to mush so quickly . . .*)

My household is abuzz again less than a week later. There's an Ebola ambulance parked outside our gate, across the road. I slip outside to observe, the cook hissing and trying to pull me back inside. I try to sound brave as I tell her I won't get too close, but my heart is a fist in the back of my throat, trying to punch through. We've never had a van this close. All the nearby houses empty as the neighbours congregate to gawk. I creep close enough to get snaps of the white PPE-suited guys bringing the stretcher out. On it is the Old Ma from the brown house opposite ours. Some of the women start wailing, hands on their heads.

Later we get the news that she died. Some say she was just sick and the clinics and treatment units were too crowded to provide her care. Others say it was indeed EVD. The wildest theory is she was poisoned by a rival in the church, a schemer with the foresight to use the epidemic as a cover for darker deeds.

Monrovia's quickly emptying out, becoming a ghost town. Everyone is leaving, and by that I mean the privileged ones who can afford to. We who have stayed are often teased, "Yor dey kwii [civilised] pipo dem. The first to leave when there's trouble, like when the war happened . . . how come yor still here?"

In that this epidemic is vividly reminiscent of the civil war, dey no lie. I feel ten years old all over again. Monrovia's aura even tastes like 1990, dense and indigo and hot-wired, like it did just before Charles Taylor marched into town and hell broke loose. I didn't get it back then. I remember being told that our family was taking "a li'l vacation" and doing twirls of rabid glee round the lounge, excited because I'd never travelled before. That vacation lasted two-thirds of my life and left behind a fragile ache where a solid sense of home should be. I've been moving, running, balancing on a razor's edge for too long. Damaged I may be, but grown and stubborn I have also become. I'm not going anywhere unless I bloody well must. My father pleads with me daily to reconsider, but I refuse—how can I leave the rest of my family behind? Besides, go where? South Africa has closed its borders to affected nationalities. Although I'm still furious over the detention, it's my first choice of refuge, and now that option is dead.

I walk. I don't know what else to do, and cabin fever from being cooped up all day is shredding my nerves. My route is Duport Road, Paynesville, and the neighbourhoods around Samuel K. Doe Stadium and Airfield Highway. Before the outbreak walking was more to air my thoughts than for fitness, but in my current state I find I'm not untangling the gnarls in my brain as effectively, whether I'm mobile or stationary. So I just trudge, and look at people, and they look back at me. We all wear "coping" expressions. On the surface, life carries on as normally and best it can, but if you're local you can't miss the undercurrent of surrealism. The usual throngs on the streets have thinned and don't look as vibrant as they did before. Hardly surprising: the death toll has reportedly reached more than a dozen a day, the infection rate over a hundred per week. For the living, fear has driven us inside our homes or outside the borders. We've changed our habits, and I compulsively take snaps of the new normal with my phone: no more mystery meat—people buy only cuts they can recognise from market stalls and barbeque vendors; pickup trucks on clean-up duty zoom down the highway to burial sites, corpses in the back covered with tarp; shoppers leave stores with arms overloaded with provisions; the new game of tag children play is "don't touch me, you got Ebola!"

Walking on Airfield Highway one day, I see high walls and a metal gate, outside of which a line has formed. In a moment of total confusion, I think it's an awareness concert of some kind and people are queuing for tickets to get in. I tiptoe to peep over the fence. At the sight of tents, a concentration camp sprawl of white, it dawns in slow-mo horror: this is a treatment centre, and that's a line of sick or suspected patients hoping to get a bed inside. My heart aches imagining all those full beds; my brain hurts trying not to imagine the hole in which all those bodies will end up.

MID TO LATE AUGUST

My birthday comes—with relief I declare myself single again—and goes. I haven't heard from Contender in almost a month; I gather he's left without a word. I tried to end it before his departure (*This really isn't working, we're too different*) and he appealed for more time, a break (*We'll work on it once your book is out of the way*). Now we've fizzled into a ridiculous unsaid, a flaccid tale of love, or lack thereof, in the time of Ebola. This was quite literally not the time or the place—there are far greater worries.

The week after my birthday the residents of West Point, a slum settlement, mob and loot an Ebola clinic in protest, stealing supplies that may be tainted with the virus. Within days, West Point is quarantined. Riots erupt and spill into central town. Two days later, I take a taxi into town and walk around aimlessly. Never have I seen Broad Street look this dead. It's humbling and frightening at the same time, witnessing how the might of man can cower when challenged by an organism only an electron microscope can see. I wander down a street opening onto Waterside Market, close to the blockades that keep the West Point residents in. Camera ready, I try to bribe two of the riot cops loafing around to let me go closer, but I'm half-hearted about it. One wants the cash; the other tells me with lazy surliness to leave or he'll take my phone and break it. In that moment, photo-diarying becomes pointless. I take one snap before my phone dies, then I go home.

My hand is forced. The Port Harcourt Book Festival is hosting the Africa39 nominees at their annual book fair, an event I've been excited about since I was selected as one of the thirty-nine laureates. Now it's all gone sour in my mouth. The organisers have been pressing for my confirmation of attendance since June. It's far from simple: if I leave I cannot return—not for several weeks, perhaps months. Against the WHO's advice opposing strangling the virus-stricken countries by closing them off from routes of assistance, not only is the border still closed, but all major airlines save one have stopped flying to Liberia.

I confirm that I'm in. A leaden sense of déjà vu sits on me as I pack. Yet again, I'm a clueless child about to be cast adrift, only this time there's no crackle of exhilaration for the adventure ahead.

I leave on the second-to-last Arik Air flight out of Monrovia. The airport is jam-packed but creepily silent. There's an international news channel filming the mass exodus; they ask a few of us for a quick interview, to share our harrowing tale with a world that wants to share our pain. I put my hoodie up and walk past them.

SEPTEMBER TO DECEMBER

THE OUTSIDE

It is the best of times as much as it is the worst.

Some weeks after I land in Ghana, it happens: my cousin dies of Ebola. He contracts it from his fiancée, and three months before their wedding the happy couple and three others close to them are gone. Everybody knew somebody who died, thousands of families were affected, yet you never conceive of a direct hit until it occurs. My family isn't big on emotional expressiveness—we cover grief with gruffness—but this numbs us all. I recall refusing to visualise where the bodies go for burial . . . now I have to. My cousin will not be returned to us, a family with Muslim roots, for final rites before sunset. We can't visit his grave with flowers on Decoration Day. His three-year-old daughter, my namesake, is fatherless.

I flit and day-trip—Accra–Kasua–Port Harcourt–Lagos–Kasua–Accra—like a nouveau brand of refugee, a fugitive of biological war, which sounds ludicrous even to me. I'm a hologram of myself most of the time, my emotions submerged, oddly calm and grateful some days, unable to get out of bed on others. People head-tilt and shoulder-squeeze me a lot, *Are you okay? We understand* . . .

Life trudges on . . .

. . . I embrace my first trip to Nigeria, although I maintain an internal chant to remind myself I deserve this, I worked for this. I am among my tribe of writers and it feels glorious. I am Liberian, I am not a virus . . .

. . . Until I confide in a fellow scribe about my loss and am told, "Oh, wow. Well, at least it was only a cousin" . . .

. . . At a literary fair, a journalist sits me down for an interview and asks nothing about my book and everything about Ebola, and how contrite Liberians should feel for killing Nigerian citizens . . .

. . . Everyone seems to have money to burn while I pinch pennies, my face hot as I turn down every deal. I "party" but never really party. Guys grin and flirt, then flinch; one actually wipes the hand that brushed my shoulder on his jeans as he walks away. No hard feelings. I never want to stay out long . . .

. . . I get robbed at Accra Mall, my passport graciously left behind. I want to leave. Why can't I leave? I'm stuck. No flights. The body count back home is now in the thousands. I wait. Read, write, sleep for two-thirds of the day. And wait.

24 DECEMBER

I've managed to wrangle a flight via Casablanca. I'm going home.

9 MAY 2015
MONROVIA, LIBERIA

"But the whole country is rejoicing. We've been declared Ebola-free. It's gone, for, like, *ever.* Why can't you be happy like everybody else?" My friend looks disappointed in me.

I sip my beer and say nothing.

2010 World Cup

Binyavanga Wainaina

> She took her own certainty along by stooping under everything: stooping under her own history of the heart, stooping under the stares in Mamprobi, and stooping under her own lowering world.
>
> —from *Search Sweet Country*, by Kojo Laing

I arrived in Accra, Ghana, yesterday. This is my first time in West Africa, on writing assignment for a World Cup anthology. Years are flying by now, as my writing career starts to take shape. It is 2006.

I spend much of the first night in a cybercafé in Osu, trying to find out as much as I can about Togo. The café is full for most of the night, full of young men, mostly, all well dressed, and, from my sideways glances, all looking for scholarships or at dating Web sites.

I am going to Togo tomorrow, to sniff around for a World Cup–related book project. Togo is suddenly in the headlines because its team, against all predictions, has qualified for the World Cup.

What a happy, happy city. People are laughing and greeting and laughing and greeting. Working, selling, building.

––––––––––––––

Many Google trails yield much information.

The French, since the days of de Gaulle especially, love fatherly African dictators who love French luxury goods, and French military bases. It makes them money, makes them feel they have their own commonwealth that gives them a feeling of international drama; it makes for good dinner-party talk and much student agitation. Omar Bongo, of Gabon, imported a French chateau; Emperor Bokassa had a Louis XIV–style inauguration and died in Bangui; Léopold Sédar Senghor died in France; and Félix Houphouët-Boigny of Ivory Coast built the biggest Catholic basilica in the world in his home village.

Gnassingbé Eyadéma, who died recently, was cut from the same market fabric. He managed to remain in power for thirty-eight years with no small help from the French, who ignored most of the abuses of his government and gave him much military aid for decades. Chirac called him a friend of France.

Nations that have cut themselves off from any way of measuring themselves against the normal transactions of their population become comical, in a crocodile-grinning, Idi Amining way. The constituency of these leaders was France, their cold war partners, their clan insiders, and the executives of the main extractors of their main overseas export. A Togo Web site reports that a former Mitterrand aide was arrested in Lomé for selling arms.

––––––––––––––

I meet Alex at breakfast in Accra. He is a carver of wooden curios who has a small shop at the hotel. His uncle owns the hotel. He spends his days at the gym, playing soccer, and making wooden sculptures of voluptuous Ghanaian women. For tourists. He shines with beauty and health and fresh-ironedness. He seems ready, fit and ready. I am not sure what for. We chat. He doesn't speak very much. I ask him if he can help get me somebody. He plays finger football on his mobile phone and finds me somebody to take me to Lomé.

Later, in the evening, we get in his uncle's Peugeot, and he drives me to meet my guide. I am struck, again, by the fluidity of his body language, and even more by his solemn maturity. There does not seem to be anything he cannot handle.

But this attitude toward me is overly respectful. He plays boy to my man. Does not contradict anything I say. It is disturbing. Before we get to the suburb where his friends are hanging out, he turns to me and asks, his face awed, and suddenly boyish, "Have you been to America?"

We find them, Alex and I, at dusk, a group of young men sitting by the road, in tracksuits and shorts and muscle tops. They are all fat-free and pectoraled and look boneless, postcoital, and gray after a vigorous exercise session at the beach, and a swim and a shower. One of them has a bandage on his knee and is limping. They are all fashionably dressed.

I ask around. They all come from middle-class families. They are all jobless, in their twenties, not hungry, cushioned in very small ways by their families, and small deals here and there.

Hubert is a talented soccer player. Twenty-one years old, he is the star of a first-division team in Accra. In two weeks he will go to South Africa to try out for a major soccer team. His coach has high hopes for him.

"I am a striker."

He looks surprisingly small for a West African football player. Ghanaians are often built like American football players. I conclude that he must be exceptionally good if he can play here.

"Aren't you afraid of those giant Ghanaian players?" I ask, nodding my head at his hulking friends.

He just smiles. He is the one with the international offers.

Hubert agrees to take me to Togo for a couple of days. He is mortified by my suggestion that I stay in a hotel. We will sleep in his mother's house in Lomé. His father died recently. Hubert is in Accra because there are more opportunities in Ghana than in Togo.

"Ghana has no politics."

I offer Alex a drink. To say thanks. We end up at a bar by the side of a road. A hundred or so people have spilled onto the road, dancing and talking rowdily and staggering. Alex looks a little more animated. They are playing hiplife—Ghana's version of hip-hop, merged with highlife. It is a weekday, and the bar is packed with large, good-looking men, all in their twenties, it seems. There are very few women. We sit by the road and chat, watching people dance in the street. This could never happen in Nairobi—this level of boisterousness would be assumed to lead to chaos and anarchy, and it would be clipped quickly. Three young men stagger and chase each other on the road, beers in hand, laughing loudly. Alex knows a lot of the guys here, and he joins in a little, in his solemn way.

I notice there are no broken bottles, no visible bouncer. No clues that this level of happiness ever leads to meaningful violence.

After a while, we find a table on the pavement. I head off to the bar to get a round of drinks. Some of Alex's friends have joined us. "You don't drink Guinness?" they ask, shocked. Guinness is MANPOWER.

When I get back, I find that a couple has joined the table: a tall man with large lips and a round, smooth baby's face, and a heavily made-up young woman with sharp breasts and a shiny short dress.

The rest of the table is muted. They do not meet the woman's eye, although she is their age. The man is in his thirties. He shouts for a waiter, who materializes. His eyes sweep around, a string of cursive question marks. People nod assent shyly. He has a French African accent.

Alex introduces us. He is Yves, from Ivory Coast. He is staying at the same hotel that I am.

Yves laughs, his eyes teasing. "Your uncle's hotel. Eh."

Alex looks down. Nobody talks to me now. It is assumed Yves is my peer, and they must submit. They start to talk among themselves, and I turn to Yves.

"So. You here on business? Do you live in Côte d'Ivoire?" I ask.

"Ah. My brother, who can survive there? There is war. I live in South London. And in Chad. I also live in Accra sometimes."

"Oh, where do you work?"

"I am in oil—we supply services to the oil companies in N'Djamena."

We talk. No. He talks. For a full hour. Yves is thirty-three. He has three wives. One is the daughter of the president of Chad. The other is mixed race—a black Brit. The third lives here in Accra. I wait for him to turn to his girlfriend by his side. He does not. And she does not react. It is as if she is worried the makeup will crack if she says anything. It is impossible to know what she is thinking. He has money. She will wear the mask he needs. Every so often, he breaks from his monologue to whisper babyhoney things in her ear.

Yves knows Kofi Annan's son. He claims to be on a retainer for a major oil company, seeking high-level contracts in Africa. He looks at me, eyes dead straight and serious, and asks me about my contacts in State House. I have none to present.

He laughs, generously. No problem. No problem. Kenya was stupid, he says, to go with the Chinese so easily.

This is the future. But most people do not see this . . .

He turns to Alex. "See this pretty boy here? I am always telling him to get himself ready. I will make it work for him . . . but he is lazy."

Yves turns to the group. "You Ghana boys are lazy—you don't want to be aggressive."

The group is eating this up eagerly, smiling shyly and looking somewhat hangdog. The drinks flow. Cuteface now has a bottle of champagne.

Later, we stand to head back. Yves grabs Alex's neck in a strong chokehold. "You won't mess in the deal, eh, my brother?"

Alex smiles sheepishly, "Ah no, Yves, I will do it, man."

"I like you. Eh . . . Alex? I like you. I don't know why. You are always promising, and nothing happens. You are lucky I like you."

Alex looks very happy.

We separate at the hotel lift, and Yves slaps me on the back.

"Call me, eh?"

Early the next morning, we take a car from the Accra bus rank at dawn. It is a two-hour drive to the border. You cross the border at Aflao, and you are in Lomé, the capital of Togo.

Gnassingbé Eyadéma was a Kabye, the second-largest ethnic group in Togo. The Kabye homeland around the northern city of Kara is arid and mountainous. In the first half of the twentieth century, many young Kabye moved south to work as sharecroppers on Ewe farms. The wealthier Ewe looked down on the Kabye but depended on them as laborers. Eyadéma made sure to fill the military with Kabye loyalists. It was called "the army of cousins" and was armed by the French. Alex is Kabye.

Eyadéma threw political opponents to the crocodiles.

Lomé is hot, dry, and dusty. People look dispirited, and the city is rusty and peeling and bleached from too much brine and sun and rough times. Hubert points out a tourist hotel to me. It looks like it has been closed for years, but the weather here can deteriorate things rapidly. The tourist industry collapsed after the pro-democracy riots in early 2005.

Hubert is not Ewe. And he supports Faure Gnassingbé: "He understands young people."

It turns out that his family is originally from the north.

We take a taxi into town and drive around looking for a bureau that will change my dollars to CPA francs. One is closed. We walk into the next one. It has the characterless look of a government office. It smells of old damp cardboard. They tell us we have to wait an hour to change any money.

In the center of the city, buildings are imposing, unfriendly, and impractical. Paint has faded; plastic fittings look bleached and brittle. I have seen buildings like this before—in South African homeland capitals, in Chad and Budapest. These are buildings that international contractors build for countries eager to show how "modern" they are. They are usually described as "ultramodern"—and when they are new, they shine like the mirrored sunglasses of a presidential bodyguard. Within months, they rust and peel and crumble. I see one called Centre des Cheques Postaux, another Centre National de Perfectionnement Professionnel.

There are International Bureaus of Many Incredibly Important Things, and International Centers of Even More Important Things. I count fourteen buildings that have the word *développement* on their walls. In Accra, signs are warm, quirky, and humorous: Happy Day Shop, Do Life Yourself, Diplomatic Haircut.

Everywhere, people are wearing yellow Togo team shirts.

We decide to have lunch. Hubert leads me to a small plot of land surrounded on three sides by concrete walls. On one side of this plot, a group of women are stirring large pots. On the other, there is a makeshift thatch shade, with couches and a huge television. A fat gentleman, who looks like the owner of the place, is watching *Octopussy* on satellite television. There are fading murals on the walls. On one wall, there are a couple of stiff-looking white people waltzing, noses facing the sky. Stiff and awkward, cliché white people. An arrow points to a violin, and another arrow points to a champagne bottle. It is an ad for a hotel: L'Hotel Climon. 12 chambres. Entiérement climatisé. Non loin du Lycée Française.

On another wall, there is an ad for this restaurant.

A topless black woman with spectacular breasts—large, pointy, and firm—serves brochettes and a large fish on a huge platter. A black chef with sparkling cheeks grins at us. A group of people are eating, drinking, laughing. Fluent, affluent, flexible. I order the fish.

When we are done, we make our way out and look for a taxi. There are more taxis than private cars on the road. Hubert and the taxi driver have a heated discussion about prices; we leave the taxi in a huff. Hubert is furious. I remain silent—the price he quotes seems reasonable—but Nairobi taxis are very expensive.

"He is trying to cheat us because you are a foreigner."

I assume the taxi driver was angry because Hubert did not want to be a good citizen and conspire with him to overcharge me. We get another taxi, and drive past more grim-looking buildings. There are lots of warning signs: Interdit de . . . Interdit de . . .

One.

Interdit de Chier Ici. No shitting here.

A policeman stands in front of the sign, with a gun.

In several hand-painted advertisements women are serving one thing or another, topless, with the same spectacular breasts. I wonder if they are all by the same artists. Most Ghanaian hand-painted murals are either barbershop signs or hair salon signs. Here breasts rule. Is this a Francophone thing? An Eyadéma thing?

It could be that what makes Lomé look so drab is that since the troubles that sent donors away, and sent tourists away, there have not been any new buildings to make the fading old ones less visible. They have gone: the licks of fresh paint, the presidential murals; the pink and blue tourist hotels with pink and blue bikinis on the beach sipping pink and blue cocktails. The illusions of progress no longer need to be maintained. The dictator who needed them is dead.

We drive past the suburb where all the villas are, and all the embassies. Nearby there is a dual carriageway, sober charcoal gray, better than any road I have seen so far. It cuts through bushes and gardens and vanishes into the distance. This is the road to the presidential palace that Eyadéma built. It is miles away. It is surrounded by lush parkland, and Hubert tells me the presidential family has a zoo in the compound. Eyadéma was a hunter and loved animals.

We drop off my luggage at Hubert's home. His mother lives in a large compound in a tree-lined suburb. The bungalow is shaped like a U. The rooms open to a corridor and face a courtyard where stools are set. His mother and sisters rush out to hug him—he is clearly a favorite. We stay for a few minutes, have some refreshments, and take a taxi back to the city center.

Driving past the city's main hospital, I see the first signs of sensible commerce: somebody providing a useful product of service to individuals who need it. Lined along the hospital wall are secondhand imported goods in this order: giant stereo speakers, some very expensive looking; a drum set; bananas; a small kiosk with a sign on its forehead: Telephon Inter-Nation; dog chains; a cluster of secondhand lawn mowers; dog chains; five or six big-screen televisions; dog chains; crutches; steam irons; a large faded Oriental carpet.

An hour later, we reach the market in Lomé, and finally find ourselves in a functional and vibrant city. Currency dealers present themselves at the window of the car—negotiations are quick. Money changes hands, and we walk into the maze of stalls. It is hard to tell how big it is—people are milling about everywhere; there are people sitting on the ground and small rickety stalls in every available space.

There are stalls selling stoves and electronic goods, and currency changers and traders from all over West Africa, and tailors and cobblers and brokers and fixers and food and drink. Everything is fluent, everybody in perpetual negotiation, flexible and competitive. Togo's main official export is phosphates, but it has always made its money as a free-trade area, supplying traders from all over West Africa.

Markets like these have been in existence all over West Africa for at least a millennium. There are traders from seven or eight countries here. Markets in Lomé are run by famous "mama Benzes"—rich trading women who have chauffeur-driven Mercedes-Benzes. These days, after years of economic stagnation, the Mama Benzes are called Mama Opels.

Most of the stalls are bursting with fabrics. I have never seen so many—there are shapeless splotches of color on cloth, bold geometrics on wax batik, pinks on earth brown, ululating pinstripes. There are fabrics with thousands of embroidered coin-size holes shaped like flowers. There are fabrics that promise wealth: one stall owner points out a strange design on a Togolese coin and shows me the same design on the fabric of an already busy shirt. There are fabrics for clinging, for flicking over a shoulder, for square shouldering, for floppy collaring, for marrying, and some must surely assure instant breakups.

We brush past clothes that lap against my ear, whispering; others lick my brow from hangars above my face.

Anywhere else in the world the fabric is secondary: it is the final architecture of the garment that makes a difference. But this is Lomé, the duty-free port, the capital of Togo, and here it is the fabric that matters. The fabric you will buy can be sewed into a dress, a shirt, an evening outfit of headband, skirt, and top in one afternoon, at no extra cost. It is all about the fabric. There are fabrics of silk, cotton, from the Netherlands, from China, mudcloth from Mali, kente from northern Togo.

It is the stall selling bras that stops my forward motion. It is a tiny open-air stall. There are bras piled on a small table, bras hanging above. Years ago, I had a part-time job as a translator for some Senegalese visitors to Kenya. Two of the older women, both quite large, asked me to take them shopping for bras. We walked into shop after shop in Nairobi's biggest mall. They probed and pulled and sighed and exclaimed—and I translated all this to the chichi young girls who looked offended that a woman of that age could ask questions about a bra that had nothing to do with its practical uses. We roamed for what seemed like hours, but these Francophone women failed to find a single bra in all the shops in Sarit Centre that combined uplifting engineering with the right aesthetic.

They could not understand this Anglophone insistence on ugly bras for any woman over twenty-five with children.

Open-air bra stalls in my country sell useful, practical white bras. All second-hand. Not here. There are red strapless bras with snarling edges of black lace. I see a daffodil-yellow bra with curly green leaves running along its seam. Hanging down the middle of the line is the largest nursing bra I have ever seen, white and wired and ominous. I am sure the white covers pulleys and pistons and a flying buttress or two. One red bra has bared black teeth around a nipple-size pair of holes. Next to it is a corset in a delicate ivory color. I did not know people still wore corsets.

A group of women start laughing. I am gaping. Anglophone. Prude.

It takes an hour for Hubert and me to move only a hundred meters or so. Wherever I look, I am presented with goods to touch and feel. Hubert looks grim. I imitate him. Heads down, we move forward. Soon we see a stall specializing in Togo football team jerseys. There are long-sleeved yellows ones, short-sleeved ones, sleeveless ones. Shirts for kids. All of them have one name on the back: Togo's superstriker, Sheyi Emmanuel Adebayor.

I pick out a couple of jerseys and while Hubert negotiates for them, I amble over to a nearby stall. An elegant, motherly woman, an image of genuine Mama Benzhood dressed in pink lace, smiles at me graciously. Her stall sells shirts, and looks cool and fresh. She invites me in. I go in and stand under the flapping clothes to cool down. She dispatches a young man to get some cold mineral water. I admire one of the shirts. "Too small for you," she says sorrowfully. Suddenly I want it desperately, but she is reluctant. "Okay. Okay," she says. "I will try to help you. When are you leaving?"

"Tomorrow," I say.

"Ahh. I have a tailor—we will get the fabrics and sew the shirts up for you, a proper size."

It is here that my resolve cracks, that my dislike of shopping vanishes. I realize that I can settle in this cool place—cast my eyes about, express an interest, and get a tailor-made solution. I point at possible fabrics. She frowns and says, "Nooooo, this one without fancy collars. We will make it simple—let the fabric speak for itself." In French this opinion sounds very authoritative. Soon I find I have ordered six shirts. A group of leather workers present an array of handmade sandals: snakeskin, crocodile, every color imaginable. Madam thinks the soft brown leather ones are good. She bends one shoe thing into a circle. Nods. Good sole.

Her eyes narrow at the salesman and she asks, "How much?"

His reply elicits a shrug and a turn—she has lost interest. No value for money. Price drops. Drops again. I buy. She summons a Ghanaian cobbler, who reinforces the seams for me as I sit, glues the edges. In seconds all is ready. She looks at me with some compassion. "What about something for the woman you love?" I start to protest—no. No—I am not into this love thing. Ahh. Compassion deepens. But the women's clothes! I see a purple top with a purple fur collar. A hand-embroidered skirt and top of white cotton. It is clear to me that my two sisters will never be the same again if they have clothes like this.

I get two outfits for each of them.

I can't believe how cheap the clothes are. Now my nieces—what about Christmas presents for them? And my brother Jim? And my nephews. And what about Jim's wife? These women in my life—they will be as gracious and powerful as this madam in pink lace, cool in the heat. Queens, princesses. Matriarchs. Mama Benzes. Sexy. I spend four hours in her stall, and spend nearly two hundred dollars.

On the way from the center of Lomé, I see an old sign by the side of the road. Whatever it was previously advertising has rusted away.

Somebody has painted on it, in huge letters: TOGO 3—CONGO 0.

We head for Hubert's home. The beach runs alongside a highway, and hundreds of scooter taxis chug past us with 5:00 p.m. clients, mostly women, who seem very comfortable.

Hubert's eldest brother has spent the day lying under a tree. He had a nasty motorcycle accident months ago, and his leg is in a cast. He is a mechanic and has his own workshop. His wife lives here too, and his two sisters. We shake hands and he backs away. There are metal rods thrust into the cast. He must be in pain. The evening is cool, and the earthen compound is large and freshly swept. It is a large old house. This is an upper-middle-class family. Hubert tells me he is uncertain. His father is from the north, and after Eyadéma died, he is not sure how safe his mother is in the capital, which is in the south.

Hubert's mother and sisters are happy to see him home, and have cooked a special sauce with meat and baobab leaves and chili. Hubert's mother, a retired nurse, is a widow. Hubert is the last born, and it is clear he is the favorite of his sisters. The rooms at the front of the house open to the garden, where some of the cooking takes place to take advantage of the cool.

We all stand around the kitchen. Clearly Hubert and his brother do not get along, but what is most curious is the family setup. His mother is the head of the household. His father is dead. His brother—a good ten years older than Hubert—behaves like a boy in his presence.

Talking about money with Hubert has been tricky. He agreed to come with me, but said we would come to an agreement about money later. He has made it clear he will be happy with anything reasonable I can afford. He is not doing this because he is desperate for the money. He seems comfortable with the arrangement I offered—and is happy to do things, trusting my good faith, and giving his. He does not eat much. As an athlete, he is very finicky about what he eats. His mother does not complain. I dig into the sauce. It's hot. Awkwardly, I make him an offer.

I find out I am to sleep in his room.

It is very neat. There is a fan, which does not work. There is a computer, which does not work. There are faded posters of soccer players. There are two gimmicky-looking pens arranged in crisp symmetry on the table, both dead. There is a cassette player plugged in and ready to be switched on, but I can see no tapes. There is no electricity—I am using a paraffin lamp. The bedroom is all aspiration. I wonder, before I go to sleep, what his brother's bedroom looks like.

In the morning, I try to make the bed. I lift the mattress and see, on the corner, a heavy gray pistol, as calm and satisfied as a slug.

Tending the Backyard: Port Harcourt

Noo Saro-Wiwa

At the end of a sleepy bus journey, I arrived in Port Harcourt (or "Potakot" as it is pronounced). I was born in this city in the mid-1970s, when its nickname of the "Garden City" seemed less of a misnomer. Now my home town was an uninviting metropolis, its grey flyovers soaring above a vista of banal concrete buildings, isolated palm trees and the tarpaulined labyrinth of the central market. Established as a coal-exporting port in 1912, Port Harcourt has barely transcended its industrial roots. Money, oil, family ties and an absence of alternatives are the main things yoking people to this dystopia, I think.

Sonny drove me back to the family house at the edge of town, along a road where soldiers stopped cars and made officious requests to see "your papers." The tensions of old came flooding back. Roadblocks like these, once common in the 1980s, no longer existed elsewhere in the country now that the military dictatorship had ended. But Port Harcourt is a tense oil city with its finger still hovering over the trigger. It's constantly expanding as its wealth sucks poor people from the countryside every year. New buildings and churches jostle for space on roadsides that were once silent.

I saw more churches here than in any other part of the country. There were so many of them they'd seemingly run out of traditional names: FRESH OIL CATHEDRAL and CHRISTIAN RESTORATION AND REPAIRS MINISTRIES placards sprouted like weeds from the roadside, the tangible signs of all manner of desperation.

We turned off the expressway and into the Igbo neighbourhood where our family home sits. The streets were flanked by high walls and iron gates, over which I caught glimpses of the rectilinear 1970s houses, painted in pale pastels or leached white, with red-headed lizards scaling their walls and corrugated iron rooftops. Verandahs looked out onto driveways planted with banana and mango trees and white lady-of-the-night flowers that wait until sundown before unleashing their fragrance into the air. I could still hear a mysterious, invisible bird that sings freakishly human-sounding melodies from the trees.

Our house used to stand on the very edge of town on a silent, middle-class street next to the bush. Behind our garden wall loomed a mysterious forest of palm trees where we would throw our banana and mango skins. Wildlife thrived there, including the infamous green snake that once shimmied into the kitchen and brushed against Zina's unsuspecting foot (her screams could be heard in Cameroon). Nowadays, we've acquired several neighbours, and sunlight streams over the wall, liberated from the dark forest canopy. Our noiseless street has developed into a little superhighway, with lorries and okadas constantly rumbling past the fruits stalls, mini supermarkets, hairdressers and countless church placards.

The house itself was more or less the same, a modest three-bedroom residence that was always too small to fit the whole family. The same portraits still hung on the walls, including the large one of my father posing imperiously with a pipe between his lips. The blue 1970s mosaic tiles in the hallway and staircase—old enough to have survived two fashion cycles—gave the house an echoey, cavernous ambience. My father's interior décor tastes weren't brilliant. He was a discerning aesthete in many respects, judging by the quality and composition of his photography, but when it came to décor or colour scheming he seemed to lose his vision completely (my mother had no say in these matters). I once had an argument with my father after he insisted—to my undying mystification—that a man's socks should always be the same colour as his shoes. Nonsensical as his sartorial reasoning might have been, I rather wished he'd applied it to the interior of the house; at least then we might have had curtains that matched the red-orange paisley carpet, not the geometric, black-and-white drapes he chose instead.

My father's only concession to good taste was the glamorous portrait of my mother, painted on their tenth wedding anniversary in 1976. From the time I was about ten, my mother stopped joining us on our two-month holidays in Nigeria in order to continue working in England. Zina and I would often stare at that portrait, wishing she were there to neutralise our father's influence and undo his decisions.

Junior had since inherited the house and had installed flooring that matched the curtains. But being boss still didn't allow him to stamp his full imprimatur on the decor: when he hired a team of men to pave the driveway in pale stone, they seized the initiative and laid down a few red slabs that spelled out the word "LOVE." Junior could only shrug at the infuriating but endearing gesture.

The living-room walls displayed photographs of us as children. Most of them were taken in England, our large-toothed faces foregrounding the lawns of Surrey and Derbyshire prep schools. The sight of it yanked me back in time and space, and confusingly oriented my mind away from this house and this country. Upstairs, my father's tiny study was the one room that felt inhabited. It was here that he typed his manuscripts and raged by telephone about Ogoni injustices, his anger interspersed with loud belly laughs. His untouched bookshelves revealed a range of surprising interests (*Jews & Arabs*; a Jackie Onassis biography) that had long since been submerged by concerns over oil spills. In these books I found common ground with him, and for the first time I regretfully imagined the kind of adult relationship we might have had if circumstances had been different. He was the type of father you adored until the age of eight, but once you grew a mind of your own, the attrition began. He could tell great children's stories, and he could talk on an adult level. But he wasn't so good during those intermediary teenage years when you had outgrown your cuteness and malleability, and his flaws materialised like a rash, and you strayed from the path of greatness he had mapped out for you. But in my twenties, I noticed our interests converging, particularly around travel. I once rifled through his old passports and was surprised to see visa stamps from countries such as Ethiopia and Suriname. Why did he go? What did he make of these places? I'll never know the full story.

After completing my tour of the house, I sat in the living room and pondered what to do with myself. This was the first time I had stayed here alone. Back in the day, our father would leave us at home all day most days while he went to work. We never did very much in Port Harcourt. During those hours of TV-less boredom, we survived on sibling companionship and Hollywood films, subsisting on the same two or three movies recorded off British TV on our Betamax VCR. Our tolerance for repetition was high: *Coming to America* and *Tootsie* were watched at least once every day, to the point that we knew the dialogue inside out. By summer's end we'd learnt to swear like Eddie Murphy and speak in a Southern falsetto, Dustin Hoffman–style.

Twenty years on, I needed a similar distraction. I felt a little lonely and abandoned, and more aware of the void left by my brother's and father's deaths. The emptiness of the house accentuated that sense of family depletion. In my childhood, my parents' strained marriage—already cleaved by geography—left me and my siblings feeling as if we were on the margins of the extended family. We were a separate appendage on the family tree, the "London" ones who never knew our cousins as well as they knew each other. My father had his own life in Nigeria, away from ours. And so this lizard-strewn shell of a house, our supposed "home," offered me little sense of homecoming or belonging, only a few shards of memory. But I was glad of it. Port Harcourt had become an undesirable place to live, and I had the option of evacuating without leaving a piece of myself behind.

My mother's predicament was rather different. She desperately wanted to live in Port Harcourt but had been obliged to raise her children in England on my father's wishes. After she had retired and self-determination, that elusive beast, was finally won, her plans to retire in Port Harcourt were tainted by the threat of violence and instability.

I felt thoroughly immobilised in this house, too. Sonny was away for the weekend, so I had no driver. The idea of travelling around by my beloved okadas suddenly seemed too strange and adventurous since my past experiences of Port Harcourt involved being driven around town to the houses of various relatives and family friends. I wanted more of the same. Home towns have a way of infantilising you like that. The elderly nightwatchman only encouraged that regression when he wanted me to "No take okada." Too dangerous, he said. And so I stood in my bedroom, clutching at the wrought-iron bars across the window like a child prisoner.

The bars had been installed to protect us from robbers, although they failed spectacularly. I still shudder at the memory of the night, sometime around 1984, when thieves attacked our house. Emboldened by their faith in police inaction, they hammered shamelessly at the metal bars, slowly prising them open, disregarding my mother's screamed insults from behind the gates at the top of the staircase. They bashed and banged without haste, squeezed through the window and helped themselves to our electronic goods. I'll never forget the chilling sound of the TV plug being wrenched from its socket.

Yet, compared with today, Port Harcourt was safe back then. Armed militant gangs claiming to fight for their indigenous right to oil wealth had turned my home town into a semi war zone the previous year, the skies reverberating with the crackle of gunfire. And kidnapping foreign oil workers and wealthy Nigerians has become big business. Abduction syndicates infiltrate all sectors of society, including the airports. Apparently, the staff at airline offices give alerts when plane tickets are purchased, then their co-conspirators, workers at the airports, track which car the kidnap target enters. One of my mother's friends was kidnapped this way. Somewhere along the road, she was asked (with surprising gentleness) to step out of her car and into armed captivity, where she briefly remained until a ransom was paid.

The tangle of corruption is woven tightly in Port Harcourt. Police are known to sell arms to kidnappers, and the navy sometimes colludes with gangs in stealing oil and shipping it. Traditional commerce no longer provides quite the same sustenance, either. Many rental properties, once tenanted by expat oil workers, lie empty, considered unsafe.

The sun was now setting and shunting me closer to the dreaded prospect of spending my first night here alone. Deebom, the cook, told me that the electricity had cut out for several days. If I wanted relief from the humidity I would have to buy fuel (or "fwell," as everyone pronounces it) to power the house generator. The price—₦3,000 for 25 litres—nearly floored me. After pointlessly protesting to him about the cost, I handed him the money to buy it on the main street.

"You must off the generator after eleven o'clock," Deebom advised when he returned.

"Why?"

"The fwell will finish if you leave it on all night."

I didn't want to believe him. The thought of sleeping in that heat without an air con was unbearable, so I kept the generator switched on until the early hours, regardless of the consequences. When, predictably, it stopped working early the next evening, I was still shocked, shocked at the perversity that so much money was needed to sustain a few hours of basic comfort. When the state supply fails, I realised, buying one's own power is not a cheap option, even for the middle classes; only the very rich can do it. If it cost this much to run a household, I dreaded to think how this expense devoured the profit margins of small businesses. Nigeria can never develop under such circumstances.

Dodgy electricity supplies took the predictability out of everyday life: drying one's hair at a salon was fraught with risk, and power cuts sometimes plunged supermarket aisles into darkness, immobilising shoppers and tempting thieves. In the nightclub beneath my hotel room in Ibadan, I remember hearing a hip-hop tune thumping through the building. When it suddenly stopped mid-song, I mentally pictured the scene: clubbers grinding and flirting to the rhythm one minute, then left in embarrassing limbo when the electricity snatched away the music and lights.

For decades, the government has done nothing to fix this situation. The previous administration sank US$13.2 billion into restoring our power network, but there's nothing to show for it. No one knows where the money went; the nation has literally been left in the dark over the issue. Yet certain politicians still like to think they can develop the economy without fixing this fundamental spanner in our daily works. They even produced a fanciful document called "Vision 2020" detailing how Nigeria plans to become a leading economy within twelve years. The concept induced wry cackles among Nigerians. How, they asked, can we build an aeronautics programme when we can't power a light bulb for more than five hours a day?

—————————

Two mornings later, with corruption very much on our minds, Sonny and I drove along the traffic-logged expressway leading out of Port Harcourt. Sticking out of the tall roadside grass was a billboard with a government message that said: DON'T BADMOUTH NIGERIA! THINGS ARE CHANGING.

We were on our way to Ndoni, a small town about 200 kilometres from Port Harcourt, the home town of Rivers State's former governor, Peter Odili. Sonny and I were on a mission to see how politicians spend their pilfered monies. I'd recently read in the newspaper that one of the worst of them, the ex-president Ibrahim Babangida, was itching to run for president again. As we waited in a long line at a gas station, I asked Sonny why the former dictator wanted to re-enter politics. Had his billions run out?

"He just wants power," Sonny said.

"Why does he need more power?"

"Because when he goes to London, nobody knows who he is any more. When he was president he went to the US . . . people over there received him . . . he went to the White House. When he came to Port Harcourt they would announce it on the TV and radio the night before. He would come here with his big entourage of cars. That is it, now . . . they want power. They like it."

Sonny's theory was that the process of enriching oneself through politics naturally creates enemies. Therefore the politician in question needs protection, which in itself requires money, which requires more power. They don't want to go the way of the assassinated former president Murtala Mohammed, Sonny believed.

Sonny said that people were particularly disgusted with Odili, a man said to have used the billions he allegedly stole in office to set up Arik Airlines, a domestic carrier. Sonny repeated speculation that Odili greenlighted the construction of three gas turbines in Port Harcourt just to receive kickbacks. The government received a big budget, built the turbines with shoddy, cheap haste, then pocketed the difference. Now the turbines have stopped working, only a few years after being built.

On the highway towards Ndoni, a minibus had parked at the side of the road, its passengers milling about and motioning for us to keep driving.

"Armed robbery," Sonny explained. The passengers reassured us that it was safe to proceed: we had missed the robbery by ten minutes. Earlier that morning Sonny had scolded me for always being late, but I suspected he was now secretly grateful for my tardiness. Further ahead of the robbed minibus, a police patrol vehicle had parked haphazardly on the roadside, its doors flung open in haste, its body perforated with bullet holes. Three officers were wading frantically into the thick bush, pushing aside tall grasses with one hand and clutching rifles with the other, chasing the armed robbers who had fled into the forest. Minutes later, a radio news bulletin reported the kidnapping of two foreigners in Port Harcourt. The dangers of life in the Niger Delta suddenly seemed all too tangible and real.

Odili was said to be partly responsible for the lawlessness. During the 2003 elections, as he ran for the governorship of Rivers State, the ruling People's Democratic Party distributed weapons to gangs in order to intimidate voters. Two gangs—the Niger Delta People's Volunteer Force (NDPVF) and the Icelanders—were hired by Odili to ensure a "positive" outcome in the elections. But soon after the polls, the leader of the NDPVF fell out with the Rivers State government, which reacted by urging the Icelanders to destroy the NDPVF. The result was low-intensity warfare, conducted freely on the streets of Port Harcourt. Ordinary streets, bars and restaurants were caught in the crossfire of explosives and automatic weapons. I read newspaper reports of gangsters operating with impunity, robbing banks, gunning down policemen, hacking at the city's stability with machetes and knives. Fortunately, no one in my family was affected, but many other blameless people died.

In 2004, President Obasanjo brokered a truce between the gang leaders. The gangs, however, never disarmed. Angered by the politicians' false promises of jobs and financial security, they continued robbing banks, and practising kidnapping and extortion. Since 2006, more than 200 expat oil workers have been abducted for large ransoms under the political pretext of "resource control."

By the summer of 2007, a faction of the Icelanders had broken away and formed a more powerful splinter group called the Outlaws, led by George Soboma. Again, the ruling party called on their services during the 2007 elections. The gangsters were seen handing out money at polling stations, becoming de facto chiefs of security in the city. Since 2003, dozens of similar gangs flourished. Again, many of them were disappointed by the government's unfulfilled promises of jobs and money. They eyed Soboma's position with envy. In time, a coalition of gangs (including the Icelanders) began fighting Soboma and his Outlaws for a bigger slice of government largesse. More havoc was visited on Port Harcourt. My brother Junior had been inside our father's former office on Aggrey Road when he heard the snap of gunfire and the screech of vehicle tyres. For a few apprehensive minutes, the street's small businesses and art shops became the backdrop to gang warfare. I felt slightly violated by it all, even from the safety of London. Though I'd had no intention of living in Port Harcourt, those months of violence made me less of an émigré and more an exile in mourning for my home town.

In the summer of 2007, the federal government sent in a military task force to control the violence. Order was restored but the leaders of the biggest gangs, having outgrown government control, were never captured. In contrast to its rhetoric, the government did nothing to punish the politicians or arrest most of the gang members. And Odili, the former governor who allegedly funded these gangs in the 2003 elections, enjoys immunity from prosecution.

Because Nigeria's oil deposits are concentrated in the Niger Delta, political power in this region (and subsequent control of oil money) is highly prized and ruthlessly fought over. Half a century of corrupt rule has done nothing to build the economy of a region that's earned more than US$300 billion since petroleum was discovered. The federal government takes about half of oil revenues and distributes it among the country's thirty-six states. Little of this money benefits ordinary people, least of all Niger Delta people, who have fallen victim to government corruption and the carelessness of the oil industry. Countless oil spills and ceaseless flaring of gas poisons the soil and depletes the rivers of their fish stocks. Age-old farming practices have been disrupted, swelling the numbers of frustrated and unemployed men.

My father tried to address this problem non-violently through his Movement for the Survival of the Ogoni People (MOSOP), which campaigned to improve the environment and ensure Delta ethnic groups received our fair share of the oil wealth. Since my father's death in 1995, several militant groups, mainly ethnic Ijaws, have adopted a similar political platform, but achieve their aims by abducting oil workers, sabotaging oil pipelines and forcing oil companies to pay "protection" money. Their actions have reduced crude oil production by a third since 2006. Gangs such as the Niger Delta Vigilantes attack oil installations to extort money or force the oil companies to create local development projects, which has placated a few people.

These gangs, including the NDPVF, are embedded in a muddy, interchangeable world of criminality and politics. One minute they're fighting the government for "resource control," the next they're cooperating with corrupt politicians and policeman to set up arms deals and oil bunkering ventures (oil bunkering involves tapping pipelines and selling the oil on the local and foreign black market).

On the road to Ndoni, Rivers State felt like a feral place. The violence had leapt from the newspaper pages and was playing out in front of me. Sleeping was the only way for me to escape the anxiety.

The road branching off the highway to Odili's home town was freshly tarmacked, and sturdy new bridges carried us across the numerous rivers and creeks of the Niger River Delta. We turned off the highway and into a sleepy village situated by the steep sandy banks of a magnificently blue river. The tidy streets, paved with interlocking stone slabs, contained only a handful of pedestrians, including a woman strolling contentedly beneath a blue parasol. A bus station under construction nearby was fronted by a sign proclaiming it an ULTRA-MODERN MOTOR PARK.

"How may vehicles are coming here?" Sonny snorted. "This was just swamp before." He pointed at a clump of trees across the street. Building a motor park seemed an unnecessary expense, considering the size of the village. Like voyeurs, we cruised around, taking inventory of the diverted oil wealth surrounding us.

"Look at it," Sonny murmured, "look at our money. Odili has turned the village into a town!" Street lights—only 4.5 metres apart—lined the roads. One or two of them were even switched on despite the midday sun, as if smugly emphasising Ndoni's constant power supply. Electricity seemed more a status symbol here than a basic requirement for the functioning of daily life.

Odili's mansion was unmissable: a big white colonnaded structure with a red tiled roof, a satellite dish and several air con units barnacling its exterior. Almost as a statement of virtue, the house stood next to a Catholic church, a fancy red-and-white building fenced off by an ornate metal gate. Other alleged beneficiaries of Odili's governorship had built mansions in the vicinity. They had two-storey, glass-fronted atriums, with the owner's names—Onyema Hall or Oshinili Villa—emblazoned hubristically across them.

"These houses look empty," I commented.

"That's because they are staying in Port Harcourt—where there's no light." Sonny sneered at the irony. People spent most of their time in the big city. Nearby was a plot of land scattered with palm trees that had been felled to make way for the construction of more houses. Sonny and I rolled slowly along the streets, past a huge house with a thatched rotunda in the garden, which Sonny suspected belonged to Peter Odili's older brother. Odili liked to spread his wealth. He is renowned for dashing people money—₦20 million here, ₦50 million there.

"You cannot get close to him and come back empty-handed," Sonny said. But what good had Odili really done for Ndoni? The town was still a quiet backwater: messy-haired women still sold fruit and groundnuts on the side of the spotless streets; the school building was a shabby confection of peeling yellow paint, and the pupils ran around in tatty uniforms. How typical that the church should be in better shape than the primary school.

"When you are in power you bring development to your village," Sonny insisted, to my surprise.

"But they should be bringing development to *everyone*. Can you imagine British prime ministers developing their home towns in England and no one else's? They don't do that."

"But you cannot be in government for eight years and your village is still bush," Sonny countered. He told me that when he and my brother Ken attended the funeral of a politician's mother at their village, he was taken aback by the scruffiness of the village. "If you are in government you must develop your village and your people. Otherwise what will they take for remember you?"

I had assumed Sonny was against Ndoni's development. In fact, he was simply annoyed that no Ogoni person had had the chance to occupy high political office and develop our villages similarly. He didn't support corruption the way Ekpenyong in Calabar did, but he was still in favor of allocating funds along ethnic lines.

"*Nobody* from the south has become a minister in Abuja," Sonny fumed. "When I was in Abuja with your father and he saw the way they were building the place, he always be angry. *Twenty-four hours* a day, he was angry."

I remember that rage. My father would grumble at the gleaming skyscrapers, venting livid clouds of tobacco smoke through his nostrils as he complained about oil money developing the north but not the south. However, he didn't believe in politicians diverting public funds to help their own village at the expense of others. He was too high-minded to delve too much into Nigerian politics, the rottenness of which I now fully appreciated. In the upper echelons of government, it isn't easy to keep one's head down and do a good job. Having principles is considered a sign of weakness by many politicians, who will punish those who try to uphold any morals. If a governor or senator doesn't help his or her friends and kinsmen, not only do they face the wrath of their nearest and dearest, but their political enemies will see feebleness in their honesty and begin sharpening the knives. In a system like this, politicians of a dishonest bent will gladly swim with the corrupt tide rather than get washed up alone on the penniless banks of virtue.

———————————

The next day, at my mother's suggestion, I visited my aunty at her shop on the other side of Port Harcourt. Known to all as Big Mama (real name Elizabeth), she's my mother's eldest sister, a large, frank, gregarious septuagenarian who once celebrated my puberty by playfully poking my breasts and cackling long and hard. Her ribaldry couldn't be more different from my mother's prim reserve, yet their faces are almost exactly alike; seeing my mother in Big Mama's every smile or frown brought on pangs of homesickness after four months on the road.

I met Big Mama at her small fabric shop across town, next to the law office of her son, Tom. I hadn't seen Tom since he was a good-looking, spirited university student. Nowadays, his handsome face was plumper and fringed with slightly greying hair. The last fourteen years had taken their toll. His father, an Ogoni activist, was murdered with three other men in 1994. The Abacha regime exploited their deaths and falsely accused my father and eight of his colleagues of inciting the murders, although on that day none of them had been allowed to enter Ogoniland where the murders took place.

It created a fissure in the family that had taken more than a decade to close. Time had passed and wounds were healing; we didn't dwell on these issues. In such family matters I still felt like a child somehow, and I naturally excluded myself from these "adult" concerns. Besides, Port Harcourt's violence seems to occupy Big Mama's thoughts these days.

"It's so dangerous now," she complained. Almost every week the streets flinched in the crossfire of gang bullets.

Tom asked me why I was in Nigeria. I told him I was travelling around the country and writing a book about my experiences.

"Why are you writing?" he said. "Junior was the one to do that sort of thing. I thought you and Zina would become doctors or lawyers."

Our cultural differences ran deep, "I don't want to be a doctor or lawyer. I'm doing things that I find interesting. I can't pursue a career just because I'm expected to."

"You should come back to Nigeria."

"I can't just come back here."

"Why not?"

"I don't know the country well enough . . . That's partly what my trip is about. I'm getting to know the place." My dislike for the country was softening into a wavering ambiguity.

"You're like one of those 1950s British women who never leave England and don't want to try new things," Tom declared.

"No, I'm not!" I retorted, irked by his inaccuracy, and a little threatened by the suggestion. "You can't just move to a country you don't know very well. I need to understand how it works. And I've left England plenty of times. I've been all over West Africa too."

"Oh," Tom said, "I didn't realise."

To bolster my case, I mentioned how expensive it was to travel around Nigeria.

"Junior could buy you a first-class ticket to Abuja if you want him to," Tom said. "He works in government."

"No, he couldn't, he doesn't have money to spend on me. And even if he did, I wouldn't expect him to."

"But you can ask him."

"Why would I? He's not my father. He should spend his money on his sons. If I want my own ticket I'll buy it myself."

"You think like a British person," Tom jibed with a smile. My family like to confront, prod, dissect and disparage with the kindest of intentions—but it rubbed raw against my diasporan sensibilities, which were more used to British-style individualism and all the ginger diplomacy that comes with it.

Changing the subject, I asked Big Mama whether her Catholic church was becoming more evangelical in the style of its services.

"Oh yes!" she said, raising her hand in approval. "We even have *prayer warriors* in our church!" By "prayer warriors" she meant worshippers who commit their lives to praying for others. "Do you go to church?" she asked.

"No," I stammered, half considering lying.

Big Mama's face crumpled into a mortified frown. Tom, who'd become a devout Christian over the years, was equally shocked. After quizzing me about the Bible and exposing every hole in my knowledge, he devoted the rest of our chat to Saving me.

He was wasting his energy. For years my mother, God bless her, tried unsuccessfully to drag me to church. Born a Catholic, she would take Zina, Tedum and me to mass every Sunday to instill the devoutness that our father—not so religious a man—strove to minimise. But a childhood spent marinating in stolid, European-style worship was enough to permanently kill my enthusiasm for church-going.

Not even the evangelical Pentecostal services that my mother converted to could sway me. When we were around twelve, she took Zina and me to an evening service, our first taste of evangelical worship. We obeyed the pastor's call to stand up and introduce ourselves to the beaming congregation. Then we watched in bewilderment as the pastor roared down the mike, touching people's foreheads and blessing them before they collapsed in spent heaps in the arms of fellow worshippers. Zina and I were soon ushered onstage to receive blessings. The pastor placed a gentle palm on our foreheads while belting praises to Jeezos. Naïve to the protocol, we resisted the growing pressure of his palm with tautened necks and heavy feet, waiting for a divine force to knock us out. But as the pastor's palm grew more and more insistent, we realised it was best to give in and launch ourselves backwards. The congregation went wild.

Amateur dramatics aside, the service was very uplifting. Had I been raised in that church from the start, things might have been different, but by age twelve I was stuck in my lapsed ways and nothing could make me attend church regularly. My mother sadly resigned herself to the situation.

My father wasn't troubled by this. He disliked excessive fixation on religion if it distracted people from their work or education. I discovered this on a Sunday afternoon in Port Harcourt when I was about nine years old. A cousin of mine, Patience, had visited our house while my father was at the office. Patience—an extremely devout teenager who didn't want to go to university—suggested that Zina, Tedum and I cut up several pieces of paper and inscribe them with phrases such as "Jesus Loves Me" and "God Lives." For us youngsters, it was a fun exercise, a chance to whip out our felt-tip pens and express ourselves artistically. We pasted the colourful signs high up on our bedroom wall and admired the results. But when our father returned home, the sight of our handiwork detonated a rage we'd never seen in him before.

"Take this off the wall!" he boomed. "Take it off *now!*" He jumped up and ripped off bits of paper himself. We scurried around the room removing the slogans, while he fumed and ranted, ordering us to speed it up. Apoplectic, he turned to a sobbingly defiant Patience and urged her—ordered her—to concentrate on her studies, not on twenty-four-hour prayer. Then he directed his wrath towards me and my siblings. We were *not* to get hooked on this "opiate of the masses," he warned. I was quaking and confused, too young to understand his anger, which appeared to be mixed with an uncharacteristic panic. My father was a proactive man who believed in action, self-sufficiency, progress. He wanted Ogonis to get educated, to become doctors and lawyers, or geologists with knowledge of the oil industry. Although, according to my brother Junior, our father became more spiritual and devoted to prayer towards the end of his life, at this point he was an agnostic who sought to fix problems, not pray for them to go away. With Nigeria in the grip of a military dictatorship, he feared that people like Patience were slipping into a religious coma.

More than twenty years on, I sympathised with my father, yet I was on the receiving end of cousin Tom and Big Mama's reverse outrage at my church absences. Tom, intent on laying all seven shades of Jesus on me, was now referring to our planned weekend get-together as an "appointment." Stiffened with a sudden rectitude, he addressed me in church-pastor tones; all jibes and grins had gone.

I sat and listened like a petrified nine-year-old, surprised at my own silence. I was unable to defend my non-attendance at church. In the face of this muscular faith, the religious defiance I displayed at Janice's house at the start of my trip had gradually peeled away after a few months in Nigeria. Tom had exposed an inner cowardice that had lain dormant and unchallenged after a lifetime in England. Up until now, I'd assumed that my father was a thousand times braver than I was. Now I realised he was a *million* times more so. He had faced up to a ruthless political and commercial system that willingly killed anyone who challenged it. I, meanwhile, was rattled by the harmless reprimands of my Born Again relatives. This certainly wasn't the voyage of discovery I'd had in mind when starting this trip.

The episode distanced me slightly from my relatives. In the years since I last saw them they seemed possessed, literally, floating away from me on a path of Righteousness. What happened to the irreverent buoyancy of the old days? Perhaps I overestimate the extent of change—children don't register adults' burdens—but there was a perceptible difference in my aunt's and cousin's spirits that alienated me. I had been warming to Nigeria over the last few weeks, but now the chill had crept in again.

The best part of the next morning was spent procrastinating in bed and staring at the ceiling. I was due to go to Bane, my family's village, to which every year during our childhood summer holidays my father banished me, Zina and Tedum for a few days. In our mother's absence, the three of us were at the mercy of our father's itinerary. My mosquito-bitten experience instilled a lifelong unease about Bane (or rural life anywhere in the world, for that matter). I always left the village with the euphoric feeling that I'd been given another chance at life.

For once, I was making this trip voluntarily. I had the power to come and go as I pleased, yet I still felt a reflexive dread, as if I were being marched towards purgatory. The morning's grey, saturated clouds bulged above us as Sonny and I climbed into the car. On the road to Bane, the abundance of buildings and church signs diminished, eventually giving way to acres of flat, tree-less farmland. In the 1980s, my fetish for perfectly shaped palm trees kept me alert on this road. I kept a constant vigil for the shapeliest specimens, with their thick round fronds and pencil-straight trunks. But now I would have been glad to see *any* tree, no matter how wretched. Farming had cleared many of them, and the fumes from oil production, coupled with the burning of fields by farmers, were choking the trees and turning some of them brown.

We passed through the tiny town of Bori, where my father was born, and where he sold palm wine on the streets as a ten-year-old boy. Bori, though growing bigger by the year, still felt like a small hamlet, a slender collection of iron-roofed buildings on either side of the road, jammed with people and okadas, mini food markets and a rainbow of plastic ware. Through the window I heard snippets of conversation in our dialect, Khana, swirling around me at unusually amplified levels, like a strange dream. In my everyday life, Khana was restricted to telephone conversations between my mother and her friends or family; it was a minority language barely heard in Nigeria, let alone England. But here in Bori, it was the dominant language. Having spent four months travelling around as an ethnic foreigner, being in a place where Khana was widely spoken carried a new and deep significance. These were *my* people—not sharp-nosed Hausas, or Efiks, Biroms or Yorubas—but Ogonis.

Most special of all, I was in a place where everyone could say my name properly. Having the name Noo (pronounced "gnaw") is a heavy cross to bear. Not only is it the same word for "crude oil" in Khana—the most unpoetic of injustices—but the specific tonality of the name makes it impossible for foreigners and most Nigerians to pronounce correctly. Barely a day goes by when I'm not explaining my name to a new acquaintance, repeating it, spelling it, repeating it again, then resignedly accepting their mispronunciation. Finally, I was in the one place on Earth where everyone gets it right straight away.

Sonny returned from a market stall and drove on towards Bane. Above the flat stretches of green acres, the sky's ashen murk became dotted with bright orange oil flares. We were nearing Bane village. My father used to point out the flares in disgust, bemoaning their environmental impact, while I would nod blankly, too young to understand the implications. The oil companies burn off excess gas, which is a by-product of oil extraction. With the correct (though very expensive) infrastructure, the gas could be captured and exported at huge profit, but instead it's burned away to pollute the skies, our wealth going up in flames.

The road leading to the village was smooth and tarmacked, an improvement on the old days when heavy rain and giant potholes—Mother Nature's speed bumps— made the last 5 kilometres of the journey take twice as long as the preceding 110 kilometres. On entering Bane, we rolled past adobe thatched-roof houses nestled between palm trees, waddling goats and small, balloon-bellied children who stared drop-jawed as our car rolled past. Bane still lacks running water or a permanent supply of electricity, but modern houses are springing up all the time. We passed one house that had a gold lion carving on the front door and the words LION OF JUDAH etched above it. Sonny, too, owns a cute red-brick and mustard bungalow. As more people build houses, the village is gradually looking less rustic.

Deeper into the village, the tarmac stopped and the road became sandy. The heat bludgeoned me as I climbed out of the car outside my father's white bungalow. It stood close to the unpainted, window-less church on the edge of his parents' compound. My grandfather's two-storey house towered above the surrounding bungalows belonging to some of his six wives, including my grandmother. All of them are dead now. Their graves filled up the compound, converting it into a graveyard of sorts. That's the tradition: we bury our dead next to their homes.

My father, however, is buried in a public field in the village as a tribute to his struggle. His body had been dumped unceremoniously in a grave after he and his eight colleagues were murdered by Sani Abacha's regime. It had taken some years to retrieve the remains: we had to wait for democratic elections, then ask the government to locate the grave, and finally the bones had to be identified through forensic tests.

In 2005, my brother Junior, sister Zina, half-sister Singto, Uncle Owens and I prepared the remains for burial. As Junior brought out the large bag containing our father's dissembled skeleton, Zina cried out loud on the far edge of the room. Singto watched silently through her tears. I decided that the situation was only as macabre as my mind would allow, so I forced myself to lift out a long bone wrapped in newspaper. Uncle Owens, a medical doctor, helped us to identify and arrange each femur, fibula, metacarpal and rib, settling our minds into a more industrious mood as we assembled the skeleton.

Before long, everyone was helping out. It was hard to conceive that these coarse brown objects we held in our hands were our father, a once energetic man with dark, stocky flesh. In vain, I searched for his face in the skull now resting at one end of the coffin. The two front teeth were missing. How and why, I didn't know. But when Junior placed a pipe between the upper and lower jaws, his teeth metamorphosed into that familiar smile.

My father was always the one who made the decisions in the family, but now we were taking charge of him, deciding the fate of his remains. When I think of the day he showed me the architectural drawings of the bungalow twenty-odd years ago ("... this is the lounge, that's the living room, that'll be your bedroom ... we'll spend summer holidays in this house ...."), I doubt he ever imagined we would be using one of the rooms as a temporary morgue. It had now made the house uninhabitable in my view, and I certainly wasn't going to spend the night there by myself.

"You fear your father's spirit will worry you?" Sonny asked.

"Sort of ... not really. I just don't like all these graves being right outside everyone's houses. We should have a cemetery."

"You cannot have a cemetery ... the place will grow into bush," Sonny explained. Cemeteries were a wholly unsuitable idea, he believed. "My brother is buried next to my mother outside her house."

"Yeah, well, I don't like it. Having a grave next to the house is like putting a bed inside the bathroom. There's an appropriate place for everything."

Sonny laughed.

My grandparents' compound was silent and empty except for the odd goat and sporadic children's game. I was used to visiting Bane with one or both of my parents, in the days when the machinery of hospitality seemed to grind into action of its own accord. But now that I was on my own, and my grandparents were all dead, there was no one to greet me or feed me. As I pottered about, examining the graves, I recalled my cousin Ketiwe once telling me that she felt little reason to visit Bane now that our grandparents were gone.

In their absence, our grandparents aroused a curiosity in me about who they were as people, the nooks and crannies of their personalities. I wondered what characteristics, aside perhaps from my sporting ability, they had passed on to me, and which parts of my character had been nurtured in England. Was my fastidiousness genetic, or the product of eight years in a dirty boarding school? Was my short temper sown in my DNA, or fashioned in the rush-hour carriages of London underground trains? Which of my ancestors was musical? I had never considered the finer details of their personalities. And this empty village wouldn't provide the answers. I chastised myself for not asking these questions when they were alive.

Sonny and I drove to the house of my maternal grandmother Daada, half a kilometre away down a sandy path. My mother and her sisters had helped to build Daada's house when they were young. It was a simple adobe structure, fitted with glass windows, wooden padlocked doors and wiring set up in endless anticipation of electricity. Daada's grave lies near the house, along with the graves of her husband and her youngest daughter, my Aunty Rose. My cousin Barisi still lived in the compound with her mother Aunty Naayira, a darker, more sinewy version of my mother. She had just finished a day of planting cassava at the farm and squealed with delight when she saw me.

They cooked me gari and soup. Its aroma triggered memories of the dilemma we faced when both my grandmothers cooked lunch for us kids. Because we always stayed in our paternal compound, we generally ate there first, meaning we were never hungry enough to accept Daada's meals at her house. The social mores underpinning the offering of food were lost on us. Turning down Daada's lunch was simply our logical response to having a full stomach, but she took it as an incomprehensible snub, which we had to rectify by stuffing ourselves in a gut-busting encore.

This time, I ate with leisurely ease. My cousin Barisi sat with me. In our younger days, she, Zina and I would tease each other and banter freely. Now she was all grown up with a husband and four beautiful kids, her natural buoyancy weighed down by money worries and other unspoken woes. Because of her new job at the local government office, she'd had to move back to Bane with her children while her husband stayed in a nearby town.

Conversation with Barisi and Aunty Naayira revolved around updates on family members ("What of Zina? What of Gian? What of Junior? What of Nene? How are your nephews?"). Then Barisi and her mother were joined by Dorcas, a neighbour. The three of them began chatting in Khana while I ate my gari and tried not to let another bead of sweat plop from my forehead into my soup. Silently I watched them. They were physically elegant women, yet hardy and blessed with practical skills like cooking, house-building and farming. My proficiencies were confined to my fingertips: tapping keyboard and flicking switches; cerebral know-how that contributed nothing to the workings of everyday village-life.

Barisi and Aunty Naayira mentioned mine and Zina's names between giggles. "What are you talking about?" I asked.

"Nothing," Barisi absent-mindedly replied, keen to continue the conversation with the others. Sensing that they were reminiscing about us, I wanted in on the chat but I was being firewalled by language. My Khana isn't fluent. The everyday basic vocabulary is buried deep in my mental hard drive, but without practice I can't hold my own in conversation. My childhood indifference towards this non-fluency gradually strengthened into embarrassment, then intense resentment. My parents spoke to Zina and me primarily in English, expecting that we would learn Khana when we were older, in the same way that they had acquired English as a second language. They mistakenly assumed that Khana could wade against the cultural tsunami of the Anglophone world. But Khana was too small a language to compete with English, which holds all the vocal tools for modern life: no Ogoni person can have a worldly conversation without importing chunks of English. So the latter became my mother tongue.

And now it made me feel small here in my relatives' house, and I was reluctant to utter even the few words I knew. I think I inherited this linguistic awkwardness from my paternal grandmother, "Mama," who I always assumed couldn't speak English until my father told me she actually knew a little bit but was "too embarrassed" to practise it on us. Hindsight makes it all clearer: Zina, Tedum and I probably came across as self-centred, toy-focused brats, subconsciously exuding a very Western disregard for their elders, which Mama possibly found alienating. Daada didn't speak English either. Our relationship with both grandmothers was a warm but generally conversation-less affair, and now, just like Mama, I preferred to stay mute than speak Khana like an inarticulate toddler. I sat back and enjoyed snippets of their nattering. Anyhow, there was little about my life that I could tell them: property ladders, career choices, publishers—they were meaningless details in this context. Births, deaths, marriages were the only news worth sharing.

As Barisi, Dorcas and Aunty Naayira chatted away, I took a walk to the river nearby, smiling wordlessly at the half-naked, hernia-bellied children whose dark, lean faces stared at mine as I ambled past. If we share fairly recent ancestors, then the lineage has most definitely forked; their poverty and my relative wealth separated not just our lives but our morphologies too, it seemed.

The river was beautiful, flowing at a lower altitude to the village, and fringed with green vegetation and mangrove swamps. We knew only vaguely of its presence when we were children, since most of our days in Bane were spent perspiring in our grandparents' houses. When Zina and I came across it again in 2005, we were in awe of its beauty, like tourists. No one else quite understood our excitement. The village boys drew little aesthetic pleasure from this place where they routinely bathed and caught fish, *bari*. Zina had asked some boys to unlock one of the fishing canoes and let us ride in it. They obeyed, bemused as to why we wanted to drift aimlessly along the water.

I returned to Daada's house and perused Barisi's photo album, feeling increasingly weakened by the sweltering air, and waiting subconsciously for permission to leave. Then I gleefully remembered that I was on my own schedule.

I decided to get going.

Returning to Bane as an adult hadn't changed my feelings about the place. There was no cathartic awakening or joyful homecoming. No matter how much my dislike of the village had diminished and my respect for my relatives had grown, any new romanticised perspectives quickly evaporated in the steaming humidity. Besides, living in the countryside seemed pointless if one wasn't getting one's knees dirty on the farm. Urban-style idleness isn't much fun without urban amusement. But perhaps one day in the future, a new world order, global oil shortages or British pension poverty might force me to live in Bane. I wouldn't be bored into complete stupefaction—the village has a large enough population to support what I like to call the "gossip threshold": enough people to sustain juicy gossip on a regular basis. I knew from past experience that talking about other people is the only entertainment when there aren't any new books to read, films to watch or web pages to surf. Life here would be tolerable in that respect. But I would have to learn Khana. And the heat—my God, it was too much.

Now I understood why my father never once spent the night here during our childhood stays. He luxuriated in the air-conditioned solitude of his Port Harcourt study while dispatching us to the village. As much as he loved Bane, his attachment to the place was an emotional one that didn't require his physical presence.

———

As Sonny drove me back to Port Harcourt, I wondered how Bane would evolve in the future. Only the old and the very young stayed here these days; migration to the cities has been draining it, and every other Nigerian village, for years. I wondered whether it would remain a quiet village, sprouting new graves and modern, fleetingly inhabited brick houses. Or would it evolve to become a town, like many villages in England? I couldn't imagine it. Urbanisation requires industrialisation and an influx of people and capital from around the country, but outsiders rarely settle in Nigerian rural areas. The land usually remains the preserve of its indigenous ethnic group. Whatever happens, Bane is the one place on earth that feels like mine, whether I want to stay here or not. I need no title deeds to this place, and found comfort in the thought that my genes alone grant me an undisputed claim to the land.

Trapdoor

Hisham Matar

arly morning, March 2012. My mother, my wife Diana and I were sitting in a row of seats that were bolted to the tiled floor of a lounge in Cairo International Airport. Flight 835 for Benghazi, a voice announced, was due to depart on time. Every now and then, my mother glanced anxiously at me. Diana, too, seemed concerned. She placed a hand on my arm and smiled. I should get up and walk around, I told myself. But my body remained rigid. I had never felt more capable of stillness.

The terminal was nearly empty. There was only one man sitting opposite us. He was overweight, weary-looking, possibly in his mid-fifties. There was something in the way he sat—the locked hands on the lap, the left tilt of the torso—that signaled resignation. Was he Egyptian or Libyan? Was he on a visit to the neighboring country or going home after the revolution? Had he been for or against Qaddafi? Perhaps he was one of those undecided ones who held their reservations close to their chest?

The voice of the announcer returned. It was time to board. I found myself standing at the front of the queue, Diana beside me. She had, on more than one occasion, taken me to the town where she was born, in northern California. I know the plants and the color of the light and the distances where she grew up. Now I was, finally, taking her to my land. She had packed the Hasselblad and the Leica, her two favorite cameras, and a hundred rolls of film. Diana works with great fidelity. Once she gets hold of a thread, she will follow it until the end. Knowing this excited and worried me. I am reluctant to give Libya any more than it has already taken.

Mother was pacing by the windows that looked onto the runway, speaking on her mobile phone. People—mostly men—began to fill the terminal. Diana and I were now standing at the head of a long queue. It bent behind us like a river. I pretended I had forgotten something and pulled her to one side. Returning after all these years was a bad idea, I suddenly thought. My family had left in 1979, thirty-three years earlier. This was the chasm that divided the man from the eight-year-old boy I was then. The plane was going to cross that gulf. Surely such journeys were reckless. This one could rob me of a skill that I have worked hard to cultivate: how to live away from places and people I love. Joseph Brodsky was right. So were Nabokov and Conrad. They were artists who never returned. Each had tried, in his own way, to cure himself of his country. What you have left behind has dissolved. Return and you will face the absence or the defacement of what you treasured. But Dmitri Shostakovich and Boris Pasternak and Naguib Mahfouz were also right: never leave the homeland. Leave and your connections to the source will be severed. You will be like a dead trunk, hard and hollow.

What do you do when you cannot leave and cannot return?

———————

Back in October 2011, I had considered never returning to Libya. I was in New York, walking up Broadway, the air cold and swift, when the proposition presented itself. It seemed immaculate, a thought my mind had manufactured independently. As in youthful moments of drunkenness, I felt bold and invincible.

I had gone to New York the previous month, at the invitation of Barnard College, to lecture on novels about exile and estrangement. But I had an older connection to the city. My parents had moved to Manhattan in the spring of 1970, when my father was appointed first secretary in the Libyan Mission to the United Nations. I was born that autumn. Three years later, in 1973, we returned to Tripoli. In the years since, I had visited New York maybe four or five times and always briefly. So, although I had just returned to the city of my birth, it was a place I hardly knew.

In the thirty-six years since we left Libya, my family and I had built associations with several surrogate cities: Nairobi, where we went on our escape from Libya, in 1979, and have continued to visit ever since; Cairo, where we settled the following year into indefinite exile; Rome, a vacation spot for us; London, where I went at the age of fifteen for my studies and where for twenty-nine years I have been doggedly trying to make a life for myself; Paris, where, fatigued and annoyed by London, I moved in my early thirties, vowing never to return to England, only to find myself back two years later. In all these cities, I had pictured myself one day calm and living in that faraway island, Manhattan, where I was born. I would imagine a new acquaintance asking me, perhaps at a dinner party, or in a café, or in changing-rooms after a long swim, that old tiresome question "Where are you from?" and I, unfazed and free of the usual agitation, would casually reply, "New York." In these fantasies, I saw myself taking pleasure from the fact that such a statement would be both true and false, like a magic trick.

That I should move to Manhattan in my fortieth year, as Libya was ripping itself apart, and for this to take place on the 1st of September, the day when, back in 1969, a young captain named Muammar Qaddafi deposed King Idris and many of the significant features of my life—where I live, the language in which I write, the language I am using now to write this—were set in motion: all this made it difficult to escape the idea that there was some kind of divine will at work.

In any political history of Libya, the 1980s represent a particularly lurid chapter. Opponents of the regime were hanged in public squares and sports arenas. Dissidents who fled the country were pursued—some kidnapped or assassinated. The '80s were also the first time that Libya had an armed and determined resistance to the dictatorship. My father was one of the opposition's most prominent figures. The organization he belonged to had a training camp in Chad, south of the Libyan border, and several underground cells inside the country. Father's career in the army, his short tenure as a diplomat, and the private means he had managed to procure in the mid-1970s, when he became a successful businessman—importing products as diverse as Mitsubishi vehicles and Converse sports shoes to the Middle East—made him a dangerous enemy. The dictatorship had tried to buy him off; it had tried to scare him. I remember sitting beside him one afternoon in our flat in Cairo when I was ten or eleven, the weight of his arm on my shoulders. In the chair opposite sat one of the men I called "Uncle"—men who, I somehow knew, were his allies or followers. The word "compromise" was spoken, and Father responded, "I won't negotiate. Not with criminals."

Whenever we were in Europe, he carried a gun. Before getting into the car, he would ask us to stand well away. He would go down on his knees and look under the chassis, cup his hands and peek through the windows for any sign of wiring. Men like him had been shot in train stations and cafés, their cars blown up. During the 1980s, when I was still in Cairo, I had read in the newspaper about the death of a renowned Libyan economist. He was stepping off a train at Stazione Termini in Rome when a stranger pressed a pistol to his chest and pulled the trigger. The photograph printed beside the article had the figure of the deceased covered in newspaper sheets, presumably from that day's paper, which stopped at his ankles, leaving his polished leather shoes pointing up. Another time there was a report of a Libyan student shot in Greece. He was sitting on the terrace of a café in Monastiraki Square in Athens. A scooter stopped and the man sitting behind the driver pointed a gun at the student and fired several shots. A Libyan BBC World Service newsreader was killed in London. In April 1984 a demonstration took place in front of the Libyan Embassy in St James's Square. One of the embassy staff pulled up a sash window on the first floor, held out a machine gun, and sprayed the crowd. A policewoman, Yvonne Fletcher, was killed and eleven Libyan demonstrators were wounded, some of them critically.

Qaddafi's campaign to hunt down exiled critics—which was announced by Moussa Koussa, the head of foreign intelligence, at a public rally in the early 1980s—extended to the families of dissidents. My only sibling, Ziad, was fifteen when he went off to boarding school in Switzerland. A few weeks later, mid-way through term, he returned to Cairo. We had all gone to collect him from the airport. When he appeared amongst those spilling out of the arrivals lounge, his face looked paler than I remembered it. A few days earlier, I had seen Mother make several telephone calls, her finger trembling as she spun the dial.

The Swiss school was remote, high up in the Alps. Public transport to the nearest village was in the form of a cable car, which operated for only a few hours in the middle of the day. For two days running, Ziad noticed a car parked on the path outside the school's main gate. It had in it four men. They had the long hair so typical of members of Qaddafi's Revolutionary Committees. Late one night, Ziad was called to the school's office telephone. On the other end of the line, a man said, "I am a friend of your father. You must do exactly what I tell you. You have to leave immediately and take the first train to Basle."

"Why? What happened?" Ziad asked.

"I can't tell you now. You must hurry. Take the first train to Basle. I'll be there and will explain everything."

"But it's the middle of the night," Ziad said.

The man would not offer any further explanations. He simply kept repeating, "Take the first train to Basle."

"I can't do that. I don't know who you are. Please don't call here again," Ziad said, and hung up.

The man then called Mother, who then telephoned the school. She told Ziad he needed to leave the school right away and told him what to do.

Ziad woke up his favorite teacher, a young Cambridge graduate who had probably thought it would be fun to go and teach English literature in the Alps, skiing between classes.

"Sir, my father is about to have surgery and asked to see me before going into the operating theater. I need to take the first train to Basle. Would you please drive me to the station?"

The teacher telephoned my mother, and she backed up Ziad's story. The headmaster had to be woken up. He telephoned Mother and, once he too was satisfied, Ziad's teacher checked the train timetable. There was a train for Basle in forty minutes. If they hurried, they might make it.

They had to drive past the car; there was no other way out. Ziad pretended to be tying his shoelace as they passed the men. The teacher drove carefully down the twisting mountain road. A few minutes later, headlights appeared behind them. When the teacher said, "I think they are following us," Ziad pretended not to hear.

At the station, Ziad shot into the concourse and hid in the public toilets. He heard the train roll in. He waited until it had come to a complete stop, counted a few seconds for the passengers to disembark and board, then ran and jumped on the train. The doors shut and the carriages moved. Ziad was sure he had lost them, but then the four men appeared, walking up the aisle. They saw him. One of them smiled at him. They followed him from one carriage to the next, muttering, "Kid, you think you are a man? Then come here and show us." At the front of the train, Ziad found the conductor chatting to the driver.

"Those men there are following me," Ziad told him, no doubt with fear rippling through his voice, because the conductor believed him at once and asked Ziad to sit right beside him. Seeing this, the four men retreated to the next carriage. When the train arrived, Ziad saw men in uniform waiting on the platform. My father's associate, who had telephoned that night, was standing amongst them.

I remember Ziad telling us these details as we sat around the dining table. I was utterly overwhelmed by a feeling of safety and gratitude, as well as by a new fear, sharp and pulsing, in my depths. Looking at me, though, you would not have known it. All the while, as Ziad spoke, I was pretending to be excited by his adventure. It wasn't till later that evening that the whole thing weighed down on my consciousness. I kept thinking about what the men had said, which Ziad whispered to us several times, perfectly mimicking the menacing tone and the Tripoli accent: "Kid, you think you are a man? Then come here and show us."

Shortly after this, when I was twelve, I needed to see an eye specialist. Mother put me on a plane and I flew alone from Cairo to Geneva, where Father was to meet me. He and I spoke on the telephone before I left for the airport.

"If, for any reason, you don't see me in arrivals, go to the information desk and ask them to call out this name," he said, and read out one of the names he traveled on. I knew it well. "Whatever you do," he repeated, "don't give them my real name."

When I got to Geneva, I didn't see him. I did as he said and went to the information desk, but when the woman behind the counter asked me for the name, I panicked. I couldn't remember it. Seeing how flustered I was, she smiled and handed me the microphone. "Would you like to make the announcement yourself?" I took the microphone and said "Father, Father" several times, until I saw him running towards me, a big smile on his face. I felt embarrassed and remember asking him on the way out of the airport, "Why couldn't I simply say your name? What are you afraid of anyway?" We walked through the crowd, and as we did so we passed two men speaking Arabic with a perfect Libyan accent. Encountering our dialect during those years was always disconcerting, provoking in me, and with equal force, both fear and longing. "So what does this Jaballa Matar look like anyway?" one of them asked the other. I went silent and never complained about my father's complicated travel arrangements after that.

It was out of the question for Father to travel on his real passport. He used false documents with pseudonyms. In Egypt, we felt safe. But in March 1990, Father was kidnapped from our Cairo flat by the Egyptian secret police and delivered to Qaddafi. He was taken to Abu Salim prison, in Tripoli, which was known as "The Last Stop"—the place where the regime sent those it wanted to forget.

In the mid-1990s, several people risked their lives to smuggle three of my father's letters to my family. In one of them, Father writes, "The cruelty of this place far exceeds all of what we have read of the fortress prison of Bastille. The cruelty is in everything, but I remain stronger than their tactics of oppression.... My forehead does not know how to bow."

In another letter, there is this sentence: "At times a whole year will pass by without seeing the sun or being let out of this cell."

In calm, precise and at times ironic prose, he demonstrates an astonishing commitment to patience:

And now a description of this noble palace ... The cell is a concrete box. The walls are made of pre-fabricated slabs. There is a steel door through which no air passes. A window that is three and a half metres above ground. As for the furniture, it is in the style of Louis XVI: an old mattress, worn out by many previous prisoners, torn in several places. The world here is empty.

From these letters, and from prisoner testimonies that I've been able to gather with the help of Amnesty International, Human Rights Watch and the Swiss NGO TRIAL, we know that Father was in Abu Salim at least from March 1990 to April 1996, when he was moved from his cell and either taken to another secret wing in the same prison, moved to another prison or executed.

———————

In late August 2011, Tripoli fell, and revolutionaries took control of Abu Salim. They broke down the cell doors, and eventually all the men crammed inside those concrete boxes wandered out into the sunlight. I was at home in London. I spent that day on the telephone with one of the men hammering away at the steel doors of the prison cells. "Wait, wait," he would shout, and I would hear his sledgehammer hitting steel. Not the sound of a bell in the open but one buried deep, like a recalled memory, ringing, *I want to be there and I don't want to be there*. Countless voices were now shouting, "God is great!" He handed the hammer to another man, and I listened to him pant, purpose and victory in every breath. *I want to be there and I don't want to be there*. They came to a cell in the basement, the last one remaining. Lots of shouting now, people vying to lend a hand. I heard the man call out, "What? Inside?" There was confusion. Then I heard him shout, "Are you sure?" He got back on the phone and said they thought the cell contained an important person from Ajdabiya, my father's hometown, who had been in solitary confinement for many years. I could not speak. *I want to be there and I want to be there*. "Stay with me," the man on the telephone said. Every few seconds, he would repeat, "Stay with me." Whether it took ten minutes or an hour, I cannot say. When they eventually broke down the door, they found an old blind man in a windowless room. His skin had not seen the sun in years. When they asked him his name, he said he did not know. What family was he from? He did not know. How long had he been there? He had, apparently, lost his memory. He had one possession: a photograph of my father. Why? Who was he to Father? The prisoner did not know. And although he could not remember anything, he was happy to be free. That was the word the man on the telephone used: "happy." I wanted to ask about the picture. Was it a recent one or an old one? Was it pinned to the wall, kept under the pillow, or did they find it on the floor beside the man's bed? Was there a bed? Did the prisoner have a bed? I asked none of these questions. And when the man said, "I am sorry," I thanked him and hung up.

———————

By October, as I was attempting to concentrate on my teaching in New York, all the political prisons, every underground secret compartment, were falling one by one to the revolutionaries. Cells were opened, the men in them released and accounted for. Father was not in any of them. For the first time, the truth became inescapable. It was clear that he had been shot or hanged or starved or tortured to death. No one knows when, or those who know are dead, or have escaped, or are too frightened or indifferent to speak. Was it in the sixth year of his incarceration, when his letters stopped? Was it in the massacre that took place that year in the same prison, when 1,270 men were rounded up and shot? Or was it a solitary death, perhaps during the seventh or the eighth or the ninth year? Or was it in the twenty-first year, after the revolution broke? Perhaps during one of the many interviews I gave, arguing the case against the dictatorship? Or perhaps Father was not dead at all, as Ziad continued to believe even after all the prisons were opened. Perhaps, Ziad hoped, he was out and, owing to some failure—loss of memory, loss of the ability to see or speak or hear—was unable to find his way back, like Gloucester wandering the heath in *King Lear*. "Give me your hand: you are now within a foot / Of the extreme verge," Edgar says to his blind father, who has resolved to end his own life, a line that has lived with me these past twenty-five years.

It must have been the story of the prisoner who had lost his memory that made Ziad believe that Father might somehow be alive. A few days after I arrived in New York, Ziad called, asking me to find someone who could produce a picture of what

Father might look like today so that we could post it around the country and online. "Someone might recognize him," he said. I spoke to a forensic artist in Canada. She wanted copies of as many photographs as possible of my father, his siblings and my grandfather. After she received them, she called with a list of questions about the conditions he endured in prison: the food he ate, the possibility of torture or illness? Ten days later, the drawing arrived. She had ruthlessly dropped the cheeks, sunk the eyes, exaggerated a faint scar on the forehead. The worst thing about the portrait was its credibility. It made me wonder about other changes. What had become of the teeth, for example, those he bared to Dr. Mazzoleni in Rome on our annual checkup? The Italian dentist used to always say, provoking in us silent pride, "You ought to be grateful to Libya and its minerals for such excellent teeth." And what of the tongue that had its own way of shaping my name, the amplifying throat and all the parts of that echo chamber, the head—its nostrils and cavities, the weight of its bone and flesh and brain—and how it alters the resonance of that gentle voice? How would this new, older voice sound? I never sent the portrait to Ziad, and he stopped asking about it. I showed it to him the next time we were together. He looked at it for a moment and said, "It's not accurate." I agreed and put the drawing back in its envelope. "Don't show it to Mother," he added.

That cold October evening in New York, I began to doubt both my ability to return to Libya and my will not to. I entered our flat on the Upper West Side and did not tell Diana about the "immaculate" idea that had occurred to me on my walk. We ate supper. I collected the plates and washed them slowly. Afterwards, we listened to music, then took a walk through the dark streets. I hardly slept that night. Never returning to Libya, I realized, meant never allowing myself to think about it again, which would only lead to another form of resistance, and I was done with resistance.

I left my building at daybreak. I was glad for New York's indifference. I had always regarded Manhattan the way an orphan might think of the mother who had laid him on the doorstep of a mosque: it meant nothing to me but also everything. It represented, in moments of desperation, the possibility of finally cheating myself out of exile. My feet were heavy. I noticed how old I had become but also the boyishness that persisted, as if part of me had stopped developing the moment we left Libya. I was like David Malouf's imagining of Ovid in his banishment—infantilized by exile. I headed towards my office at the college. I wanted to immerse myself in work. I tried to think about the lecture I was going to deliver that afternoon, on Kafka's *The Trial*. I thought about K's tenderness towards the two men who come to execute him; his dark and heroic surrender; the words he thought to himself:

"the only thing I can do now is keep my mind calm and analytical to the last"; and the corrective, regretful discovery of: "I've always wanted to seize the world with twenty hands. . . ." I told myself it was good that I had the lectures to think about. I crossed over a grille in the sidewalk. Beneath it, there was a room, barely high enough for a man to stand and certainly not wide enough for him to lie down. A deep gray box in the ground. I had no idea what it was for. Without knowing how it happened, I found myself on my knees, looking in. No matter how hard I tried, I could not find a trapdoor, a pipe, anything leading out. It came over me suddenly. I wept and could hear myself.

About the Contributors

Chimamanda Ngozi Adichie is a Nigerian novelist and short story and nonfiction writer. She earned a bachelor's degree in communication and political science at Eastern Connecticut State University, a master's degree in creative writing at Johns Hopkins University, and a master's in African studies from Yale University. Her novels *Purple Hibiscus, Half of a Yellow Sun*, and *Americanah* received critical acclaim.

Doreen Baingana is a Ugandan writer and editor. Her book *Tropical Fish* won the 2006 Commonwealth Writers' Prize for best first book, Africa Region, and the AWP Award for Short Fiction. She also won a Washington Independent Writers Fiction Prize and was a finalist for the Caine Prize for African Writing. Her fiction and essays have appeared in journals and newspapers such as *Glimmer Train, African American Review, Callaloo, The Guardian*, and *Kwani*. She has an MFA from University of Maryland and was a writer-in-residence there.

Boris Boubacar Diop is a Senegalese novelist. He has become a prominent contemporary Francophone writer and has published several novels, essays, and plays. His novel *Murambi, The Book of Bones*, a fictional account of the Rwandan genocide, was nominated to the Zimbabwe International Book Fair's list of Africa's 100 Best Books of the twentieth century.

Nuruddin Farah is a Somali novelist and professor. He was exiled by Mohamed Siad Barre, the dictator of Somalia from 1969 to 1991, and currently resides in Cape Town. While in exile Farah taught in Germany, India, Italy, and the United States. Farah's literary work is known for its feminist and nationalist themes, and he is a scholar of Somali studies.

Hawa Jande Golakai is a Liberian writer and clinical immunologist. She earned her BS from the University of Cape Town and her MS from Stellenbosch University. Her debut novel, *The Lazarus Effect*, was shortlisted for the 2011 Sunday Times Fiction Prize and University of Johannesburg Debut Prize. In 2014 she was included in the Africa39 anthology of the most promising sub-Saharan writers under forty.

Heidi Grunebaum is a poet, author, and senior researcher at the Center for Humanities Research, University of the Western Cape, South Africa. Her research focuses on aesthetics and politics. In 2011 she published the monograph *Memorializing the Past: Everyday Life in South Africa after the Truth and Reconciliation Commission.* She collaborated with curator Emile Maurice on the "Uncontained" project, which included an exhibition, a writing project, and the book *Uncontained: Opening the Community Arts Project Archive.* She also worked with Mark J. Kaplan on the documentary film *The Village under the Forest,* which was awarded Best South African Documentary Film at Encounters International Documentary Film Festival.

Emmanuel Iduma is a Nigerian writer of fiction and nonfiction as well as an art critic. He has an MFA in art criticism and writing from the School of Visual Arts, New York City. He is the cofounder of *Saraba,* an online literary magazine. His first novel, *Farad,* was republished in the United States under the title *The Sound of Things to Come* in 2016. His travelogue *A Stranger's Pose* was published in 2018.

Abu Bakr Hamid Khaal is an Eritrean novelist currently residing in Denmark. Khaal fought many battles against the Ethiopian occupation as a member of the Eritrean Liberation Front, and spent several months in a Tunisian refugee camp during the Libyan revolution. Khaal has published three novels: *The Scent of Arms,*

Barkantiyya: Land of the Wise Woman, and *African Titanics*, which is his first novel translated into English.

Hisham Matar is a New York–born Libyan writer and professor of creative writing at Barnard College, Columbia University. To date, he has published two novels: *In the Country of Men* and *Anatomy of a Disappearance*. The first was shortlisted for a Booker Prize in 2006, while the second book's publication coincided with the Arab uprising of 2011 and subsequent toppling of Muammar Gaddafi. *The Return: Fathers, Sons and the Land in Between* earned him a Pulitzer Prize for biography and a PEN/ Jean Stein Book Award in 2017. *A Month in Siena* came out in 2019.

Achille Mbembe is a Cameroonian philosopher, political theorist, and writer on African history and politics. He earned his PhD in history at the Sorbonne in Parris and his DEA in political science at the Institute d'Etudes Politiques. He has taught at Columbia University, the University of Pennsylvania, the University of California, Berkeley, and Yale University. Mbembe is a staff member at the Wits Institute for Social and Economic Research at the University of Witwatersrand.

Hassouna Mosbahi is a Tunisian writer, literary critic, and freelance journalist. He has published five collections of short stories, eight novels, and some nonfiction in Arabic. In 1986 he won the National Novel Prize (Tunisia) and in 2000 the Tukan Prize (Munich).

Yvonne Adhiambo Owuor is a Kenyan writer who was named "Woman of the Year" in 2004 by *Eve Magazine*. In 2015 she won the Jomo Kenyatta Prize for Literature for her book *Dust* on the violent history of Kenya in the second half of the twentieth century. Her second novel, *The Dragonfly Sea*, was published in 2019.

Zachariah Rapola is a South African writer and filmmaker. His short stories and poems have appeared in *Tribute Magazine*, *The Boston Review*, *Serendipity*, *Oprud*, *Witness*, and *Discovering Home*. He has published literature for young adults: *Stanza on the Edge*, *Stanza and the Jive Mission*, and *Stanza's Soccer World Cup*. His television dramas include *Hola! Mpinji*, which he created based on characters from the Stanza novel series. His collection of stories *Beginnings of a Dream* won the Noma Award in 2008. He mentors emerging young writers in rural parts of South Africa.

Noo Saro-Wiwa, born in Nigeria and raised in the United Kingdom, is an author and a journalist. She holds degrees from King's College London and Columbia University in New York. Her highly praised *Looking for Transwonderland: Travels in Nigeria* won the Albatros Travel Literature prize in Italy. Her work is included in *A Country of Refuge, An Unreliable Guide to London*, and *La Felicità degli Uomini Simplici*.

Taiye Selasi is a novelist and photographer. Her fiction debut, "The Sex Lives of African Girls," published in the literary magazine *Granta*, appears in *Best American Short Stories 2012*. Her first novel, *Ghana Must Go*, was named one of the Ten Best Books of 2013 by the *Wall Street Journal* and *The Economist*.

Véronique Tadjo is an Ivorian poet, novelist, and artist. Among her works translated into English are *As the Crow Flies* (1986), *The Shadow of the Imana* (2000), and *Far from My Father* (2014). In 2005 she was awarded the prestigious Grand Prix Littéraire de l'Afrique Noir for *Reine Pokou* (Queen Pokou).

Binyavanga Wainaina was a Kenyan novelist, short story writer, and journalist. He was the founder of the East African literary magazine *Kwani?*, which has featured several Caine Prize-winning writers. In 2002, Wainaina won the Caine Prize for African Writing for his short story "Discovering Home." He was a Bard fellow and the director of the Chinua Achebe Center for African Literature and Languages at Bard College. His memoir *One Day I Will Write about This Place* was published in 2011.